CAGED

CAGED

A STORY OF JEWISH RESISTANCE

DAVID J. LANDAU
alias
Dudek, Janek and Jan

PAN
Pan Macmillan Australia

First published in 1999 by the Landau Family.
First published in 2000 in Macmillan by Pan Macmillan Australia Pty Limited
First published in 2001 in Pan by Pan Macmillan Australia Pty Limited
St Martins Tower, 31 Market Street, Sydney

National Library of Australia
Cataloguing-in-Publication data:

Landau, David J., 1920–1996.
Caged: the story of a Jewish fighter.

ISBN 0 330 36285 2.

1. Landau, David J., 1920–1996. 2. Warsaw (Poland) — History — Uprising of 1944 — Personal narratives. 3. Warsaw (Poland) — History — Warsaw Ghetto Uprising, 1943 — Personal narratives. I. Title.

940.534384

Typeset in Bembo by Midland Typesetters
Printed in Australia by McPherson's Printing Group

You can visit the *Caged* website at:
http://www.cagedbook.com

To all our dear and precious friends — who we have met through private or business life.

To Jan Karski, Jacek Eisner, Janek Kostański, Władysław Bartoszewski, Rutka P.

To Terry S. and Sam N. who showed that different backgrounds are respected and elevated when we all choose to live in peace.

To the doctors who were so kind to David.

To Michaels everywhere,
to our family,
to wives, husbands and families everywhere,
to soldiers of peace, the bravest mission of all.

To Noemi,
to Luba,
to you.

Foreword

David (Janek) Landau is one of my heroes to whom I looked up to during and before the Warsaw ghetto Uprising. I, a sixteen-year-old boy, scared, hungry, yet wanting, desiring to fight back, to avenge, not go like a sheep, needed an example to look up to.

David was one of those who humanity, and the Jewish people in particular, are proud of.

We were the first of all the occupied nations in April 1943 to rebel against the German barbarians openly, in the streets of a big city. But David Landau went further, to persist and resist the vicious German occupier one and a half years later — in August 1944, in the Uprising of Warsaw. He survived.

I have the greatest respect for him.

An Israel *Chai*! *Kol Hakavod*.

Jack Eisner
Author of *The Survivor of the Holocaust*

Contents

Preface

My parents arrived in Australia as refugees. They found themselves without the structures of history, family and environment that the rest of us take for granted: the street we know intimately, the city we can navigate, the language we grew up with, the people that are our own. They were without context.

How strange it must have been for these two young people from secure homes full of love and laughter, whose families had been large and energetic, to arrive as refugees in Australia, their lives a blank canvas stretched over black and burned boards.

David was disabled from his war injuries; my mother was a young bride. Both were traumatised beyond our comprehension, yet somehow managed to re-create a life. They gathered up what family they had: Luba's uncle and cousin, whom David had once brought to Russia; her brother, his wife and baby, who had arrived in Australia a few months earlier. Cousins already in Australia provided a semblance of what had been. They also created a new family, a family of friends.

Before the war, their families had owned businesses, homes and agencies throughout England, Europe, Scandinavia, Canada and Australia, yet my parents could not muster the energy and spirit to reclaim what was rightfully theirs. Their efforts went into re-establishing human ties and feelings of community, into starting their existence again and making life meaningful. This was their priority and they did it well.

I was their only child, born in this new land. In our home, love was ever present. I grew up knowing that love was the central theme of my parents' lives and that I was witness to a love story that had endured trials and tribulations beyond belief.

Their respect of each other as individuals strengthened these bonds. They were honest, dramatic and witty, yet protective and loving. Independence was encouraged and expected. They were friends as well as parents. Trust, openness, humour and love were our way of life. And my parents passed the same blessings on to their extended family and friends.

For almost fifty years, David maintained a wall of silence around the earlier years of his life, the years that are recounted in this memoir. But time and time again he was hurt by the inaccuracies appearing in the written records about the Warsaw ghetto, particularly with reference to the role in the Uprising of the ŻZW (Żydowski Związek Wojskowy), the Jewish military organisation with which he was most closely associated.

It was understandable that the communist regimes in Poland and the Eastern Bloc would not look kindly on a non-communist organisation that sought to discredit their myth that all organised resistance to Hitler was left-wing. Once the ŻZW had been declared an enemy of the state, its role in the Uprising was rapidly excised from the history books.

David knew that his own first-hand account of what had gone on in the ghetto would help later historians redress this imbalance. Preparing this account was a very difficult task for my father. It was painful and traumatic to revisit the enormity of his loss, and a space of fifty years had barely brushed away the hurt. Yet he committed himself to the task, as many others have done. He would discuss details, dates, identities and locations with my mother for hours, preferring to recall the truth in this way than rely on published documents, which he had learned to mistrust. He wanted to place his story on record without the influence of other stories.

Sometimes he would arrive at dates from careful deduction and sequential analysis of lengths of time, climate, light or darkness. Other dates were indelibly etched in his memory. I remember his difficulty in describing the Jews, Christians, Seventh Day Adventists and Gypsies of Poland. He wanted to stress that they were all Polish, all connected through the suffering of their homeland, all had a duty to help defend and save each other.

To complete this difficult work David was as disciplined and organised as he was in everything he did. He set aside a certain number of hours daily to dictate the material, then a further, and greater, number of days and hours to edit and check the material with my mother. He was pedantic in the extreme, always careful to state what he remembered and never to add what he could not be sure was correct.

My father worked at his task of remembering while keeping up a flurry of community, social and working activity. Even while battling severe illness, he worked with a will that constantly surprised his doctors.

When David called me and said, in an unusually weak voice, that he had finished the memoir, I knew we had to prepare for his passing. The memoir was the task that had been keeping him alive and, in some understandable way, hastening his death. Mercifully, he lived to receive the Medal for Warsaw ten days before he died. The doughty fighter rose from his deathbed to attend the presentation, which was, in a way, the opportunity for all of us to say goodbye. My father predicted his date of passing within a range of ten days and joked, 'I'm glad they've chosen the fifth of May, because I told them I wouldn't be here on the sixth!'

He was awarded the medal by Her Excellency Dr Agnieszka Morawińska, the Ambassador for Poland, on behalf of the ex-President of Poland, Lech Wałęsa, and the past and present Polish governments, and received a letter of salute from the Israeli Knesset (Parliament). At the ceremony, my father, speaking through me, expressed his deeply held view that people could live in harmony if only they respected each other's beliefs, for beliefs are private and personal, and belong in the heart of each individual. He warned that only through peace, reason and liberty could the lot of humankind be improved.

David became apolitical and often reminded me that he had joined the ŻZW, rather than some other group, merely because it had been the first to organise armed resistance.

It is four years since my father died, yet I have had enormous difficulty finalising this book. Not because writing can be difficult, but for a simpler reason. I guess that I have still wanted to shield my father from the hurt and pain he experienced at the end of his life when he finally spoke out. It was so surprising to hear critical comments and words spoken by people who were not even in the ghetto, let alone involved in the Uprising. David eventually let go of the hurt; he understood the ignorance that their comments displayed. But this only made him all the more determined to speak up for those comrades-in-arms who could no longer speak, who did not survive. He believed that whoever did survive should tell their story.

My father knew that each person's story is their own. He knew that others would take issue with some of his recollections and that these were natural responses when there were so few survivors of his group in the Uprising. He also knew about all the stories that will be never told and the assumptions people believed as facts. The great Australian lawyer, Louis Voumard, often advised my father, the young lost refugee: 'Remember, David, when the years go on, you should never be surprised when you tell your story if people don't believe you, you'll scarcely believe it yourself.'

Speaking about his life in Australia, David said that, 'People who were not in the camps or the ghetto didn't believe my stories or didn't want to listen, as they felt overwhelmed. In the end, I became very lonely. Others, who fought for ŻOB, are still so political that they don't adequately acknowledge the contributions of rival resistance groups. After the war, the left-wingers in Poland declared us [ŻZW] the enemies of the state. All our fighting and our achievements were ignored and wiped out of official accounts. This sentiment continues today in some instances. The left-wingers are not interested in me, some still see our party as revisionists, as "baddies". I read the things people have said about places where I was at the time and I know they are distorting reality. It disturbs me. It's wrong information which is being conveyed and as such it is disrespectful to those who died for the cause.'

Surprisingly and mercifully, when my father did finally speak, there were other first-person witnesses who came forward; people who persuaded him to record his story, such as Jan Karski, Janek Kostański, Jacek Eisner, Eddy Jagodziński and Władysław Bartoszewski (the former Polish Foreign Minister and the most prolific chronicler of Warsaw history in the Second World War). There was also corroborating evidence in the writings of Chaim Lazar, Jan Kostański and other writings revealed to be written about David.

To my way of thinking, when one reads or views writing or films on the Holocaust, it is important to keep in mind that Jews did not go 'like sheep'. It is also important to remember that there were survivors. Their very existence has taught all thinking humans to say, 'Never again!' A combination of factors created a survivor but most strongly and foremost, fate. Then there were looks, age, friendships, means and tenacity, and so many other factors too complicated and capricious for our imagination. To be a survivor was a lottery with very few chances and to 'win' was to carry a legacy of pain.

To be a child of these survivors or any survivors of genocide is to learn much about inner strength and to be in constant awe, shock and respect for those who have survived.

There were so many who did not survive. My father's family was active in the Resistance. His brothers, especially Joziek, became active in the Uprising. His cousin, Joseph Borenstein, was a leader of the desperate Uprising in Auschwitz from which many escaped, while he threw himself on the wire. Joseph's brother Maurice was a member of General de Gaulle's men.

People will ask why my father, with his 'Christian looks', his means and incredible daring, did not leave the ghetto permanently? Why did he always return to the ghetto after his forays on the Aryan side? Why go back to be part of the Uprising, knowing he would almost certainly die? When asked what he was thinking, whether he was afraid, my father would just shrug and answer, '*Masada.* I wanted to be with my people. I simply saw no other way.' Peace was the only salvation.

You will be reading a book that was written and first published for a grandson and for our extended family and friends. As a person, my father David was complex and intense. The overriding memories others have of him are of humour, laughter, strength, an enormous capacity and joy for life and a special sensitivity towards others in need. He was never afraid to state his case, to demand and expect what was fair. He could easily sense deception, laziness and falsehood and was intolerant of such behaviour. Never a snob, he was shy, yet flamboyant, and was open to all, regardless of position, race or background. He was, in the words of my godson, 'a champion'. A champion because he successfully balanced family, friends, duties and responsibilities and managed them all with determination, energy and, at most times, a grin.

This book is simply written, but my father's story is so tragic, so incredible, that, as his daughter, my heart breaks knowing it to be true.

Yet my father, David, never allowed himself to be called a hero.

Miriam

David's Introduction

IN the late evening hours, I sometimes catch myself contemplating the past. In such moments I also plan for the future. But at my age I have to admit that much more has accumulated in my past than will ever accumulate in my remaining years. My memories have begun to outweigh my plans, and there is nothing abnormal in that. What is out of the norm is the cage I find myself locked in. A cage made out of the past. A cage in which I am locked for the rest of my life. This cage has no physical presence, but it is as real to me as if it were made of steel rods set in concrete and fenced with barbed wire.

I am not the only one trapped in such a cage. I belong to a breed of people unknown before my generation, a breed that will be extinct within the next ten to twenty years. Our entire breed suffers from the same aberration. We survived. We cheated the sprawling German killing machine of death camps and ghettos, and came out alive from places we were not meant to survive. We live in a time warp from which only death will release us, and each of us carries within their mind a mental cage which dominates their life.

Those who have become my friends or have known me after I passed the age of twenty-five, consider that fate has always smiled on me. This is not the whole truth. They do not know about my younger years when fate and I were locked in the one cage and I lived a constant knife fight; fate against me and I against fate. But fate gave in. Instead of making me its victim it befriended me and I became a survivor. But the cage has remained. The bars have become overgrown with normal life in a free country, but it is still a cage.

I welcome you as a visitor to relive with me the years in which fate and I fought the battles of life and death with unsheathed knives. After my generation has died out, you will not be able to learn about it through hearing first-hand accounts.

Three large cities found a special place in the history of the Second World War. They suffered the worst form of torture at a time when torture was the norm, starvation was endemic and cruelty, deprivation and death visited tens of millions of people. Stalingrad was the first of these cities. Its name became a synonym for bravery and death. At Stalingrad, a fateful decision for the world was made. The human will to live overcame the powers of evil in their push to enslave the world for a thousand years. Berlin was the last of the three. From that city, the evil beast began its murderous conquest, until in Berlin it was finally put to death.

Between these two cities lay an innocent sacrifice: Warsaw, my home town. Like the other two, it was also destroyed and, like them, rose from the ashes. But unlike them, Warsaw suffered not one but three destructions before it, too, lay in total ruins. Unlike the other two, where soldier fought soldier, Warsaw was first raped by the German military attack on its defenseless civilians. Three and a half years later, it was once more tested beyond the limits of endurance, when the Jews in the ghetto fought the unequal but heroic battle behind its besieged walls. Then a third test, when my home town stood at the gate of liberation and wanted to win its freedom for the price of its blood. It would have won that honour if Warsaw had not been betrayed by Stalin, who gave the order not to tilt the scale of the battle towards our victory and not to let anybody else do it. Thus, for the third and final time, Warsaw was left completely destroyed. Three cities. But there was only one Warsaw, the home in which I lost my entire family.

Since the war I have been drawn to return to Poland at every opportunity — even during the communist regime. Like the invisible cage in which I live, I am bound with a thousand invisible cords to Warsaw. Not even the knowledge that Warsaw was being ruled from Moscow by the followers of Stalin could kill my longing to return there. My desire was not to live there again but to relive an unknown something, a past which no longer existed. I returned to Warsaw and found it a changed, colder city than the one I had grown up in. I began returning each year to commemorate the ghetto Uprising. Over the years I marched the blood-road of my younger times. I marched with those who were no longer visible to the many who had not been there with us in 1943. To my comrades of the ghetto fights I could speak words I could not speak to the living. With them I could share memories that were locked under seven locks when I spoke with the living. This I could do only in Warsaw and only during these commemorations, when the dead heroes walked beside me and we were surrounded by thousands of strangers who had come to pay homage to our deeds, but knew nothing of our days of fire.

For close to fifty years I lived without knowing how to begin to speak about Warsaw, where almost five hundred thousand Jews had been murdered for the unforgivable crime of having been born Jews. After forty-six years I have found my voice and words. I do not know how this miracle has happened. It is tragically late. Much too late for the whole story to be told and confirmed by the living. Of those who survived, only a handful is still alive. And I could not find or remember all of them.

The Jewish people were not the only victims of Hitler's regime. Russians, Poles, Czechs, French, Belgians, Dutch, Luxembourgers, Gypsies, Italians and others suffered and died in hundreds of camps, along with the many thousands of Germans who actively or passively resisted the German evil. But it was the Jews who suffered the most universal victimisation and who, including babies, children and the very old, were threatened with total annihilation, even from birth.

To all of these victims I pay my respects. They were victims not only of Hitler but also of his murderous henchmen and their helpers, who betrayed their own country and came to the service of the most heinous crimes.

To all of these victims I say, I salute you!

1

My early life

I was born in Warsaw in 1920, about a year after Poland was reborn, when it threw off the yoke of one hundred and twenty years of foreign subjugation. I was the middle child of four boys and a girl. My family, although it had a strong, full, Jewish identity, was far from typical. We did not celebrate the Jewish holidays, or keep kosher; nor was I sent to a *cheder*, a religious school. And whereas in most Jewish homes in Warsaw, Yiddish was spoken, in our home we spoke Polish.

Another way in which we were not typical was that we did not know poverty, unlike the vast majority of Warsaw Jews who eked out a precarious living. By the standards of our day we belonged to the upper middle class. Our father's reputable tannery Hilan supplied Polska Spolka Rymarzy for the Polish Army as well as clients such as Bata and others. We were also involved in real estate.

We lived in the Jewish district of Warsaw at 17 Muranowska Street, which was later the site of some of the most ferocious battles of the ghetto Uprising. The large building belonged to our parents. Of the one hundred and ten tenant families (around seven hundred people) we had only some eight or ten who were able to pay their rent regularly; the others just lived there. My father, who had capitalist leanings, once told my mother that maintaining the building was a huge financial undertaking considering the amount of rent that came in. Mother, who was rather more socialist-minded, replied, 'Make the tannery pay for the losses on the building.' To the best of my recollection, my father never again mentioned the subject of rent.

One of our tenants was a shoemaker who made his living repairing the worn-out shoes of his neighbours. He was an artist in reviving shoes which should have been discarded long before they were brought to him for repairs. He used to 'buy' his leather from us and, like the rent, sometimes paid for it and sometimes didn't. My brother once asked my father why he never demanded the money the shoemaker owed us.

'He cannot pay for the leather because he needs the money to pay the rent,' my father explained.

'But he doesn't pay for the rent either!' my brother exclaimed.

Father allowed a silence to hang in the air before responding, 'You have just answered your own question. For if he doesn't have the money to pay the rent where could he find the money to pay for the leather?'

Looking back on our home I realise how hard the older generations worked at keeping the family together. My mother's family were all passionate socialists, at least in theory. My father's side were business people who had little time for socialism. When Grandpa from our mother's side visited us, my mother always managed to have other guests and, without fail, she would arrange it so that my father and his father-in-law would sit at opposite ends of the extended table. Any danger of a serious clash over 'class interest' was thus neatly avoided.

Although our home was without any religious affiliation, most of our friends were Jewish. The capital of Poland had a population of approximately one million, of which around a third was Jewish. Keeping our Jewish identity was thus an easy and natural inclination.

We were an unusual family. I cannot recall ever hearing my parents raise their voices to each other or their children. They never spoke to us in a tone of parental authority. They disciplined us only by example. If we arrived late for a meal, the girl who worked in our house knew not to serve us or let us help ourselves to any food. Mealtime was for those who came to the table. Once, when I was twelve or thirteen years old, I came home late after visiting a school friend. Dinner was almost finished and the family was being served dessert, which was all I was given. Afterwards I remember using my pocket money to buy a buttered roll with herring which, following so soon after the sweets, made me feel sick. But I had learned my lesson and was never again late for a family meal.

These childhood years laid down a firm foundation for my personality. Often during the trials of war, I depended for inner strength upon this foundation and was grateful for my childhood environment and upbringing.

However, I was lacking in school discipline. Once our geography teacher asked me to point out where Paris was on the large map hanging at the front of the class. I had no idea, but instead of feeling helpless, I played up to my classmates. 'I don't need to know where Paris is,' I boasted. 'If I ever want to go to Paris, I'll go to the station, buy a ticket and let the train take me there. The driver will know where Paris is.'

As a result of such behaviour, I did not stay at any school for long. This did not upset me, though, as my interests lay in other directions. When I was fifteen I attended my last school, Żuchowski. There, I joined the army cadets, which taught me discipline. When the year ended, I left Żuchowski and studied at home after hours with tutors. During the day I worked in our tannery and building company. I also joined Walka Młodych ('The Struggles of the Young'), a left-wing youth organisation. My mother did not say anything about this but I could feel her approval.

At sixteen I became a part-time organiser for a branch of Walka Młodych called Pajorg ('The House of the Worker'). Pajorg was in the Tatry Mountains in southern Poland. It was my duty to organise accommodation, food and programs for the 'delegates' of Pajorg when they visited Warsaw. During tense May Day demonstrations I led one hundred and fifty Pajorg members in the march. We carried flags and called out slogans which the police did not like very much.

My involvement in this kind of political activity was very much in keeping with the tradition of my mother's family. Her cousin Finkelstein and his son from Lublin were the Head and Secretary of the Polish Communist Organisation. My first serious political activity took place a year later, when I decided to support the republican struggle in Spain. Franco's army had overthrown Spain's elected government in July 1936. I felt it was my sacred duty to come to its rescue. With no passport and only the money I had saved from work, I crossed illegally into Czechoslovakia. Once there I made contact with the Socialist Party of Czechoslovakia, which directed me to the Basque region of Spain. Feeling proud of myself, I made my way to the Spanish border. Initially, I was turned back because of the pact of non-aggression that had been signed by several European countries. Even when I succeeded in making contact with the republicans, my sacrifice was in vain. The office which recruited volunteers rejected me on the grounds of my youth and military inexperience.

I returned to Poland with the last of my savings. I was a social idealist without much concept of the real world. For me, at the dawn of the Second World War, socialism meant sacrifice and poverty.

2

Autumn, 1939

FOR many people, the story of the Second World War begins on 3 September 1939, when Neville Chamberlain announced to the British people that Germany had failed to withdraw its armies from Polish soil and that 'England is therefore in a state of war with Germany.'

But for Poles, the Second World War began two days earlier, on 1 September, when the murderous German *Luftwaffe* invaded the Polish skies, in particular those over Warsaw, and terrorised our people, who were not aware that war had started. For us, the Second World War began with Hitler's speech the year before, when Poland was put in the sight of German guns. This speech turned the sun-filled calm of a Polish spring into a nightmare. Fear began to smoulder under our feet, over our heads, in us and around us. Throughout the late spring and the hot summer of that year we tried to steel ourselves for an unknown fate. In retrospect, none of us came close to imagining the horrors ahead. But already, by September 1939, we had endured eighteen months of war, a war of nerves.

My second-oldest brother, Mietek, was in the middle of an officer-training course. He was to finish in the summer but by late June it became clear that his release had been deferred.

My oldest brother, Eliezer (Lutek), had already done his military service. When he saw our mother's eyes filling with fear of the impending war, he tried to turn the situation into a joke. 'Mum, please understand they can't start a war without me and the other officer reserves. Without us they can't start anything!' he explained.

I had not been called up for service as I was nineteen and the call-up age was twenty-one. However, I believed I knew what war was even though I had never carried a gun other than as a cadet.

I spent the beautiful summer days of that year enjoying life as much as possible and spending every free hour in the company of Luba Gutrajcht, my childhood sweetheart. In the last two years, she had blossomed into a beautiful young lady.

We worked long hours in the factory producing leather for the Polish Army. But Luba was constantly in my thoughts. If anything about the possibility of the war occupied my mind, it was not the fate of our family but the fate of that young girl who had slowly grown into my heart and taken residence before I knew she was a tenant. I felt no fears for my family. I had been brought up in secure surroundings and felt emotionally protected by the way our mother ran the household. My father was a successful man. Important people often came to his office and it was easy to sense the respect his staff held for him. If there was to be a war I could leave it to my father to organise the family. Mother, too, seemed secure. She ran a strict but very warm home and now she had only the three youngest children on her hands.

I had known Luba since the time when our different ages were a chasm between us. I had started coming to her house when I became friendly with her brother, Meir. I was nearly eight years old and Luba was a child of five. Culturally, we came from different worlds. While our home had no Jewish tradition, Luba's parents were observant Jews.

I came to know her brother through our tannery. Their family firm, Gutrajcht Brothers, was one of the largest fur dealers, manufacturers and suppliers in Poland and the surrounding Eastern European countries, as well as many countries outside of Europe. Our tannery bought hides which the Gutrajchts rejected. Between the young Meir Gutrajcht and the young David Landau a friendship grew. If, at the age of eight, somebody had told me that I was destined to share my life with his little sister, I doubt I would have believed it.

Mr Alexander Zisha Gutrajcht had been known as a highly successful merchant and manufacturer, and a man of great generosity. One act of generosity cost him his life. On a freezing winter day he was standing on one of Warsaw's main thoroughfares chatting with someone when he noticed a pious Jewish man passing in a thin coat and trembling in the cold. Not thinking of the consequences, he called the fellow back, removed his warm fur coat and handed it to the stranger. The man was concerned about the unusual generosity and asked his benefactor what he himself would wear home. But he took the gift and left. Mr Gutrajcht didn't notice as his body chilled in the freezing air. By the time he arrived home he was feverish and he died a few weeks later, leaving a widow and eight children. Luba was the second youngest.

Thousands of mourners came to walk in the funeral procession and the streets around the Gutrajcht home were packed. Christian and Jewish businesses along the route to the Jewish cemetery closed out of respect. The honour of carrying this noble man to his eternal rest was shared by as many as possible. While the hearse travelled empty, pall-bearers took turns to carry the black-draped coffin along the road.

As time passed and we turned from children into youth, my friendship slowly shifted from Meir to his sister, Luba. It was so natural that I never felt anything else than brotherly concern for her until she became a striking young woman. The one who first noticed the change in our relationship was her mother, Gitele Deborah, a noble and refined widow. Gitele kept a strictly kosher household. I loved to go there on the Sabbath and experience the atmosphere of the holy day. I felt that Gitele was responsible for this special atmosphere and I was thankful to her for it.

But Gitele did not like me very much. In her eyes I was not

traditional enough and therefore endangered the religious faith of her youngest daughter. However, as her own boys had also become less observant after the death of their father, she accepted the inevitable. After all, she did not demand religious observance. Her often-quoted attitude was that the first religion was to be good and to follow the Ten Commandments.

I was in the tannery early on the fateful Friday morning when the phone rang. There are times when intuition knows something before the mind becomes aware of it, and this was one such instance. Lutek, who had said the war would not start without him, had been called up two days ago. Now it could start. My mother was on the phone, her voice full of fear.

'Is everything in order at your end?' she asked.

'Why shouldn't everything be in order?' I said, though I had already guessed. As the war planes began to scream their noisy descent right outside the tannery, it was Luba who concerned me most. Nobody else but me could be entrusted with her well-being. I nominated myself at that moment as her guardian, dismissing her brother-in-law, the husband of her oldest sister, who had been the surrogate father of the family for some years.

We worked on, but in a chaotic way. The air-raid sirens shrieked and people ran into the long, narrow rows of open-air shelters that had been dug during the past weeks. Every few minutes we heard an announcement over the radio. 'The Commander of the Air-Raid Defence announces an air-raid over Warsaw' or, 'The Commander of the Air-Raid Defence announces the end of the air-raid over Warsaw.'

As the Polish Army had insufficient radio communication of its own, the civilian program began to be interrupted with coded announcements, which only those concerned could understand. 'Attention, attention, arriving, arriving. Be six end twelve.' Or, 'Attention, attention, passed, passed,' with the coded details.

When I left the factory that evening, the city was no longer the same. The streets smelled different. The faces of the people had changed. Even the warm air of the late summer had become permeated with the smell and taste of war. While I had tried to maintain a normal working routine during the day, Warsaw had been turned upside down. Boys were running down the streets selling the extra edition of the newspaper: big, fat letters announcing the first casualties.

In this unreal air I read in the newspaper that the German Army had crossed our borders and had been repulsed by our heroic Polish soldiers. While our own losses were vaguely described as light, the losses of the enemy were given in detail. We had shot down forty-four German war-planes and destroyed more than seventy tanks in the first hours of the war. The enemy casualties were very heavy and more than one thousand German soldiers had surrendered to the Polish forces near an unnamed border. They had declared that they didn't want to fight for Hitler, who had taken food from the people's mouths and was building guns and tanks instead.

That night the streets of Warsaw were in darkness. As soon as a spot of light was seen in a window the occupants were ordered to cover it. The usual noise of a living city had been stifled. As if fearing to hear their own sounds, those who had to be out in the street spoke in hushed voices. At the evening meal my father said, 'Who knows if we will all sit at this table next Friday night?' I saw my mother holding back her tears.

The absence of our two eldest boys also brought the war directly into our home.

The first days of the war are engraved in my mind as a mixture of hallucination and reality. As I try to recall them I find myself wandering half lost in my own thoughts. There is a touch of early autumn with sunny skies in these images. My father was supervising the factory but very little was being produced. He instructed me to take care of our other interests, especially our building business. I was also running messages to buy the basics as our maid had left us. But this was not easy; bread had become scarce within two days.

On the third day of the war I found myself in front of the British Embassy, in a crowd of thousands, cheering the British Empire for declaring war on Germany. A similar crowd cheered the French Ambassador, who stood on the balcony of his residence. Balconies were in fashion for such occasions. Hitler and his fascist friend Mussolini delivered their world-shattering speeches from their balconies. Now our allies came out onto their balconies to let us know in person that they were on our side. We sang the Polish anthem and those who knew the words of the English and French anthems sang them when they were played. For a few hours we rejoiced in the belief that the war was nearly over.

It is strange how the mind plays tricks with the passing of time. Sometimes I can visualise myself speaking to Luba over the phone during those surreal days. The conversations are long and serious. At other times I can see myself in the dark streets of Warsaw, passing bombed-out houses, some still burning or smouldering. Or I am going, at some late evening hour, to see how Luba and her family are faring. Conversations merge into one repeated moment. The only thing that is quite clear is that, except for the provision of basic necessities, I left the worries of the tannery and our home to my father while I worried about Luba.

For five days we tried to acclimatise ourselves to the war; less than the time it had taken God to make the world. On the sixth night came the total collapse of everything that had been built up over generations and centuries. It began around midnight.

I was coming home through a dark street where a small group of people was gathered outside a bombed-out house. Someone pointed a torch in my eyes and asked what I was doing there. I explained where I had come from and where I was going. My answer must have satisfied the man because he sent me on my way.

When I arrived home my parents were already asleep. I heard strange sounds outside, so I switched off the light in my room and opened the drapes. A stream of people in carts, on foot — leaving by whatever way they could — was moving in the middle of the road. Something out of this world had happened. I left the apartment and went down into the street.

Three young men passing our building stopped me and one asked in surprise, 'What are you waiting for? Start moving.' Before I could speak, he said, 'Don't you listen to the radio? A general mobilisation has just been announced. The government is leaving Warsaw. We will take on the German pigs on the River Bug. Better hurry up or the Germans will catch you.'

When I came back inside my mother was up. She was extremely agitated. 'Thank God you are here. I heard the noise and went into your bedroom, only to find you were not at home. What is happening in the street?'

After I told her, she woke my father, who came out of the bedroom as alert as if he had been awake for hours. I repeated my story and we all looked out. The whole width of the street was taken up; it was like watching a parade. But this was no ordinary parade. It was a midnight march of a nation heading eastward from somewhere unknown to somewhere unknown. Men and beasts, women and children, merged in the shadows. My father opened the windows and the noise of the street penetrated.

'The world has lost its senses,' he said as he closed the windows and went over to the telephone.

He dialled and I heard him mention his own name and ask for someone who was very high up in the defence department. I had seen that man's signature on the formal orders we used to receive at the factory from the government. The man came on the phone, my father greeted him and then, for quite a while, he listened while his face grew more and more strained and grave.

I looked at him and at my mother, and realised that nothing was left of the security I had always felt in the house. When he put down the phone my father found it hard to speak. 'In two hours the government will be leaving the capital. Hitler will be forced to move part of his attacking armies to the western front where the French are at this moment making preparations to break out of the Maginot Line into Germany.'

It was a chilling report and fear filled my mother's voice as she asked, 'What does it all mean?'

'It means that every able-bodied man should leave Warsaw for Lublin as soon as possible if he doesn't want to finish up in German hands. The Colonel I spoke to said that if I had phoned half an hour later I would have missed him. But he advised me to stay on in Warsaw and not to abandon the tannery. He said he is confident the Polish Army will be back in Warsaw within a fortnight, three weeks at the latest.'

For the first time in my life I saw my father unable to make a decision with his usual confidence. His words sounded as if he were waiting for one of us to reply. My mother found her strength. 'I am not sure it is a good idea for David to leave right now. This may be the time when he is needed here more than anywhere else. The family is already split enough, why split it further? Besides, where would he go and to whom?' She turned to Father. 'You said yourself the army will come back in three weeks, why run away and then have to come back? And what will happen if the German planes do to the people on the road what they have been doing to Warsaw?'

She stopped and waited for an answer but Father didn't say anything. We could hear the throng growing noisier, and slowly the arguments started for and against my leaving. It was not a time for sleep although the discussion and the action out on the street tired us to the bone.

By the time the first rays of the autumn morning had pushed through the drapes we had decided that I should leave, and my mother had taken complete control of the situation. She had packed a suitcase and produced from somewhere a sum of money for me.

'Be careful, my son,' she said, 'don't spend the money the way you have been used to in normal times. There will be no more on the road to replace it once you have spent it. In the meantime, it will be there when you need it and remember, we will pray that every time you open a door on the road, it will be as friendly to you as if it were the door to this house.' I had never heard my mother mention the word 'prayer' before. Its use now brought home to me the true heaviness of this moment.

I prepared to leave, but as I picked up the small suitcase my mother asked in surprise, 'Are you really leaving?' Desperation flickered in her eyes.

I decided to have a cold shower and as the icy water cascaded over me I felt as if I were coming out of some nightmare. 'Do I have to join that hysteria and run? Do any of the people below know exactly why they are running and to where? Where will I have my next wash? Will it be in some river with thousands of others, like cattle?'

I came out of the shower and told my anxious parents that I was not going. We would stay together and whatever happened would happen to us as a family. My mother was relieved that I had made up my own mind.

The youngest two of the family had slept through the night peacefully. When breakfast was ready they cast a curious glance out the window, expressed mild surprise about what was going on in the street, then they came to the table.

As we ate we listened to the radio. There was little to cheer us in the local news. The government had been transferred during the night and in spite of the sudden move, there was to be no interruption to the functions of the ministries. The front was being stabilised along the line anchored on Lublin and the ambassadors of our allies remained in Warsaw. In a joint statement, the news reader told us, the French and English representatives had informed the Polish Defence Forces that Great Britain was sending an expeditionary force to strengthen the French forces and to open a joint attack on Germany's western border. 'Germany may think they are going forward fast, but it will be nothing compared to the speed with which they will have to run back to Berlin when our allies begin to destroy them in the west!' the news reader concluded optimistically.

By midday the mass exodus had slowed noticeably. German planes kept up their continuous bombing and we watched the destruction growing around us. After each bombardment more buildings were left in ruins and the injured and dead had to be dragged from the rubble. Civilian nurses and doctors with Red Cross armbands worked in the decimated streets in a futile attempt to save those they could. Tram traffic, normally the communication line of the city, began to falter, and electricity was interrupted for long periods. On the third day of the government's absence from Warsaw, a new phenomenon appeared: groups of desperate people fell on the bodies of dead horses lying on the road and dismembered them within minutes. We quickly became accustomed to the sight.

On the morning after that first night's chaos, the Mayor of Warsaw, Stefan Starzyński, a major in the Polish Army, called on Warsaw's citizens to defend their city. He appealed to the soldiers in the city and the stragglers of forces that had already been destroyed to remain in Warsaw to defend the capital. His calm voice, the words he used and the way he made his appeal bonded Jew with non-Jew, civilian with soldier; all following his call. While the soldiers held the German forces at bay, the civilians did all they could to protect the soldiers. It was no secret that Warsaw was surrounded by the enemy. But the radio news bulletins and the few papers that still appeared endeavoured to keep up morale by reporting the changing fortunes of war in other parts of Poland and of loyal forces battling to relieve the besieged capital. We held on in hope.

In the second week of the siege the struggle was no longer for victory but for survival. The trams had stopped running; their carriages were used to build anti-tank structures at the end of the lines. The Mayor kept up his encouraging speeches, but every day hundreds of people left our bombarded, thirsty city and headed east.

Within a week my parents had changed their minds and pleaded with me to leave. This was after the building next to ours had been destroyed and more than a third of its inhabitants killed or injured. Members of the civil defence force told us not to bother pulling the dead from the ruins but to help the injured. My father was among those who attended to them. When he came back to our apartment he had decided. 'You heard what the orders were,' he said. 'If we should be killed you will not be permitted to waste your time on us. Go and save your own life.'

3

Spies among us

GERMAN forces were already established in pockets on the eastern side of Warsaw, but with care one could avoid them. The landscape outside the tragic city had barely been touched by the ongoing war. Peasants still toiled with their harvest; Polish money still bought basic goods, although prices had risen sharply. On the road, people joined up with groups leaving the city, then left them again without plan or reason. We were wanderers without a firm destination or purpose.

We ignored the horse-drawn military wagons that we passed on the sandy roads, but tried to hitchhike whenever an army vehicle drove by. I heard the sound of a truck approaching and ran into the middle of the road waving my arms. The driver pulled up and indicated for me to sit on the left-hand side of the cabin where usually the driver would have sat. I had seen right-hand drive cars in Czechoslovakia, and the driver told me that this one had been made there by Škoda. He was glad to have company, the weather was good and my luck was in, as he was going to Lublin.

My luck was in, but not the driver's. From his side of the road a plane appeared. He managed to stop but not to escape. A row of bullets pierced the side of the truck and he was killed. The whole action took seconds. I jumped out before the shock set in. When I came to my senses I realised the meaning of luck. The steering was on the wrong side for Polish roads and that was the only reason I was still alive.

I joined a man of my own age who was pushing his bicycle. He had been riding but he was tired so he decided to walk for a while. The German Army had already arrived at the small township where he lived, so he had set out and the soldiers had not bothered him. He was heading for Kovel, a township to the east, where he had relatives, and he invited me to come with him. Why not? I thought.

We had walked some kilometres when we saw a parked limousine with a chauffeur in uniform standing beside it. He lifted his hand, indicating for us to stop. I was no longer interested in hitching a ride but my companion stopped. 'Wait a moment,' the chauffeur said, and opened the rear door. I recognised the man who stepped out. He was Julian Glass, a steel magnate from Warsaw whose pictures had appeared in the papers every few days. He ignored me and turned to my new friend. 'I will give you this vehicle for your bicycle. It is all right but I have no gas for it.'

For a moment I struggled to believe the exchange. Glass already had his hand on the bicycle as the chauffeur asked him what he should do with the suitcases in the boot. He didn't answer but set out on his way, pedalling without looking back. The chauffeur handed my friend the keys to the vehicle. 'If you know how to unlock the boot you'll be able to dress yourself in a real shirt with a real suit.' His own words must have triggered something in his mind, because he grabbed the keys back from the new owner and opened the boot himself. He took hold of one suitcase and was about to walk away when my friend stopped him and demanded, 'This belongs to me!' I could see myself getting involved in the situation and left.

An hour later, I sat down in a ditch, wondering whether to keep going until I reached the village I could see on the horizon. Then I heard a voice and looked up. It was my friend carrying one of the suitcases. He was wearing a clean suit with a new shirt and tie. 'We made a deal. I took this new suit, the shirt and what was left in the suitcase, and the chauffeur got the car,' my friend told me.

It is a pity I cannot recall the name of my bicycle friend. Within minutes of our meeting we had found a common language, although we came from completely different backgrounds. The only thing my new friend may not have known about me was that I was Jewish. I could not tell if it would have made any difference to him, but it was not in my interest to disclose this to strangers. The few days we walked together were full of drama, although in our situation one would hardly have considered this out of the ordinary. Drama was the daily routine of people who had left their homes and gone off to meet their fate.

I cannot remember many of the names of the people I met during this time on the road. Like the clouds above us, groupings changed constantly. One could walk into a barn in the evening with five people and wake up in the morning to find them all gone, their place taken by a dozen strangers. Changing one's mind from minute to minute was not unusual, and the right of each person to do so was accepted without question.

The weather remained beautiful, sunny and mild. At any other time it would have been paradise to spend days like these in the countryside. The villagers were mostly friendly; they had not yet been spoiled or become greedy. The prices they asked for a glass of milk, a piece of bread or for a simple meal were still reasonable. Often food was given as a gift and with understanding. Most barns had been turned into free lodgings for the weary to spend a night.

My friend had seen a small formation of Polish soldiers taking a break on the road and had noticed that they had a field kitchen. 'If they have a field kitchen they must have food,' he reasoned. He suggested that we should join them to enjoy some free food, but I was not so sure.

'What makes you think they will let us?' I asked.

My friend said he had seen civilians sitting in the group, including two priests.

Nobody asked us any questions as we joined the file. We fell in near the priests, who made way for us to move in front of them. They were young men, carrying a single suitcase between them, and they kept to themselves a short distance back from the rest. At intervals, one of the officers would go over to talk with them.

The Captain who led the group of a hundred or so soldiers and civilians was friendly and fatherly to all. We stopped at a late hour in a field and he and three soldiers distributed two thick slices of bread and a big spoon of white cheese to every person. We had to queue some distance from the distribution centre and, after receiving our ration, move off in the opposite direction. Only when everyone had filed past did he and the three soldiers take their own rations.

The Captain asked for any civilians who would like to join the next day's march to raise their hands. He explained that they intended to walk about forty kilometres to arrive in Kovel the following day. Not all hands went up, but the priests standing next to my friend were eager. 'We will have to start before sunrise tomorrow,' the Captain explained. 'On the last three mornings German planes have visited us early, as if they had been informed precisely where we were.'

We slept in the field. The lucky ones were given blankets to cover themselves, two to a blanket. My friend and I, though, were considered young and healthy enough to withstand a night in the field uncovered.

My friend woke me just before dawn. He was afraid and whispered that he had something very important to tell me. I got up and we made our way carefully among the sleeping. He led me in the direction of the priests, but two guards pointed us towards the place that was to be used as a toilet, some two hundred metres away. As we walked, my friend told me something which I found hard to believe. 'A short time ago I saw the two priests get up.

One went over and walked with the guards while the other turned away and kept playing with a torch. He kept switching it on and off, on and off. When he had finished playing with the torch he came back to his place, lay down and went back to sleep. The one who had gone over to the guards, returned a short while later and lay down next to his friend.'

We went back past the two priests, who were fast asleep. Before the blue of morning began to dawn, the soldiers called us to get up. 'We will walk now,' the Captain began, 'and food will be distributed —' He was interrupted mid-sentence by somebody calling out, *'Samolot!'* (an aeroplane). A small plane flew over us and within seconds, members of our group lay dead or wounded.

The plane returned several times. When at last it flew off there was panic among the civilians and shock among the soldiers. While the Captain organised whatever help he could, the priests put on their sacred stoles and went among the dead and the wounded anointing them and giving them the last rites. I looked at them and something dawned in my mind. My friend did not want to tell his story to the Captain. He feared high-ranking officers and priests even more. I was not going to say anything for the simple reason that I was not sure of the truth. But a few minutes later the Captain and several soldiers were running towards the priests with their guns drawn, calling to them to raise their hands. We discovered that the Captain had planted some civilians at the rear of the columns, to observe the priests' suspicious behaviour. Later, during a brief and formal trial, it was revealed that the priests were German spies.

It was with some bitterness that we watched the spies being led away by an officer and four soldiers. The army men returned alone. After this, most of the civilians were sent on their way. My friend and I were among those who were allowed to remain.

Tomorrow morning which of these people in this barn will still be here? Before daybreak we will begin the final leg on the road to Kovel. And then?

What is my brother, Mietek, the brand-new officer, doing now? Is he leading a group like this on to some other place? Is he still alive? And my brother Lutek? You said the war could not start without you. You never told us that they had trained you to promote nightmares.

I am thinking of you, too, Luba. Of Friday evenings, of the candles in the silver candelabra which your mother will have lit before sunset. Is it Friday tonight? I have counted the people here. Seventeen. Seventeen strangers sleep tonight in a strange barn which belongs to somebody we do not know, another stranger. It's crazy. Tomorrow we will go our separate ways and never remember any of the faces. Perhaps I will remember this one who sleeps next to me. He and I have been together now for three days. We have eaten the same things and I have watched him changing the hiding place where he keeps the fifty złoty that he earned by selling his limousine. At present he has it in his left shoe.

It is raining and I have no coat. I am feeling the cold. Tomorrow in Kovel, the first thing I will do is get myself a new raincoat. I washed my shirt when we stopped at the river but there was no time to dry it in the sun. I am wearing it now, hoping my body will dry it. Good night, Father. Good night, Mother. Good night, my brothers and sister.

Good night, Luba. When I come home I shall say something to you I've never said before. I shall say how much I love you. I never understood it before.

When I come home now, if I come home, if there will be a home, we will be together again. Good night from the barn outside Kovel. Good night. Sleep in peace, my family.

I awoke to a nightmare of screams and the sound of machine-gun fire. It took me a minute or two before I could make sense of it all. A sudden burst of heavy autumn rain on the tin roof had woken people up, but they could not orientate themselves in the dark and had panicked. Their screams had alarmed the soldiers on guard who had switched on their blue-light torches to investigate. The torches didn't do much for the lighting but their narrow beams in the long, dark barn had helped to spread panic among the already strained nerves. Only the booming voice of the Captain, who appeared at the barn door, prevented the situation from getting completely out of hand.

The roof had seen better times and could not protect us from the downpour. The soldiers used their torches to pick out the dry areas where the roof didn't leak and we huddled there in groups as the rain came down. We had no thought of lying down anywhere; the straw was soaked through and cold. My shirt was wet again and making me freeze. I pulled it off and stood in the dark, surrounded by others like myself. We leaned on each other like a stack of timber poles, and thus, standing upright, we slumbered.

I was awakened later by the movement around me and heard the Captain say, 'Please do not follow us.'

The soldiers had decided to travel forward without us. It didn't take very long before the civilians, too, began to melt away, leaving in twos and threes in the dim light of a cloudy dawn. My companion was also preparing to go. He had his suitcase in his hand and asked if I wanted to accompany him to his relatives. But I had something more immediate to worry about. During the panic, someone had stolen my suitcase. For the first time since leaving Warsaw, I had forgotten to guard it. My friend left without me but I am sure he was not the one who had taken it.

The rain had stopped but the road was wet, chopped up and muddy. The water leaked inside my shoes, soaking them, and I felt cold, lonely and miserable. It took some force not to give in to the despair inside me. Walking made the situation feel less miserable. I tried to pretend I was out on a walking tour, enjoying the adventure, but the illusion didn't last long.

The distance to Kovel was shorter than I had thought. Within an hour I was at the outskirts of the town. The old timber houses looked as if they too had become war victims and refugees. They stood huddled together with bent backs and in need of a wash. One had a hand-painted sign out the front, proclaiming it to be a restaurant or coffee house.

It was dark inside, with warm steam hanging in the air. People sat on long benches at bare tables with worn timber tops, eating thick slabs of bread and drinking tea out of glasses. Nobody looked up as I entered. A woman in an apron pointed to an empty place. Before I sat down, she quoted the price of a breakfast. It would cost more than a meal in a first-class restaurant in Warsaw before the war. When I asked what breakfast consisted of, she pointed to the others. They were all eating herring and onion. She offered me an egg instead of the herring but when she mentioned the price, the herring became very reasonable.

I felt better after breakfast and went into the town to buy a change of underwear, some new shoes and an overcoat. The township, with its neat brick houses, looked much better than the rundown outskirts but the stores were empty and shoddy. However, I found the items I needed and the prices turned out to be affordable.

The proprietor of the store told me about the Russians, who were expected at any moment. 'I'll keep most of the stock at home until I know where we stand. Besides, what use is my clothing stock to them when what they want is food?'

The sun came out and I strolled around. Turning off the main street I found myself outside the synagogue; a few men were standing outside at the gate. They looked at me with apprehension, but their faces cleared when they realised I was Jewish. The introduction was short. They knew already that Warsaw had been taken by the German Army. Now they were waiting for the Russians like everybody else, but with less patience. The women and children were hiding inside the synagogue. 'We need young men like you to protect us,' one of them hinted. 'Stay with us, we may need young people.'

I assured them I would be around, then left to explore the rest of Kovel. The town was bordered by a river and a small wooden bridge led across it into an open field. As I approached the bridge, I noticed two men in military uniform lying low on the other side.

One had his rifle hanging over his shoulder, while the other had some kind of old machine-gun on two small wheels. Both weapons were pointed in my direction. The distance between us was no more that forty metres. When one of them ordered me in Russian to go back, I knew who they were. In a few hours they would be in the town.

At a food store in the main street a queue had formed to buy herring and pickled cucumbers. When I heard the prices I left, returning to the cafe at the end of the town. Suddenly the prices there seemed quite cheap. The woman was friendlier than before. This time a meal of soup, bread and vegetables cost me less than I had paid for the herring in the morning. Before nightfall I was on my way once more, this time to Vilno.

My first contact with Red Army soldiers puzzled me. One minute they were friendly, like trusting children, and the next they were suspicious, like wild creatures. They were poorly dressed and seemed malnourished, yet took great pride in being soldiers of the Red Army which had liberated eastern Poland from the 'slavery of dictatorship', as they called it, where people had been living in constant fear and hunger. I soon realised that the Polish soldier was, by comparison, an aristocrat.

I met a major who had escaped from Poland to Russia in the early twenties and was with the Red Army. He didn't realise that I was Jewish and he poured out his heart to me, telling me about the tragic mistake he had made in running away to Russia. He warned me not to say a single word that could be considered offensive or negative about the 'liberators'. I understood.

In the two days that it took me to tramp from Kovel to Vilno, I learned how to conduct myself. In a small town on the way, I saw how the Soviet Union dealt with 'capitalists'. The owners of pickled-herring shops and shopkeepers who sold rusted nails and hammers and called themselves hardware dealers, had been rounded up and brought to the market. The people stood around and an officer of the Red Army gave a fiery speech, in Polish, about how capitalists were dealt with in the republics of the Socialist Union. The storekeepers were duly shot.

After a few hours in Vilno, I felt a sense of relief. It was hard to see any sign of war except for the refugees who filled its streets. The Jewish community seemed the same as it had been before the war, and the doors of Jewish homes were open for us at any time of the day. The town had been torn away from Poland by the Red Army, which was there preparing to retreat and hand over the city. It had been given to the Lithuanians, who claimed it as their capital.

I had already spent half of my money when I met up with a Jewish fellow somewhat older than me, who said he knew how to make soap. He was looking for a partner who could finance him. Having experienced how it feels to be clean after two weeks of wandering, I knew how badly soap was needed. I pictured myself as a successful entrepreneur and manufacturer of the most popular item on the market as soap was unobtainable. We went into partnership. We found a neglected place to work in, bought the raw materials and made our first batch of beautifully coloured soap. It was also our last.

The soap was like glass. Although it looked attractive, it would not foam. After a few hours in the market I cut my losses and decided to return to Warsaw. I was lucky to get out of that business alive. I could have been shot for making and trying to sell the product, which was hard enough to pave roads. This kind of life was surely not for me. I recalled my mother's words, 'There will be no other money when this is gone.' It was gone.

I sold my watch in Vilno for a good price to a black-market dealer who specialised in supplying the senior officers of the Red Army with goods they had never seen in Russia. A truck driver who carried cattle legally between Vilno and Białystok agreed to engage me as his helper for a reasonable price. We were on the road for only one night, arriving in Białystok as the first, light snow began to fall on the city.

I was looking for lodgings and was given an address where

refugees usually gathered to arrange such things. To my joy I met an old and close friend from Warsaw, Mietek Grynglas. We embraced as if we were brothers who had found each other after years. He had left Warsaw long after I had and he could tell me news from home. Now I heard from Mietek words that chilled me to the bone. 'If you decide to return there, go at once. Your mother is very ill.' She had not felt well when I left but she had put it down to stress. He could not or would not tell me what the illness was, but he left me in no doubt that her condition was serious.

He found me lodgings and the next day, as we parted, he handed me a letter for his parents, beseeching me to deliver it. We said a sad goodbye and then I turned my face to Warsaw.

I had to sneak through the new border between Germany and its new ally, the Soviet Union. I managed it quite easily. Within two days of leaving Białystok, I stood at our house at 17 Muranowska Street, Warsaw. The bricks were the same as those I had left but the world in which the building was standing had changed completely.

4

Homecoming

MY mother's tears are still wet. After more than half a century, I can touch the spot where I felt them on that late autumn afternoon, when I was yet to have my twentieth birthday. I can recall the pain mingled with the relief in the first minutes of looking into each other's faces and realising that we were together once more. The shock of seeing how much my mother had changed in a few months drained away much of the joy of my homecoming. The two youngest in the family, my brother Joziek and sister Sala, joined in my welcome, their young faces speaking a language of suffering their words could not express.

After my first real bath in many weeks and a light meal we sat at the table and my mother held my hand in hers, as if afraid I would disappear. She suggested that I go and sleep, but I could hardly restrain myself from talking about the last few months. The apartment had changed. It looked poorer and sadder than I remembered it. The invisible hand of fate had wiped away the easy life I had known.

The Germans had destroyed the soul of Warsaw. Hitler had visited and taken the salute of victory in our beloved city. Every day the press, radio and wall posters proclaimed new anti-Jewish laws. Breaching any of these laws had one penalty — death. The curfew hour was more restricted for Jews than for Poles. Our tannery had been closed since the second day after Warsaw fell. A large sign outside the gate warned that trespassers would be shot without warning.

That evening, Mother went to bed early and I sat with Father in the drawing room. He told me the doctors' prognosis, that there was no hope for Mother. She had developed the worst kind of cancer and it was progressing rapidly. The diagnosis was no secret but Father had never brought himself to speak with her about it. He was not even sure she knew her true condition but believed she knew her time was short. He was hoping that Mietek and Eliezer would return from the wherever they were while their mother was still alive.

My father spoke of different kinds of mourning. Until then I had not known that he was as much a philosopher as a businessman. He spoke to me in a new way, as if I were no longer his third son, but an equal. 'There is a difference between the way parents grieve for a child,' he said, 'and the way children grieve for parents. A third sort of grieving is when a head of state dies. That is full of pomp and tradition, with death-marches and national days of official mourning. But the most difficult mourning is for the losses of war.'

He let the silence take over and, in it, I understood him better than in his words. I knew he was grieving for Poland, for Warsaw, for the Jewish tragedy inside the national one. Above all of this was his inconsolable personal grief, which I felt in the echo of his words, suspended in the silence. He went on to say that we were lucky to have our apartment in the Jewish area. The high brass of the new order had confiscated many luxury apartments by simply walking in and throwing out the people who lived in them. Daily arrests were common and people disappeared without trace.

In the middle of Father's litany the phone rang. He went into the other room to answer it. When he came back, he was a changed, happier man. I asked him who had called, to which he replied, 'First, let me tell you what's going on in the factory, then I'll tell you who called.'

'The factory?' I said. 'I thought the Germans had ordered it closed?'

He smiled sadly. 'Yes, you're right, but that doesn't mean nothing is happening. I haven't given in to everything the Germans have ordered. You know the baker who operated behind our tannery? I mean, the wall that was always warm when he heated the oven? He has become very useful. I have made a business arrangement with him, to knock a small hole in the wall, from the tannery to the back of his oven.'

'But what use is that?' I asked. 'A man could hardly fit through it, and he would still have to crawl the whole length of the oven on his belly.'

'Precisely. You remember our caretaker, Fidelzajt? He's a small, thin man, and he is able to crawl through the oven. Via him and the oven we have been able to distribute lots of finished leather. Fidelzajt is happy as he is well paid. The baker is happy as he makes in a day what the bakery would bring him in a week, and we are happy as we have been able to preserve several tonnes of leather.'

He waited to make sure I had understood his success and then continued. 'Now, if I ask you to guess who that caller was, I bet you won't be able to come up with the right name.' He waited, but I excused myself, protesting that I was too tired to guess.

'Josef Franke,' said my father, strangely triumphant. 'He told me he has been made an official in Warsaw and that he would like to see me. He didn't ask if I wanted to see him, but said he would be here tomorrow morning at ten.'

'Let's wait and see what he wants,' I said, suddenly weary. The emotional exhaustion of my homecoming, this talk with Father, and now the mystery of Franke, had worn me out. 'I think I've had enough for one evening. And you too, Father, let's call it a day.'

But I was too tired to fall asleep. My mother's now haggard face, the way she had aged in the last few months, kept running through my mind. The way Father had smiled his sad smile about having outwitted the Germans and, on top of this, the phone call from Franke, all kept me awake for some time.

I remembered Franke. He had been an employee in our tannery — a good worker, with clean, quiet habits, who kept to himself. Unlike the other workers, who just washed their hands before sitting down to their meal, Franke would remove his apron, tidy himself and wash his hands and arms thoroughly. He made no secret of being a German of Polish citizenship. But there was one mystery surrounding him. At meal breaks he would often walk into the office and ask the switchboard operator to dial one of his sisters' or brothers' numbers, every time in a different place. We decided that he must have had about forty brothers and sisters in as many towns in Poland! He always paid for the phone call as soon as he had finished, and we sometimes joked that he was giving away factory secrets to his friends.

Now he had become an official, appointed by the Germans, these phone calls came back to my mind. I could not help smiling, wondering if the calls were still being made. I understood; Franke must have been a German spy.

Precisely at ten o'clock, Josef Franke arrived. He was wearing a uniform with the insignia of the SS. He was polite and greeted my parents in a very respectful manner. In a more jovial tone, he turned to Father and said, 'I know your people have difficulty obtaining food in the open market, so I have brought you some. Herr Landau, would you do me the honour of inspecting these supplies?' He noticed the worried expression on my mother's face and quickly added, 'Do not be alarmed. It is just downstairs. You are welcome to come too, Frau Landau, and so are you, Master David.'

We went down to find a large cartload of sacks filled with basic foods. A young driver was waiting for instructions. Franke was glowing with pride. 'I am sorry, Herr Landau, for many things but most of all I am sorry for Jews like you. If it was up to me I would have made you and your family Aryans, but unfortunately this is impossible.'

The driver unloaded the sacks into one of our sheds and out of courtesy we invited Franke up to our apartment. He was pleased to accept the invitation. Over tea and biscuits, he explained his visit. 'The food was my own idea. I had the opportunity to show my appreciation for all the years that I worked for you and I was glad to do it. But I am here also about business. We knew that you were an army supplier and therefore we had to close the tannery as soon as we could. I have been made SS *Untersturmführer*, not a very high rank but I am now in charge of all tanneries, including leather and fur stock in Warsaw. Unlike other Jewish factories, which have all been handed over to German trustees, I have convinced the authorities to let you run your tannery as before, Herr Landau, except that you will be now working for the German Government. I have presented you in a very special light to the authorities in Berlin and they are willing to leave you untouched, even though you are a Jew. You would be free to come and go when you want. Your bank account could be reopened and you would be able to employ the same people you had employed for the Polish Government, regardless of whether they were Jews or not, so long as they were not politically implicated.'

My father thanked him for the offer in the same polite manner that Franke had made it. 'I feel honoured, Herr Franke, that you have kept such a good opinion of me. I am sure that, if it had depended on you, things would have gone differently for us, but now, as things are, I cannot go back to the tannery. It would no longer feel like mine or my family's. Please understand, Herr Franke. My family and I have lived here with our fellow Jews since childhood. How could we allow ourselves to be treated differently from them? I can't put us in such a position in the present circumstances.

'But we are very grateful for this food and even more so for the goodwill you have shown by offering it to us. But if you really have such a good opinion of me, Herr Franke, please let me reimburse you for its cost.'

Franke was truthful. 'Herr Landau,' he said, 'this food didn't cost me a pfennig. Will you accept that?'

'Then may I know how you obtained it?' Father pressed him. Franke smiled, almost apologetically.

'I confiscated it,' he said, 'and saved it for you. As you know, all Jewish goods and machinery not needed for daily survival are now confiscated. They have become the property of the German Reich, administered by trustees. That is why there is now a sign over your tannery warning that trespassers will be shot, as they are now trespassing on property belonging to the Reich.'

Father opened his mouth.

Franke paused. 'Yes, Herr Landau?'

But my father decided to say nothing. 'I am sorry, I have forgotten what I was going to say. Probably nothing of importance.'

Franke carried on. 'As I was saying, everything belonging to Jews is now the property of the Reich and I am the trustee for the property that is in Warsaw. Yesterday, I closed one of the largest dry foods warehouses in the city. As chief trustee I had to be there in person to take possession of the goods. The size of the warehouse reminded me of your own tannery, which is also large and well stocked.

'We do not begin the stocktake until tomorrow, so as yet there is no official record of that warehouse's contents. I therefore authorised a charity requisition for some of the goods, the ones which I am giving to you. So you see, no cost has been incurred. Even the driver is temporarily employed by me, transporting stock from the holdings of other trustees. So please accept it all with my compliments.'

Laughing, he stood up and saluted my mother. A few seconds passed before my father responded to his outstretched hand. 'Not used to shaking hands with your former employee, eh, Herr Landau?' Franke said jovially. 'Yes, times have changed but I will always consider you and your family as different from other Jews. You were always a decent man, Herr Landau, and I shall always remember it.'

We did not keep the food to ourselves. Within three days my father had organised a communal soup kitchen for most of the tenants in the building. For weeks, the neighbours were talking about the generosity of Mr Landau. They never knew that the food had been donated by the SS.

The weeks I had spent away from home had been a hard lesson. But within days of my return I had fitted in with the new situation as if I had lived that way all my life. On the first day at home, I realised that Mother was aware of her condition and had decided to carry on her normal routine as long as possible. I saw how much the two younger siblings had taken to helping her run the house. Father left home in the mornings and returned before the curfew. By the third day I knew that I could not sit around waiting for something to happen.

I had visited the Gutrajchts on the first morning after Franke had left. Luba was as sweet as ever. In these few weeks she had grown up and now understood that these were not the times for frivolous games. Our commitment to each other had taken on a serious meaning: to stay alive for each other and to care and help each other with all our might and all our love.

I made it my business to organise food for our family and for the Gutrajchts. For Jews in Warsaw, food had become a problem. There were queues everywhere, and Jews always received an unfriendly reception when they joined them. Mostly this was from the Germans, who kept order and threw the Jews out of the lines. Some Germans were unable to distinguish between Jewish and non-Jewish faces, so they bribed Polish boys with sweets to point out the Jews to them.

In my search for food throughout the city I came to realise how hard Warsaw had been hit by the Germans. I saw that in every street there were houses lying in ruins; the faces of the people had taken on a hardness I had not seen before. Motorcycles carrying uniformed German officials crisscrossed the city. The soft autumn hue of Warsaw had given way to a strange and harsh landscape where Jews tried to make themselves invisible.

As I walked through the city streets, I considered getting out of Warsaw to the countryside where the food shortage was less severe. While I was thinking about this somebody took hold of my arm from behind. Before I had time to be scared, a friendly voice said, *'Serwus przyjacielu'* (Greetings, friend). I turned around and came face to face with my Polish school friend, Zygmunt Zawadzki. He had passed me, he said, but he hadn't been quite sure that it was me. 'Have you got a minute?' he asked earnestly. I had more than a minute, and said so. 'It is not good to stop in the street these days,' he said. 'Let's go somewhere, I want to talk to you.' We entered a building nearby and stood by the staircase. His eyes told me that he was genuinely pleased to have met me. He began by reminding me that we had been in the same group when we were cadets at high school. 'Have you done any military training since then?' he asked. I said no. 'Never mind that, what are you doing now? I know how hard it is now for Jews. Can I be of any help to you in any way?'

I told him how matters were and he immediately gave me the name of a man, Paweł, and his address only half an hour from Warsaw. 'Go there and say that I sent you. Tell them what you told me and stay in touch. I know you are a patriot and that the war is not yet finished. We may need you. Would you be ready to help if we should call on you one day? In the meantime, good luck. Go and get some food, it will be waiting for you.' As we shook hands, he added, 'I know you have a telephone at home. May I ring you sometime? If I say this is Zygmunt, without saying Zawadzki, you'll know I need a favour from you.' He went out first and I followed a few seconds later.

The address he sent me to was correct, although at first I was greeted with suspicion. In my eagerness, I had introduced myself without giving my name, saying only, 'Zygmunt has sent me, he told me you have food for sale.' Paweł denied having any food. His eyes were sharp and I was sure he didn't like me, or Zygmunt for sending me. He asked me who I was.

'David Landau,' I said, 'a school friend of Zygmunt's.'

He was surprised. 'Landau? Are you Jewish?'

I was just as surprised by his question. 'Of course I'm Jewish!'

He moved back and looked in my face. It dawned on me that he was not the first one who had made a point lately of underlining that I didn't look particularly Jewish. 'Well, Mr Landau, if Zygmunt sent you, he had his reasons. Please come inside.'

When I left I carried with me a large suitcase filled with butter, eggs, a chicken, some cheese and other goods which our family had probably not seen since the beginning of the German occupation. I also carried a new interest, the opportunity to become involved, to help in some way to fight the Germans. Paweł gave me three addresses of people living east of Warsaw, saying they would help me when the need arose. 'But if I were you, I would go and see them as soon as you can. Go, and when you meet any of them, say you have spoken with Paweł and Zygmunt. And don't tell strangers that you are a Jew, it will bring you no benefit.'

'Not even those people?' I pointed to the names on the piece of paper in my hand.

He answered reluctantly. 'Is it important that they know you are Jewish? Now I know who you are, and that Zygmunt will vouch for you, leave it at that. If there should ever come a time when it will be necessary for them to know, they will know it. For the moment, don't make a point of it.'

'And if they ask me?'

Paweł looked at me once more closely. 'If they ask you, laugh and say nothing. But I am sure they will not ask you, not with a face like yours.'

Smuggling was a serious offence. For Jews it meant being shot on the spot, without trial. For Poles it meant a long jail sentence or even disappearing into a concentration camp. People had already been sent to concentration camps for smuggling a suitcase like mine. But the risk was outweighed by the health benefits these luxury goods could bring to my family. I was willing to gamble.

Zygmunt telephoned within two days and we went by tram to an outer suburb, Żoliborz. At the tram terminus we turned into a side street and Zygmunt pointed to a building. 'Take notice of that place. If you should ever be in trouble and need an address quickly, go up there. On the first floor there is only one door with a bell. Don't ring it. Knock on it four times and wait. You may have to repeat the knocking a few times, but don't change the knock. And now let us go in here.'

We had been standing in front of a small shoe shop. Inside, Zygmunt asked for somebody named Heniek. The lady pointed to the back of the shop. A middle-aged man was obviously waiting for us. Zygmunt presented me to Heniek and excused himself, saying he had to attend to some important matter. I could see that Heniek was expecting the excuse.

He came right to the point. 'I know who you are and I know your father's tannery. It is still closed, I know. From now on you will be known as Janek, not David. Your old friends may still call you that if they like, but to me, Zygmunt and Paweł, and whoever else you meet through us, you will be Janek.

'Yes, Heniek.' I grinned.

'You learn fast, which is good. Let's hope you don't forget fast as well.'

I assured him of my willingness to join one of the partisan groups. He, in turn, gave me the name of a young woman, Krystyna. She was most helpful in finding peasant farmers who would sell me eggs, meat and dry food. Whenever the need arose, she also organised places for me to stay overnight.

I waited for a few weeks then finally contacted Zygmunt, who told me that they had hoped to send me to the Puszcza Białowieska ('The Dense Forest'), but this had failed.

Years later I discovered that I had been speaking not to Heniek, but to a man also known as Bystry. His real name was Henryk Iwański, and he helped the Jewish people in a vital way: he was an Underground co-ordinator for fledgling partisan groups. I had been one of the first to meet him in this capacity. He was a great aid, one of the greatest, to our Jewish Armed Union, the ŻZW, as well as a passionate supporter of the Jews in general. Unfortunately, he paid very dearly for this support. His brother and son lost their lives while fighting alongside the Jews in the ghetto.

I also discovered why I had not been sent to Puszcza Baiłowieska. It was to protect me from anti-Semitic elements there; the same ones that later called themselves 'Narodowe Siły Zbrojne', or NSZ. These elements had penetrated 'The Dense Forest' and were trying to eliminate Jews from the partisan movement.

5

A hard winter, 1939

DURING the first months of the German occupation, the Jews of Poland, like European Jews for centuries past, had hoped to wait out this new wave of anti-Semitism.

The first winter of the war was long and brutal. At the end of November, the season was in full force. The snow had already hardened and the temperature was always below freezing. The winter was particularly hard on the Jews in that part of Poland which Hitler had decided to annex to Germany. In Berlin, an elaborate plan had been made to deport some of the Polish population from the annexed land in order to create *'Lebensraum'* (living space) to settle Germans. This area had been renamed Wartegau. The Polish population was to be resettled in the part which had been named *Generalgouvernement*, 'General Government'. As for the Jews of Wartegau, discussions were going on about creating a Jewish reservation near Lublin, in the General Government. Wartegau was to be made *Judenrein*, cleansed of Jews, as quickly as possible.

This issue was the subject of a discussion between my father and one of my friends, Salek, which I vividly remember. Three of my Jewish friends had come over to stay with us one night. They were members of the right-wing Zionist youth movement, Betar, which before the war had maintained reasonably good relations with the Polish military. Through various 'whispering channels', my friends had learned about the arrest of a Polish officer who had lived for some weeks in Warsaw disguised as a civilian, in order to escape arrest by the Germans. My friends had connections with this officer and feared that they might be arrested too. They had been warned not to sleep at home for a few nights, until any possible pursuit had died down.

I had heard about their predicament earlier in the day and wanted to ask Father whether they could stay at our apartment. I couldn't find him, so I decided on my own authority to let my friends stay, stipulating only that they pretend, for my mother's sake, to be staying somewhere else in the building. Once she had retired to bed, which she did very early, we could stop the pretence.

The closest of these friends was Meir, Luba's brother and my childhood friend. He always accompanied Luba on her daily visits to our house when she came to prepare our meals. He did this in order to escort her home afterwards, before the curfew started. On this particular evening, Luba understood that she would have to return home on her own.

The other friends were Salek Geller and Sevek Bekerman, both brilliant boys. Salek was politically orientated and well informed. He had been the first to say, before the war had even started, that the fight with Germany would be a matter of life or death. Under the guidance of two older leaders of the Zionist Revisionist Organisation, the patron organisation of Betar, he was establishing an Underground military organisation of Jewish youth, to be guided by ex-officers of the Polish Army, both Jewish and non-Jewish. Meir had invited me to join the organisation but I had refused, believing I would never be considered an equal to others in Salek's plans.

Father came home minutes before the curfew started, looking pleased with himself. The people he had been working with had managed to get a considerable quantity of high-grade leather out through the bakery. He was even more pleased because the leather had been delivered and paid for in gold.

He was surprised to find that we had guests for the evening meal but, when he heard that my friends would be sleeping elsewhere in the building, he relaxed. Mother hardly ate at all. She took her pain-killing drops and retired immediately after the meal.

Later we sat in the lounge room. The oven had been well tended and was radiating a comforting warmth. A stranger would have taken us as armchair politicians talking about the theoretical problems of other people in far-off places. Father joined in after he had finished his work. He had known my friends since our childhood and he had the gift of understanding our way of thinking without interfering or belittling our inexperience. When the discussion turned to the danger in which we Jews were now living, whether we acted legally or illegally, my father said, 'It would be impossible for Jews to survive if we obeyed the German orders and restrictions. If we have to die in the end, we might as well make ourselves as comfortable as possible in the meantime.'

Salek Geller reacted to this with restrained anger. 'Mr Landau,' he said, 'you talk about *making ourselves comfortable* as if you don't believe the Germans are capable of carrying out their threats to exterminate us. Well, I have better reasons than you to believe that one day Hitler will consider the elimination of all Jews a necessity. I have said it before and I say it now, our fight with the Germans is one of life or death. What we see now is just the beginning.'

My father remained calm in the face of this rebuke. 'You have got me wrong. Just like you, I believe that the Germans would not hesitate to get rid of us one way or another. I have not had my eyes or my brain shut to anything that has happened to Jews under Hitler since 1933. But as a businessman I have learned something about the limits of production. Do you, my friend, realise that it would take at least three-quarters of the entire German Army to round up the Jews everywhere? And do you believe that the Jews are Germany's main priority, now that it is at war with such world powers as the British Empire and France?

'I believe the only thing the Germans are interested in is to bring us to our knees financially, so that then when they offer us bread and water to work for their war industry, we will be glad to do so. Killing all of us Jews is something only a sick imagination would bother to conjure up.

'I have always been willing to consider your proposition that Germany might kill us all, and not only theoretically but as a real possibility. But as a real possibility I cannot see it happening. It is clear to me that you are debating this proposition not from reason but from a religious position, and I prefer never to debate with people who base their arguments on belief.'

Salek looked puzzled.

My father continued. 'Religion doesn't have to be about God. Your religion is that the Germans are willing to put their anti-Semitism before everything, even success in the war. But this is irrational, only a madman would do that. And as that is the basis of your argument then we have nothing more to say.'

With this Father excused himself and left us alone to our deliberations. We sat around for a long time after he had left, debating the situation in our own way. I remained less certain than my father.

I had become a smuggler. My business was to act as a private postal exchange, charging twenty American dollars for a two-way letter exchange across the German–USSR border. It was more rewarding to smuggle in provisions from the Russian side, but this had led to trouble.

A Russian guard had stopped me near the border in a restricted part of the forest. Luckily, I had no food with me. He asked where I was going. I knew from experience to point in the opposite direction from the one I planned to take, as the Russians usually sent people back in the direction they had come. I pointed eastwards. He considered this with suspicion, then asked where I had come from. From the west, I said, pointing to Germany. He hesitated, then let me go east, smiling oddly. To this day I don't know if the smile was meant as a sign of friendship or to show that he understood the game of smuggling and believed he had outsmarted me.

After leaving him, I had to walk many kilometres out of my way before retracing my steps and meeting the peasant who was to guide me across the border.

I decided that smuggling in winter was too dangerous. Snow betrays everybody and everything that passes over it, and the Russians had started to take harsh measures against those who violated their border. The Germans, too, were now looking for smugglers, especially Jewish ones.

I felt relieved when I was on the German side and reached a place named Treblinka. It was a small rail-line established before the war by the Polish Government together with the Warsaw district authorities. The line had been built to serve a newly opened gravel quarry. I stayed overnight with a Polish peasant around two kilometres from Treblinka.

On my return to Warsaw I was greeted by my brother Mietek, who had been back home for just four days. We embraced and looked each other over before I asked him about Mother.

'Oh, David, you have no idea how glad I am to have come home in time. Mother collapsed on the afternoon I returned. We called the doctor and he confined her to her bed. She asked to be put up in the last room. She is there now.'

When I saw her I was struck with how she had changed in the six days I had been away. She looked at me without moving, her head on the pillow and tears running down her face. I promised her that I wouldn't go away again, that I would stay with her always, if she wanted.

'No, don't do that,' she said. 'Go about your work, only don't stay away so long. If only Eliezer, too, would now come back.'

Her voice trailed away. I sat at the foot of her bed and she took my hand the way she had done when I returned the first time. She spoke quietly, calmly and seriously. 'I am glad we brought you up to stand on your own feet. You will have to do without me, and you'll manage, but I would be so very glad if Eliezer would come home in time. I haven't very much left in life now, except to wait for him.' I walked out of the room like a mourner.

Eliezer returned the next day. My father went into Mother's bedroom and in a few minutes she came out in her dressing gown, frail and emaciated, but with the light of joy in her eyes. We had warned Eliezer how sick Mother was. She held onto him, her oldest son, with all her strength, crying silently. Finally, after a considerable time, we took her, totally exhausted, back to bed.

Luba had begun to prepare lunch when there was a sharp knock on the door. Before we could open it, three Germans entered. Two were in officer's uniform. The third, a civilian, spoke first. 'Landau, isn't it?' he barked. The officers stared at Eliezer and we were sure it had something to do with his homecoming. 'Your furniture,' continued the civilian, 'where is it?'

'Through there, in the other rooms,' said Father.

They entered the lounge room and examined the paintings on the wall. The civilian looked at the officers, who nodded in agreement. He turned to Eliezer. 'Take the paintings down,' he ordered, 'and be careful how you do it!' He didn't have to repeat the order.

'Bring the paintings to me,' said one of the officers. 'One at a time.'

The civilian went into the dining room, followed by the three of us. We left the officers alone in the lounge, examining the paintings.

There was a lot of furniture in this room, which Mother had kept under cover as the dining room had not been used since the beginning of the war. The civilian grabbed at the white covers, threw them aside, and told us, 'The furniture will come down. All of it!'

'The covers will be needed too,' he added, 'as the furniture is not going to a synagogue but to the home of a German officer. So, one of you, fold the covers.'

Next he walked into the main bedroom. Since Mother had moved to the back room, the bedroom had not been used. Father had been sleeping in the lounge room, on a sofa which opened up as a bed. The man murmured something under his breath then turned to us and commanded, 'The bed will come too,' he walked on, then stopped and added, 'with the bedding.'

So far, he had not spoken a single sentence which was not an order.

All day long, we carried the furniture downstairs and loaded it onto the waiting trucks, supervised by the three new owners of our property. When all was done, the officer who had asked to examine the paintings turned to our father and said with a serious face, 'For a Polish Jew you have unusually good taste. But Jews no longer need beautiful things. Comfort yourself with the thought that your paintings and all this furniture are going to a person who deserves nice things. A person with good German taste.'

As if to finish the matter properly he pulled a piece of paper from his sleeve, handed it to my father and said in the same calm way, 'When the war is over, present this paper to the German Treasury and they will compensate you for the materials we have commandeered for war use.'

We went back upstairs shaking with rage and fear. Luba was sitting in the empty lounge room on a kitchen chair, which had obviously not been good enough for German taste. Her face was chalk white, she was biting her fingernails and her eyes were wide open and dry. I felt that we had become strangers in our own home and that nothing belonged to us anymore. Eliezer and Mietek stood together at the entrance to the dining room, both still catching their breath.

Suddenly Mietek burst out laughing. 'I think this is the first time I have seen what our furniture really looked like,' he said. 'While

I was in the army camp, all I could recall was the shape of those damned white covers.'

His comment broke the tension and we all started to laugh. It lasted only a few seconds, but long enough for Father to regain his composure.

'If it were only a question of money,' he said, 'we could buy all the new furniture we need from the proceedings of yesterday's leather sales. But I believe that German officer was right. For the moment, we Jews don't need luxurious furniture and expensive paintings on our walls. What we need is what we already have, each other. As long as we have that, we haven't lost much.'

The real shock of what had happened occurred hours later. The threat to our security as a family had been too great for us to fully understand while the German robbers were in the house. From the moment they opened the door until hours after they had gone we felt their presence overwhelming us. The naked walls and the empty rooms were of secondary consideration while the personal shock was working within us physically. When that side of the drama began to subside, our helplessness started to surface.

The security we had felt in the house since our birth was gone, as though security depended on covered walls. We saw that the paintings and furniture had hidden from us a truth which was now revealed, that we had no right to call anything our own.

We were sitting in the kitchen discussing how to tell our mother what had happened, when the door of her room opened. We all stood up, each unconsciously trying to prevent her from noticing the disaster. But to our surprise, and before we had worked out how to tell her, she asked simply, 'Have they gone already?'

She took note of the empty rooms and naked walls, but showed no emotion. Father embraced her. She pushed him away and looked us all over. 'They have not hurt any of you, have they?' From some unknown well Mother had drawn up strength and calmness. We had been afraid of what the shock might do to her, yet there she was, cool and collected, considering the whole matter as nothing more than a child's fall.

After that, she seemed to recover a little. Our sense of family grew much stronger. We felt a heightened awareness of the unity we represented.

As soon as the weather began to improve I went to Bartosze to get food for my family, as it was cheaper there than in the Jewish sector. One of the leaders of the Underground had asked me to see if I could also get food for the members of the ŻZW and I had agreed. Transport was not a problem and my trip was successful.

My second trip to Bartosze nearly cost me my life, and could have endangered the Polish family I stayed with. It was in the spring of 1940.

In the small settlement of Bartosze five peasant families lived together in a farming colony. They knew me well; I bought their farm produce and delivered supplies to them from Warsaw. We had become friends who understood and trusted each other. On this trip I had to wait for the delivery of some produce and so was invited to stay the night.

The following morning we noticed some Germans approaching the colony. We could not let them find me there, so with the family's help I climbed into the loft, crouched in the far corner and waited.

At first, everything appeared to be going well down below. I heard questions being put in German and then translated by somebody into Polish.

'Has anybody slept here overnight who does not belong to this household?'

'Nobody.'

'Has anybody been here yesterday during the day?'

'Somebody passed on the road while I was in the paddock, but I cannot say if they went into somebody's house or not.'

'How many were there?'

'One person, as far as I could see. From where I was I could not tell if it was a man or a woman, because of the heavy winter clothing and the dimness of the day.'

'Without going outside could you show us through the window how far you were in the paddock?'

There was a short pause and then, 'I was near the tree where the two motorcycles are now. More to the left.'

'You are sure you didn't see any other strangers around here yesterday?'

'I am absolutely sure.'

'And you have nobody in the house who does not belong here?'

'You are welcome to search for yourself.'

'We will. But if you lied and we find anybody here who does not belong in the house, we will take you outside and shoot you. If you tell us the truth we will spare you. So I ask you again, is there anybody in the house who is not a member of your family?'

'No.'

And then I heard the order. 'Two of you, see the opening to the loft? The lid is not straight. Get up there and check thoroughly. If you find anybody hiding in the loft, don't shoot. Bring them down here, we may need their information.'

I realised the game was up if I could not get out through the thatch roof. At the same time I was afraid that the noise of moving the straw might be heard.

Downstairs they were shifting furniture so the Germans could climb into the loft. I took advantage of the noise they were making to push myself deeper into the thatch. I wondered if somebody would look up and see me. Outside the thatch, at the end of the roof, I found a stork nest large enough to hide in. The German put his head through the thatch but did not want to walk on the insecure roof, so he could not see me. From my hiding place I watched, frozen, as the Germans went into the next house then, finally, returned to their motorcycles and left.

When I came down, my hosts wanted to know how I had managed to disappear. They were sure I would be caught but they had been committed to the lie that there was no stranger in the house. The head of the family had realised that any change to the story would only bring harm, so he let fate take its course. My hosts said that the storks only lived there in summer and that they had left their vacant house for me. We laughed.

'The pair has been coming back to the same place for a number of years. We have named them Kazik and Wanda. Kazik after King Kazimierz the Great and Wanda as the soul of the Legendary Polish Princess Wanda, the one about whom the legend says, Wanda lies in Polish soil because she didn't want the Germans to be there ever.'

After that experience I decided to stop travelling outside Warsaw for provisions.

6

The farm

THE winter gave way to warmer, longer days while we lived on, 'clinging to an ice float', as the saying goes.

I went to see Sevek Bekerman, who told me about the British landing in Norway and their defeat by the Germans. But it was all just talk and I wanted action. It was the same at Salek Geller's place. 'We must prepare for a fight of life and death,' he said. Talk, talk, talk.

In the meantime, Jews were fleeing to Warsaw from Łódź. The Germans had decided to let the Jews stay in Łódź, which had been renamed Litzmannstadt. But they were building a barbed-wire fence around part of the poorest area of the city, and by the end of April all Jews would have to move there or leave Łódź. Hundreds of Jews had been shot in night raids because they had not moved out of their apartments in time.

Surely, we argued, things would never get this bad in Warsaw. Even in wartime, Jews would always be safer here, because Warsaw, though occupied, was still open to the eyes of the world. The Germans might restrict our rights, but the situation would still be better here than in the provinces. But this did not alter the chaotic routine which had become part of our daily existence.

Eliezer and Mietek had found interests outside the home. Father was busy with his business or with retrieving the stock from the tannery and making a fortune from it. He had guaranteed work for at least another year to two, even if it were, technically, illegal. It seemed I was the only one who lived without a plan. I seldom made plans even for one day ahead and I was not happy about this. Something had to change.

One of our tenants, a carpenter, came up to our apartment one evening to offer us his advice and assistance. His son had been working with a German firm which was about to take on more workers. The work was on a farm named Agryl, outside Warsaw. Agryl had been made the supplier of primary products to the German Air Force in Warsaw. Its manager was a low-ranking SS soldier who had turned the place into his own semi-private gold mine. For five hundred złotys, the carpenter told my father, I could be engaged at Agryl. The work would not be strenuous and, as the carpenter considered me capable of dealing with people, he thought I might be able to obtain at least a small share of the manager's profits.

The next morning, the carpenter's son took me with him to Agryl and presented me to the manager, whose name I have forgotten. He introduced me with the strange words, 'He is one of our kind. I can vouch for him.'

The manager's reply was just as strange. 'You vouch for him with your head,' he said, and the carpenter's son said, 'I know.'

The manager sent him off to work and took me into his primitive farm office. He sat down behind a simple table and told me that I was allowed to sit down, as I had not yet been engaged. He was going to interview me first and wanted me to feel comfortable. He assured me that if I should get the job, I would be treated like a Jew, but not yet. I sat down on the only other chair in the room.

He began by telling me about himself. 'I am a German and you are an *Ost Jude*, a Jew from the east. I can therefore afford to put my cards before you. If you should think of blackmailing me after you have heard what I have to say, or betraying me, you had better think again because I am an SS soldier and you are a stinking *Ost*

Jude, even if you wash yourself every day with cologne and powder yourself with baby powder.

'Well then. I am a thief by profession. I have been in jail for gross larceny, if you know what that is. I am not ashamed to tell you because your friend has given me his word that you also are a professional thief.

'I do not pay any Jew who works here any wages. If you want to earn wages here you will have to work for it on the private side of my business. Understood?'

I assured him it was all very clear. 'Good,' he said, 'then you can start work as a farm hand. But before I kick your ass out of this office to make you do some useful chores, let me give you some of the rules I have laid down to keep you Jews on the straight and narrow. First of all, now that you have been engaged by me, get your ass off that chair!'

I jumped up. 'What is your name?' I told him that it was David. 'A good name for a Jew. I have rules here. You are not allowed to eat anything. Not when I see it. You are not allowed to cook any vegetables from the place unless I turn a blind eye to it. Clear?'

'Yes, sir.'

'We milk a hundred and fifty cows here with the peasant women's help. Have you ever milked cows?'

'No, sir. But I am a quick learner.'

'We will find the appropriate work for you. Now, if I don't see you taking a gulp of milk, you are lucky and will get away with it. But if you think the same goes for cream, I warn you right now, don't make such a dangerous mistake! Jewish stomachs are not good enough for cream.'

My mind raced to make sense of this new world I was joining.

'You will probably be working with the chickens in the other yard. We have over a thousand chickens here. They are for the German Air Force, not for you. However, if a chicken becomes sick or breaks a leg or a wing, I have decided that you Jews are permitted to cook it and eat it. So you see, I am a generous man.

'It is forbidden to mistreat the chickens, but your friends have remarkably good eyes and always seem to find a bird with a broken leg or wing. But, I repeat, don't go and break the limb of a chicken, it is forbidden and punishable. Just keep your eyes open and you'll probably find one from time to time. The only thing you'll get from me is some bread and soup, which you may consider your payment, if you like.'

The speech continued. 'To earn money for yourself, you will have to first earn money for me. From the money I'll earn through employing you privately, I may in the future pay you or not pay you. It will depend on how good you are.'

'Yes, sir. I will make sure I do my best for you.'

'You mean you will make sure you do the best for yourself. I don't believe people are generous enough to work for others. Jews have never worked for anybody but themselves. I am not stupid enough to work for the glory of the Third Reich unless there's something in it for me. We always work for ourselves, always. My professional honour as a thief would be insulted otherwise. So be careful. Never try to cheat me with words. Be as honest as the honour among thieves requires. I'll let you steal within reason from whatever there is to be stolen, and in exchange you'll bring me back what I tell you to bring back. I'll let your friend explain the technical side of how this will be organised. I will take no part in the stealing or the transport of any item until the end of the transaction. Should you ever be caught, you will say you have been stealing for yourself. Is that understood?'

What was there to misunderstand?

'You will keep your mouth shut. Not all the Jews employed at Agryl are employed by me. They are happy to work for Agryl without pay for the privilege of being of service to the Third Reich and not being beaten too often. I give them an additional privilege of letting them steal some vegetables, making out that I don't see it. So you see, I am basically a good man.'

Of course. Here was a thief who was a good man. More

importantly to me, he was an excellent SS man. He was unproductive and therefore undermining the German war effort, and I wished that there were more like him.

'Now, to help you in your work, you will be issued with a special permit which will allow you to move about freely. This is a great privilege given to you by Agryl for the benefit of your work here. We deliver our produce to the air force in Warsaw every day. Sometimes we make more than one delivery. I always accompany the cart to the air force depot, to make sure you Jews don't help yourselves to the goods reserved for the fighting forces of our glorious Führer. Tomorrow you will come with me on a delivery. Your friend will tell you what you will need for the trip. Is that clear?'

'Absolutely clear, sir.'

'Just one more thing. Your Polish compatriots have their lousy cows running free just outside our farm. If any of these cows should chance to cross over into our territory, what will you do?'

The question was sudden and something told me that I was being examined. I was supposed to be a knowledgeable thief, so replied, 'I would make sure it never returned from whence it came.'

'Good. If you were not a Jew, we could really start something big. It's a pity you are not a German, right?'

'Very true, sir.'

'Now go and make yourself useful for the rest of the day and ask your friend to give you instructions for tomorrow.'

The instructions my friend gave me were clear and precise. Among my many tasks I was to bring eggs, some butter and other things 'designated for the air force' and put them in the manager's office. The next day, they would be delivered as a separate parcel to the officer-in-charge, as a bribe. The main air force delivery would be considerably less than that shown on the official papers.

The work at Agryl turned out to be educational and profitable. We had a very good supply of provisions for ourselves and for our families. It was a shame the arrangement lasted only six weeks.

The private business of this SS man was too successful. He was told that Agryl was to be audited and he was asked to prepare the documents for it. His first action was to liquidate his private undertaking. As a result, I lost my job along with others, including our neighbour who had been the manager of the private side of the business. But I couldn't complain. It was well worth the five hundred złotys we had paid and I had become an accomplished thief, at least as far as my boss was concerned.

At the beginning of summer, 1940, I was back at square one, with no work, no income and no real prospects. Mother's condition had worsened and Luba was helping run the household more than ever. The weeks I had been with Agryl had taught me that food and American dollars were the best businesses for a survivor to be in, though they also carried the greatest risks. I had to weigh up each job on its merits and decide whether the risk outweighed the return.

I had been the food provider for our household and for the Gutrajchts even before Agryl. Now I had to carry on independently. Open black markets in primary products were working in different parts of Warsaw. The German authorities looked the other way where Poles were concerned. Germans were making the greatest profits anyway. Food on the black market that did not come from Polish small holdings originated from the confiscated stock of Jewish businesses that were now owned by Germans, as well as from army stock. Other goods stolen by the Germans came from their own government for their private benefit.

For Jews, the black market was a triple danger. The Polish underworld frequently robbed Jewish traders of their goods and money, knowing that nobody would defend them. Robbery was common, often accompanied by force. However, the greatest danger came from the Germans.

I began to visit the various markets in Warsaw in the company of my Polish friends. We bought together and nobody asked us any questions. When I became known to the main traders, who brought their goods from the surrounding townships, I branched out on my own. I quickly gained the confidence of some important traders and established a less risky way of dealing in primary produce. The transactions were made before the purchased goods even came to Warsaw. I began to travel once more, but now without smuggling. I paid for the goods in cash in the villages and smaller townships, then the sellers would make a single delivery to an address in Warsaw. It suited the sellers as much as it suited me.

One such purchase, in Żelechów, was for five hundred killed and dressed chickens. By that time I had learned to make deals with retail sellers. The currency I requested was vodka (known in the trade as '*bimber*') or dollars. Dollars came in two qualities, 'soft' and 'hard', paper or gold. One seldom mentioned the word 'dollar', referring mostly to 'soft ones' or 'hard ones'.

I paid for the chickens in advance, the greater part in *bimber* and the rest in German marks and 'soft ones'. The goods were delivered as agreed and each of my clients received their purchases. I collected soft and hard currency, *bimber*, German marks and other stock. By the end of the transaction we had butter and eggs for ourselves, beef, chicken and veal in the ice boxes, dry food for months, and a nice profit as well.

The black market, Mother's sickness and other matters had forced me to give up plans of becoming an active member of the Underground, but only for the moment. I could have had financial help from Father but never liked to ask for it. All my life I tried to be independent. Also, smuggling food to the Jewish sector was the only way to avoid hunger.

However, in one day two things happened which revived my intention to volunteer for Underground work. Salek Geller brought us the information that in France, which had been occupied by the Germans for only a few weeks, the Resistance was already at work. The BBC had begun to transmit coded messages to the French Resistance and had broadcast the news that a military train had been derailed somewhere in France. It also announced the death of the Betar leader, Vladimir Jabotinsky, at the age of sixty. Salek gave me some leaflets announcing this death, and wondered if I might paste them up (illegally) in my district. Of course I was not going to refuse such a request.

I finished this job quickly and without incident. On returning home, I found an ambulance outside our building and two orderlies carrying Mother downstairs on a stretcher, followed by Father, Mietek and Luba. When the ambulance had gone, we returned solemnly to our apartment. I didn't even ask what had happened. I had seen that Mother was alive, but only just.

The incident shook me out of my trance of buying and selling, wheeling and dealing. I decided that I had to escape from the hypnotic world of food and dollars. Fortunately, there was no longer any need for my economic contributions. Father had converted his tannery stock, literally, into gold, which he kept, of all places, in the attic. We considered it to be the safest hiding place. The attic floor was made up of rows of grooved boards which had never been nailed down. Father started to hide the bars under these boards, spacing them in rows to avoid pressing too heavily on the ceiling below. By the time the attic was half full it contained a few thousand small gold bars, each one stamped and verified by the prewar Polish mint or some other authorised body. Gold, *bimber* and dollars were considered the three best financial securities at the time and we had at least two of them.

Mother was in hospital for four days. She begged us to take her home. 'I don't want to die in hospital,' she said. 'I want to die in my own bed.' We did not lie to her about her condition, she was too intelligent for that. The next day we brought her home. A few days later she died.

It was no longer possible to give her a full traditional funeral, which even non-religious Jews observed. The hearse came, we wrapped Mother in a white sheet and carried her downstairs ourselves. The hearse attendant helped us place her in the coffin.

We arranged with the undertakers to bury Mother and we followed the hearse to the graveyard. Our mother was buried in a private ceremony. Later, we smuggled in a simple headstone with her name carved on it. We could not arrange to bury her in the family mausoleum.

After our mother's death, family ties began to loosen. A stranger would have thought us good tenants living under one roof. We had all grown and gone our separate ways. Father was still looking after the two youngest ones but we each had our own interests.

Around the time of the Jewish High Holidays, in September 1940, rumours began to circulate that the Germans had decided to create a ghetto in Warsaw like the one in Litzmannstadt. Some people denied this. They said that a body called the Committee of the Jews, set up by the Germans when they entered Warsaw a year earlier, had been told that no such ghetto would be created. But this was generally considered to be wishful thinking. Rumours were rife and the situation was tense.

Some of the Poles were indifferent to the rumours, as if the Jewish situation had no part in their lives. Some, who had kept up contact with Jews over the last year, began to separate themselves from us. Others began to make plans with us about what to do if the rumours were true.

During this uncertain time, I visited Luba and her family daily. On my way to her apartment one day, two German soldiers asked me in fluent Yiddish, 'Are you a Jew?'

I turned in astonishment and looked at them, feeling sure I had misheard. They stared back. 'I asked you if you are a Jew?' one of them repeated, while the other jerked his head and said in the same Yiddish dialect, 'Come here.'

Even if I had been a Pole, I could not have mistaken the jerk of his head for anything other than an order to move closer. I walked over and the conversation continued in Yiddish.

'Have you any "soft" or "hard" ones?'

'I don't deal in such things. It is illegal.'

'We know that it is illegal, but we can see from your clothes that you are not living like the stupid ones. Don't be afraid, we are not interested in finding criminals, we are looking for "hard" and "soft" ones.'

'I told you, I don't do anything that is illegal. Besides, I must apologise for my Yiddish which is not as good as yours. In our home we speak Polish.'

'We come from Bałuty. Have you heard of it? It's the former Jewish district in Łódź, where the ghetto is now. A few Poles and Germans used to live there too, before the war, including us. We grew up surrounded by Jews and all our friends were Jewish. If Bałuty wasn't sealed off now, we would have bought the money we need from our friends there. But with the ghetto and its barbed wire, it's impossible.'

'Why are you dressed in German uniforms?'

'Because although we speak Yiddish like the Jews, we have *goyishe* heads and calculated that, as we are not circumcised, we could use our knowledge of Yiddish to pretend that we were *Volksdeutsche*, or Polish Germans. We thought it would give us an easy life, but two weeks later we were drafted into the German Army. We are not trusted completely and so we have been sent here for a special course, before being sent to the front. Now that you know all this, can you find us some money? We will buy whatever you can bring. Marks mean nothing to us. We are from Bałuty and can help ourselves to German goods whenever we like. We will buy from you at a premium and can pay you in marks, if you prefer. We have enough money to buy big.'

I deliberated before answering. 'Wait here by the gate. Whether I can find what you want or not, you have my word that I will be back within ten minutes.'

I ran to Luba's house and sought out David Korn, a boyfriend of Luba's older sister, Helena. David dealt in foreign currency. When I told him my story and asked if he had any dollars he looked at me with astonishment. 'Have you gone mad? Germans who speak Yiddish are the most dangerous of them all. They are used as spies. If you bring them even a single dollar you'll never come back alive.'

I did not agree with him, although I feared he might be right. In the end I convinced him to act against his better judgement. He gave me ten dollars, saying, 'You are going to your own bitter end, but I don't want you to live with the thought that I didn't want to help you.'

The soldiers were disappointed that it was such a small amount, but paid up as agreed, including the premium. They promised to come back the next day at the same time.

David Korn decided to play it both ways. He gave me fifty dollars in small bills and told me to offer the soldiers only twenty dollars initially. If they bought the twenty without any questions, I was then to offer the rest. I got to the rendezvous early and watched the soldiers as they approached. They walked cautiously, making sure they were not observed before entering the courtyard in which we had arranged to meet. I offered them the whole fifty dollars, saying I had collected it from two friends. They quickly checked out the notes, paid for them and arranged to meet me the next day.

I made sure every day that the soldiers were alone. They, too, checked that nobody was watching us. They never asked where I came from or for any other information. They bought over two thousand dollars from me in less than a week.

I waited for them one day as we had arranged, but they didn't show up. I did not see anybody snooping around or anything suspicious. I waited at the same place each day for several days, but the strange pair never returned.

7

A man called Guzik

LITTLE has been written about the Jewish people who were officially exempt from the virulent anti-Jewish laws of the Third Reich. Jews who held citizenship of neutral countries were protected by law and through the representatives of the country of their citizenship.

There were quite a number of these people, but perhaps the most interesting of all was Guzik, a Polish Jew. He was a Swiss citizen who worked for the American Joint Distribution Committee, better known throughout the Jewish world simply as Joint. Still active today, Joint provides financial help to Jewish individuals and institutions around the world. Its main beneficiary before the war had been Poland, and Guzik had been the director of Polish operations for Joint, based in Warsaw. He was a well educated and respected man of small stature but high ideals. The way he performed his work won him recognition and respect from all shades of Jewish society, and his name opened many doors.

Before the war it had been a simple matter for Joint to transfer American dollars to Polish banks. But by the late 1930s Joint had become reluctant to transfer money to Germany because of its anti-Semitic laws and, by 1939, long before Hitler had declared war on the USA, the transfer of American-Jewish money into German-occupied countries had completely dried up. The offices of Joint in occupied Poland were closed for lack of funds.

It was at that time that the respect in which Guzik was held came into its own. He approached wealthy Polish Jews to raise funds for the poorer Jews. In return he gave his personal assurance that any money handed over to him for this work would be repaid in full by Joint after the war, and adjusted for inflation. People trusted him, receiving for their fortunes only an official receipt of Joint, signed by Mr Guzik.

Two days before the Jewish New Year, 5701, which fell in September 1940, Mr Guzik came to visit my father. The Landau family had been one of the donors to the Joint annual appeal for many years. Now he came not for a donation but for a loan on behalf of Joint, to be repaid in American dollars after the war. We knew what the situation was like for the majority of Jews in Warsaw, now that the Germans had confiscated our means of making a living and closed our bank accounts. Our family had managed to live in reasonable comfort for a year, but only through enterprises that the Germans would have considered illegal.

Guzik told us about the severe conditions of the other Jewish communities in German-occupied Poland, particularly the Jews interned in the ghetto in Łódź , where Joint was no longer allowed to operate. He told us of the impoverished state of Jewish institutions, which carried on their work illegally under the threat of death. I heard for the first time that in Warsaw nearly twenty illegal Jewish religious schools were operating, teaching Jewish subjects and giving the children a warm meal every day.

He told us about the thousands of Jews who had fled the Gestapo at the beginning of the war or immediately after the German occupation. They had come to Warsaw but had no hope of establishing themselves in business and had been forced for nearly a year to live totally on charity. 'The charity pot is shrinking and the number of needy is growing,' Guzik told my father.

It was years before I realised how sensitive Guzik had been to the feelings of his fellow man. He smiled as he said to my father, 'I know that you, thank God, have not yet registered among the new clients of Joint. Unfortunately, many of our former large donors have had to turn to us for help. I feel not only pain but also silent shame that I cannot reward them even ten percent of their former generosity.

'It is hard for anyone to say what the financial standing is of any Jew today. I do not know where you stand, Mr Landau, and I have come to find out. I know you recently suffered a personal loss and I feel your grief. But from where I see our fate under Hitler, I only pray that, by the New Year, we do not all envy the dead. But now let me ask you quite openly, Mr Landau, can I count on your help?'

I was touched by the simplicity of his question. My father replied that he was still able to help.

Guzik's face lit up. 'Mr Landau, may you enjoy your good fortune from now on, if only because of the joy which you have just given me. How much are you able to offer us?'

As if it were the simplest thing in the world, my father asked, 'Can I consider your signature acknowledging receipt as the equivalent of a cash deposit in an American bank?'

Without the slightest hesitation, Guzik replied, 'Yes, but such deposits will only be open to draw upon after the war.'

My father offered his 'deposit'. 'Let us open the account in the Joint Bank with two hundred and fifty grams of gold. My son Eliezer will make delivery of the deposit to you sometime tomorrow. I am not able to offer you dollars, as the few I have are needed for living expenses, but if gold is good, I may make additional deposits at a later stage.'

Between 1940 and the end of 1942 we obtained a number of receipts signed by Guzik. Unfortunately they were lost during the ghetto Uprising.

Guzik borrowed and gave away probably millions of dollars over the years on behalf of Joint, until he was forced to stop. He used his freedom of movement to bring the limited help that was still possible to the tormented Jewish communities of occupied Poland, often endangering not only his freedom but also his life.

Regrettably, he was killed in an air catastrophe soon after the war ended.

All nasty things were ordered for us on the High Holy Days. On the sacred day of Yom Kippur, 12 October 1940, the Germans, having previously denied the rumours, proclaimed that a separate area in Warsaw was to be handed over to the Jewish community 'as a gift'. The area, officially named *Juden Viertel*, or Jewish Quarter, was soon to be known, simply, as the ghetto. To distinguish it from the rest of the city it was intended that it would be surrounded by an eighteen-kilometre long brick wall.

By the end of October all Jews in Warsaw had to be residing inside this area. Those moving into it were forbidden to bring furniture or other possessions from their old homes. All they could carry were small bundles of bedding and clothing.

Non-Jews in the ghetto had to be out by the same date. They were allowed to take all their furniture and possessions, although it proved impossible to organise the necessary transport in time. As a result, the deadline for the transfer of populations was postponed until 15 November, by which time one hundred and ten thousand Poles had left the ghetto and one hundred and thirty-eight thousand Jews had entered it.

Our building, 17 Muranowska Street, stood near the north-eastern border of the ghetto. Muranowska Street and Plac Muranowski (Muranowski Square) were fated to play an historic part in the ghetto Uprising, but this was in the future, a future which few could foresee.

When the rumours about the ghetto started I recall the long conversations about how we could transport all the gold bars that Father had stored in the attic, if we had to move into the ghetto. That is why, when the rumours became official, we were relieved to find that our building was already inside the designated area.

With their usual perfidiousness, the German authorities had promised that the ghetto would remain open to what was now called the Aryan, Christian side of Warsaw. But even before 15 November, permits had been introduced, issued by the Jewish ghetto authorities, and guards had been posted at the ghetto entrances.

The permits were not difficult to obtain and most of them were group permits, allowing a designated number of people to work outside the ghetto. I joined one of these working groups. As we left, the guards would look at the document our leader gave them, count the number of people leaving and then let our unit proceed. Other work groups left each day via Nalewki, Żelazna, Nowolipki and the other gates in the ghetto's brick wall. Our job was to stack bricks and usable timber from the rubble of destroyed houses. The work was not excessive and with a reasonable effort the task could be finished in half the available hours. This left time for the real reason for leaving the ghetto.

It had become clear early on to me, and to many others, that the ghetto was to be nothing more than an open grave. The food rations were set so low that signs of starvation showed from the first day. If we were to survive, it would have to be by illegal means, by bribing guards and developing smuggling to a high art.

It was not difficult to establish contact with the 'Aryan' Poles. We had no German supervisors and our Jewish overseers were in the same boat as we were. Within a few days, exchanges between the ghetto and the outside began to function in a meaningful way. The ghetto offered dollars, gold, clothing, art works, underwear and other goods, in exchange for food and, once trust was built up on both sides, small arms.

The custom was for Poles to approach us, as we Jews were too visible to risk leaving our work sites. At all times, under penalty of death, we had to wear a white armband bearing the blue Star of David. Because of my 'good' Aryan looks I sometimes risked taking this band off and walking away, but I had to be careful. An exchange would be agreed but no goods would change hands. Instead, the routine was to bribe the guards at the gate before leaving the next day, to allow us to take the requisite goods out of the ghetto and, in the evening, return without a body search. If a search was carried out it initially involved only the loss of the smuggled goods, so long as they were not arms. But soon, being found with smuggled goods led to beatings and, soon after that, instant death.

In addition to these planned exchanges, we were sometimes offered goods 'on the spot'. To take advantage of them we needed ready capital on hand. The more enterprising of us entrusted money or valuables to contacts we had established outside the ghetto, thus forming a sort of 'bank'. We also hid in the ruins goods we had brought from the ghetto but been unable to sell on a given day.

Through my contacts, I was one of the first to be offered 'hot' goods, meaning small arms. Following instructions from my Betar friends I accepted the offer and bought two Polish hand grenades, known as 'potatoes'. Although I had bribed the guards, I remember the terror I felt that evening as I returned to the ghetto. I thought my heart would give me away if I had to undergo a body search. My standing in the Betar was sealed with that first purchase. On that day I became one of the few insiders. At a later stage many people would obtain arms for the organisation, but in the winter of 1940–41 little had been organised in this respect.

I was very familiar with the types of small arms offered for sale and concentrated mostly on revolvers, although I did not shy away from buying hand grenades. The black market offered three types of hand grenade: Polish, British and German. The first two were similar but the German had a handle shaped like an ice-cream cornet, which made it extremely easy for a recipient to grab the grenade and hurl it back at the thrower. I avoided buying these ones as much as possible.

In the first months of buying arms, the prices were steep and the risk high, but the supply of all varieties was considerable. Once the trust between seller and buyer was established, business was business and our common enemy became the same — the cursed Hitlerite.

I would be offered anything up to a light automatic machine-gun. Although such a treasure could cost a small fortune. The delivery was made in parts, each individually greased and packed. We smuggled the parts in with the help of many of the Jews who worked outside the ghetto.

No one in my family knew of my work. We all smuggled, it was the only way to survive, but the smuggling my family knew about consisted of money, food and medicines. My father would not have approved of my arms smuggling and I never discussed it in his presence. Like everyone of his generation, he believed there was some hope of surviving the war and that resistance, especially armed, would only make things worse. But Salek Geller had managed to convince me otherwise.

As well as buying arms, each of us working outside the ghetto made his own deals with the Poles. Sometimes we would form a partnership to purchase a particular item, but in general we acted together only to bribe the guards. My main capital for exchange was Father's gold bars, but these were much too big for day-to-day purposes. Each time I had to change one I had to assemble a group of buyers and sell them part of the value of the bar. This required some organisation. I learned, out of necessity, to accept many things in exchange, including food, American dollars, German marks and even, at one stage, American twenty-dollar gold coins.

Each day the brick fence around the ghetto grew higher. This jail that we were building around ourselves was paid for with Jewish money, built with Jewish labour and supervised by the first recruits of the now infamous Jewish police, the *Ordnungs Dienst* or 'Keepers of order'.

In January 1941, the call went out for bottles and glass. For some unknown reason they had become scarce in the ghetto. The mystery deepened when broken glass also became sought after. It didn't take long to discover the reason for the shortage. By now the ghetto wall was three metres high and the Germans demanded that it be topped with broken glass. Like the other resources used in its building, the Jewish authorities had to find the glass from within the ghetto. When the wall was finished, the shortage of glass was over.

8

The Warsaw ghetto

How does one measure time? When one lives through a life day by day; when one can plan for the future while enjoying the present, that is one measure. I have had fifty years of such time. But how does one measure time when the future has no plan, no image, and the present is not consumed but pushed out of the way by the desire to survive? Is the minute an hour and the day an eternity? I don't know how that time should be measured.

My grandson's generation would probably describe the time of the Warsaw ghetto as something seemingly closer to the time of Babylon than to the present. Although our daughter was born in Australia, the story of the Warsaw ghetto was familiar to her because we talked about it often. The smell of the ghetto was in her parents' flesh and she became used to it. She absorbed this smell as her parents held her in their arms, as they dressed her, as they fed her and took her to school. To her the ghetto was a natural part of childhood.

Do I still live in the ghetto or does the ghetto still live in me? It is a riddle. We have not separated, although I have gone from one end of the world to the other, and from one end of life to the other. Sometimes I know quite clearly that I have remained caged in that ghetto, in the war years. At other times I am just as sure that the war years have remained caged in me. And so these fifty years since then have become both an eternity and no time at all. How does one measure time?

There was the Warsaw ghetto where people, who had been dying for weeks or months, died at night in our streets and were covered with newspapers. Death had waited like a vulture at their homeless door, as they made their last meal from the flesh of their own bodies. They consumed themselves. They left for Death only skin and bones to chew. There was the Warsaw ghetto where people without a soul sought out the pleasures of the flesh. The nightclubs where nothing was forbidden, the food, the music, the girls. One need not ask where their money came from. It came from the quarters of the Devil, who had for their benefit taken the human form and dressed in the uniform of the Gestapo. The money the Devil handed over in Warsaw's ghetto came from the blood sale, and it could only be used for pleasure and for the deadening of the soul.

There was the Warsaw ghetto where people, who had not lost the Divine image in which, according to the Bible, they had been created, cared for others with whatever had been left to them. They built schools, helped to keep the hospitals open, organised shelters for the old and did not wait to be thanked. Their work was a poor caricature of humans in real life. But their devotion filled this caricature with beauty and goodness which still casts its light within me.

There was the Warsaw ghetto where people resisted. It took us a long time to become the resisters. We lived in the secret ghetto within the ghetto. The risks we took honed our pride, the knowledge we shared gave us a bond of friendship, and the preparations we went through for the ultimate test made the smallest of us ten feet tall. We made the words 'Warsaw ghetto' into a glorious icon of human faith and our deeds affirmed against all odds the liberty of man.

The Warsaw ghetto was all of these and more.

Autumn turned to winter, winter to spring and spring to

summer. Yet there were no seasons inside the ghetto, only a waiting time. But waiting for what?

One person waited for bread, another for deliverance. A third waited for the German guard to look the other way as he or she crossed between the two worlds separated by gates. Some of us waited for the time when our revolvers could be used effectively. We all waited for a future that would belong to us for a moment. We waited for the right time.

9

The ghetto summer of 1941

FOR the younger generations of non-Jews it may be hard to differentiate between ghettos, concentration camps and death camps. In terms of goals, there were no differences. They were all intended to destroy innumerable victims. All served to subjugate and reduce the enslaved to a state of willingness in which they co-operated in their own destruction. The only differences were in the methods used to achieve this end.

The ghetto was considered by the Germans to be the best and subtlest system. In it Jews could be made to administer all the necessary stages towards their own destruction, in the belief that by following the German orders they might be saving themselves. The ghetto was presented by the Germans and accepted by the Jews as nothing worse than a separated, enclosed area where Jews could continue to administer their own lives, only segregated from non-Jews.

As the ghetto was meant to minimise contact between Jews and non-Jews, the Germans decided to select a single Jewish man in each ghetto as their go-between. This man was called the *Juden Altaester*, or 'Eldest of the Jews'. His task was to receive the German orders and ensure that they were carried out to the letter. His authority replaced all other Jewish institutions, which were dissolved by the Germans and declared illegal. And this authority was to be supported, if need be, with German might.

The *Juden Altaester* in Warsaw was Adam Czerniakow, an engineer and an honest, sincere fellow. He was not a particularly staunch man and not very bright, but he willingly undertook to lead his brethren at a difficult time. As a man of liberal upbringing, he was, unfortunately, too weak in character to be a forceful leader. He delegated his authority with little discretion. When, after three years, he discovered the true aims of the Germans, he chose to take the easy way out of his difficulties by committing suicide. He did not share his knowledge with his advisers or with the Jews he was supposed to lead.

Czerniakow took a personal interest in the selection of candidates for the Jewish police force which was set up to assist him in the running of the ghetto. Most of those accepted for police work were university graduates. Czerniakow believed graduates would be better able to serve the people. The Germans, however, had other plans for these police, forcing them, gradually, to abandon their honest intentions for the sake of their own survival. Their deterioration began with the accepting of bribes, which corrupted their moral standards. The second stage followed quickly. Instead of working for the good of the *Juden Altaester*, they became, unwittingly, instruments of the German plan. They became human robots, used by their German masters to round up close to three hundred thousand Jews and bring them by force to the wagons that were to carry them to the death camp of Treblinka. But this was to happen later.

The German authorities in Warsaw wielded two main weapons in their battle to subjugate and break the will of the Jews. The starvation-level diet and the fear of leaving the ghetto illegally, as any Jew found doing this would be shot. Thus the instinct to live led either way to death.

The non-Jews who had moved out of the ghetto had often stripped their apartments. Floors had been ripped out, toilet-pans removed, even doors and windows had been taken from the vacated apartments. At the same time, some one hundred and thirty thousand Jews had been evacuated from other parts of Warsaw to the ghetto and needed a roof over their heads.

The newly created police gave the best apartments to their own families and relatives. The richer Jews quickly learned that only through bribing these men could they hope to obtain reasonable accommodation for their families. As a result, those who had joined the police force had discovered a gold mine. The salary quickly became a minor consideration, the position everything.

In the meantime, the stripped premises, which could have and should have been repaired, fell into disrepair. Some became rubbish tips and toilets, others the final resting places of the weakest. The pavements outside these buildings were the first to be decorated with emaciated bodies, frozen in the cold Warsaw nights.

The police were basically trained by outside authorities who stood behind them. It was therefore important to be on the best terms with members of the force.

When the first small rations were allocated to the ghetto, the people in the food department behaved in exactly the same way as the police. They looked after themselves first. Only a tiny portion of the small allocation reached the non-affiliated inhabitants of the ghetto. It was the same with those in charge of coal and winter fuel. The bread people gave extra rations to the coal people who supplied them with extra coal in turn. And both bribed the police, and so the vicious circle grew. Those organisations that still believed in basic morality fought a losing battle.

During the first winter, death by starvation was rife. Night after night the streets filled with bodies to be collected in the morning. These bodies were naked, as their clothing had been sold for money to buy food. A department of the Jewish administration, the 'death collectors', was set up to collect the bodies and bury them in mass graves. Ghetto inhabitants learned to ignore this morbid phenomenon. Sometimes bodies were placed outside nightclubs in protest, but the underworld characters merely stepped over them as they left the clubs in the early hours of the morning.

When starvation began to reach epidemic proportions, the *Juden Altaester* requested a slight increase in the food ration. The German authorities ignored it completely.

Another request, for soap, had unfortunate consequences. The Warsaw Health Department, Jewish Section, came back with a strict order from the German command to establish 'hygiene units' to delouse 'the dirty Jewish population', which seemed incapable of looking after its own cleanliness and hence presented a danger to the clean Aryan population. The Jews were to be deloused in communal disinfecting baths. If even a single case of typhoid or typhus was reported, the whole building involved was to be disinfected.

During the spring and summer of 1941, these units became the new scourge of the ghetto. The 'disinfectors' would appear at a given street, seal off a building with police help, then go from apartment to apartment, forcing the people out and marching them under guard to the disinfecting bath. While the inhabitants were away, the disinfectors or the police, or both, would rob the dwellings while disinfecting them. The deloused inhabitants would come back from the 'bath' stinking of one kind of disinfectant, to apartments stinking of another and robbed of most of their belongings. The people feared the police and the disinfectors more than the plagues of typhus or typhoid themselves. And there was no authority to which they could turn. The targets of the disinfectors were mostly larger buildings, where there were many tenants and more to steal.

The health problem was made worse by the dearth of doctors in the ghetto. We discovered early on that the Germans were assassinating doctors, mostly by night. It was an attempt to undermine our ability to treat the ill, and we feared that one day there would be no more doctors left in the ghetto. To counter this, some Betar members, myself included, with the approval of Betar leaders, joined a first-aid group. Our teachers were top doctors such as Rubinstein-Jezierski, Flatau, Anastazy Landau and Rapke.

Unfortunately, when the disinfectors appeared, we feared being drafted as their helpers and decided to disband the group.

To complete the hell of life in the ghetto, the German authorities installed loudspeakers on the street corners. They broadcasted news of German victories, information about new orders and music, and they were never turned off.

As the winter eased, smuggling grew in spite of the dangers, particularly over the wall where it ran between the Jewish and Aryan graveyards. The German soldiers and their Polish police helpers did not guard that area as closely as they did other parts of the ghetto wall, believing the collective graves were rife with typhus. Thus the exchange of goods and people between the two graveyards blossomed.

On the Jewish side the daily collection of bodies kept the graveyard busy.* The death collectors were known as *pinkierts*, the name given before the war to the head of Jewish funerals. They came and went constantly in groups of three, wheeling a flat wagon which carried five or six bodies. One person pulled and two pushed, and thus they would wheel their load to the graveyard and return in the same formation. A bitter joke made the rounds among those who risked their lives by smuggling. 'The best place to make a living in the ghetto is the graveyard.' This was true.

* On a trip to Warsaw in 1993, David pointed at two large grassy depressions in the Warsaw cemetery divided by a path. 'Here we buried over ten thousand, and the Germans? They brought their children, covered their mouths and noses and, standing them in a truck, allowed the older youth to pick up the little ones to show them where they threw the Jews.'

10

Bystry, the beginning of ŻZW

There are few popular accounts of the role of the Jewish Armed Union ŻZW in the Jewish Resistance in the Warsaw ghetto. Academic accounts do exist, in the archives of Yad Vashem, in the military history of the Polish Underground and elsewhere. But outside these, the little that has been written is considerably less than deserved, unlike the detailed history of the Jewish Fighting Organisation ŻOB and its Commander, Mordecai Anielewicz.

Let me try, then, to redress the balance.

Warsaw fell one month after the beginning of the war, which had started, without a formal declaration, on 1 September 1939. Many of the soldiers defending it were Jews. Not wishing to fall into the hands of the Germans, many of these Jewish soldiers went 'underground', changed into civilian clothes and became, effectively, invisible to the Germans. In October, the Germans ordered all Polish soldiers involved in the recent defence of the capital to report to German military quarters. Those who declined would be dealt with under war regulations, if caught. That is, they would be shot as spies.

A Polish captain, Henryk Iwański, has left a record of what happened soon after. Four Jewish officers of the Polish Army visited him at the St Stanisław Hospital at 37 Wolska Street. One of them, First Lieutenant David Mordechai Appelbaum, had fought in his regiment. These officers were members of the Irgun Zvei Leumi (IZL — 'Organisation of National Army'), which had been led before the war by Menahem Begin, future Prime Minister of Israel.

They told Iwański of three Underground Jewish officers, Paweł Frenkel, Leon Wajnsztok and Dr David Wdowiński, who by German law should have been reported to the German *Offlag*, or prison camp for officers. But somehow they were still free. With Iwański's help they wanted to organise a Jewish youth movement and train its members to resist the Germans.

Iwański, in turn, did two things. He told the officers that he should be referred to by his code name 'Bystry', and he handed each of them a Wis 9 mm pistol with the compliments of the KB Security Corps of the recently formed Polish military Underground. To the best of our historical knowledge, these four pistols were the first arms Jews received for the future ghetto Uprising. The four officers resolved then and there to create the ŻZW. All historical documents agree that the ŻZW was not lacking in armaments at the beginning of the Warsaw ghetto Uprising in 1943.

The same is true of the ŻOB. Historian Dr Joseph Kermish has been recognised as the foremost authority on the history of the Warsaw ghetto. In 1946 he interrogated the SS General who led the destruction of the Warsaw ghetto Uprising, Major General Jürgen Stroop. Dr Kermish wrote: 'It is also known that some days before the outbreak of the revolt, the arsenal of the ŻZW was full of various arms — machine-guns, carbines, pistols, hand grenades, bombs — as well as rucksacks full of ammunition, German uniforms, which were used during the fighting, and so on.'*

The youth movement, which Appelbaum had spoken about, was the Betar. In January 1940, the KB gave the officers an additional twenty-nine Wis pistols, which the Polish Underground organisation Świt had approved during its monthly meeting in December 1939. The older members of Betar, who belonged to

---

*See reference in Yisrael Gutman, *The Jews of Warsaw*, Midland Books, USA, 1989.

the IZL, began training as soon as they had twelve members who could be trusted. The ŻZW's leaders were as follows: Paweł Frenkel, Leon Rodal, Abraham Rodal, Advocate David Shulman, Gdalia Zylberman, the Łopata brothers, David Mordechai Appelbaum, Moshe Wainstok, Kalman Mendelson, Henryk Lifszyc and Dr Josef Celmaister.

The Betar members who joined the ŻZW leadership were Simcha Witelzon, Eliahu (Alek) Hilbersztein, Yitzhak Bilawski, Natan Shultz, Pinchas Taub, Josef Goldhaber, Dr Michael Strykowski, Lee Leizerowitz, the Rosenfeld brothers, Moniek Złoto, Yitzhak Binenkorn, Samuel Luft, Dr David Wdowiński, Heniek Feberbusz, Leon Wajnsztok, Jan Pika and Salek Hazenszprung.

The training sessions always took place at night, at three places: in the basement of Karmelicka 5, at Nalewki 15 and at Nalewki 29. The first headquarters of the ŻZW were at Miła 10.

From the first days of the ghetto, Betar had begun building bunkers. They were not intended to be used as places for survival. Instead, they provided a safe place to store illegal arms and to train recruits in the use of revolvers, carbines and rifles.

Betar remained in the Zionist movement, even when it had cut its affiliation with the World Zionist Organisation (WZO). Our aim was much wider and larger than the compromise which the WZO had been ready to accept. The founder of Betar, Vladimir Zev Jabotinsky, was convinced that the land of Israel would return to the Jewish people only through the same means that it had been lost nineteen hundred years earlier, through a military campaign. It was a conviction later confirmed by history.

Jabotinsky's determination spoke to the heart of the Polish leaders, who wanted to see as many Jews as possible fight the Germans. They were willing to train Jewish youth for the coming fight. Therefore, even before the war, close relations developed between Betar and members of the Polish Army. Because of this it was impossible for our organisation to work in the same way as other illegal Zionist youth movements in Warsaw.

The Hashomer, to which Anielewicz belonged, and similar Zionist youth movements were organised on virtually the same basis as before the war. Of course their work, too, was illegal, but it was not as dangerous to the Germans as what we were doing.

There were even some German 'ideologists' who were all for letting the Jews organise themselves internally to carry out all sorts of activities that did not pose a danger to the Germans. Their logic was that as long as the Jews were busy with internal matters, they would not try to resist the German plan. The Germans saw the Zionist youth movement within the Warsaw ghetto as one such activity. They knew that, if necessary, they could liquidate the organisations with the help of the internal Jewish traitors who worked for their Gestapo.

Betar could not afford the luxury of recruiting young people by going out into the ghetto streets. The secrecy we had to keep was strict and total. When I became officially accepted as a Betar member I was not told, and officially never knew, who the leaders of the organisation were. When I was eventually trusted with their names it was on the understanding that I must never acknowledge them to their face. On one or two occasions I spoke to the organisers of military training, such as Frenkel, the Łopata brothers and Rodal, but resistance was never referred to, until the days of the Uprising. They came to our meetings only as Zionists, and talked to us about Eretz Israel, the theory of Betar, about the aspirations of Zionism and so on. Only our direct leaders, their superiors and the Haganah — or head leadership — discussed training progress and organisational matters connected with it.

New recruits were accepted only on the personal recommendation of members, but this too was not easy. When I was recommended, Luba's brother, Meir, who had been a member of Betar for some years, Sevek Bekerman and Salek Geller, who had been my friends almost since youth, all had to approach me first on their own behalf and report on me to the organisation. Knowing that I worked outside the ghetto, they asked me to buy small arms for Betar, but through their representation. I had known 'Bystry' for a long time. However, when he told me that he had been appointed the liaison officer between the Polish Underground and Betar, he had already received the report from Betar about me. His trust in me through the channels of Zawadzki was a separate matter.

These facts explain why the ŻZW could not easily afford to co-operate fully with ŻOB. We could not risk jeopardising our own position with the Polish Underground even if we, as Jews, believed otherwise. It was also a question of having the agreement of our Polish partners, the Underground Army, the KB Security Corps, who kept training our fighters and supplying us with arms. We could not risk even asking if they would agree to us establishing close relations with the ŻOB as it would have made them wonder what activities we were getting up to behind their back and whether they were dangerous to their own work. We therefore kept ourselves as a separate body, while co-ordinating our anti-German activities with ŻOB, supposedly without the knowledge of the Polish side.

The changing political map of Jewish life was ignored by most of the illegal Zionist youth organisations in the ghetto. Like the socialist-Zionists before the war, they were less than friendly to Betar, knowing little or nothing about what was taking place in the ŻZW organisation. Even the leaders of these organisations probably considered us to be on the fringes of society or simply crazy. Unfortunately, we could not risk exposure by correcting this distorted view. We went on with our work as best we could, hoping that one day we might be better understood by our brethren in the ghetto. One or two leaders, perhaps, knew about our activities, but they were sworn to secrecy.

History has sometimes belittled the importance of the ŻZW. I now trust that its role and that of other smaller groups will be recognised for all time. We must remember and understand that the enemy did not differentiate, they did not ask to what organisation one belonged before carrying out their heinous crimes. We fought for all Jews, our country and peace.

11

The end of our home

BEFORE the Germans attacked their Russian allies on 22 June 1941, there was nothing to indicate the imminence of such an action. The German–USSR pact was being hailed in the German press and radio. Friendship was blossoming between the two peoples, or so it was said. But in the Underground, an attack was considered likely, even more so when reports filtered through that German forces were moving towards the Russian border by night. But these reports had no effect on us. We were sure that, in the case of an attack, the Russians would win. Also, we had other, more immediate problems to consider.

Our family home was slowly disintegrating; ties were breaking. With Mother gone, Father was the only one for whom the place was still really home. Our love for each other did not diminish and the treasure of belonging remained, but it became like jewellery that is seldom worn. The perspective of years has helped me to understand the trauma and tragedy which caused this disintegration and the separation which was its result.

Mother's long sickness helped prepare us for what was to follow. But Father was still badly affected by her death, of course. He was to remain in a virtual emotional void for the remaining two and a half years of his life. Some months after Mother's death, a friend from Father's childhood arrived to take care of the house, and her presence helped Father to maintain his daily routine.

Luba was missing out on the sweetest years of her life. Like all Jewish teenagers under Hitler, she was not allowed to enjoy the fresh taste of adolescence. Until Father's friend arrived, she would travel to our home each day to put the house in order. She spent more working hours there than at her own home. Later, when we hired a lady to do the housework, it was Luba who kept her finger on the pulse. She was our housekeeper in every sense.

By 1941 it had become clear that Luba and I would share whatever was left of our lives. We hoped that fate would leave us sufficient time to make that sharing complete. My two older brothers had married and left home many years before, though they remained close and their wives had become part of our family.

I admire the simplicity with which Father remained human in those years. Unlike many people who closed their fists and their hearts, Father found it easy to share his fortune with strangers who were in need.

His generosity helped to protect us in an unexpected way. One of the plagues in the ghetto were the street youths who snatched parcels from passers-by. These 'snatchers' had a sixth sense for parcels of food, soap and money. They never touched Luba and me, though. In fact, the opposite often happened. Most of these snatchers knew us as the 'voluntary givers'. If they saw us coming they would offer us their protection for part of the way, warning others of their kind that we belonged to those who should not be disturbed, the voluntary givers. When I bought provisions for us I often gave something to these street youths, who received it without ever requesting more, sharing the goods among themselves as I had asked them to do. They understood how difficult it was to acquire provisions and what it meant for us to share with them.

Father had little to do outside the home, and he spent his time quietly. Mr Guzik from Joint visited every few weeks. When he left, Father would give a receipt to his sons, repeating these words each time, 'Keep it and don't lose it. After the war these receipts will give you enough money to begin a good life.'

He remained interested in ghetto matters. When we suggested fleeing and hiding outside, Father's old strength re-emerged. 'I am not moving from here! If I cannot be safe here, I will surely not be safe on the Aryan side. I am too old to live in fear. The constant strain of living just for the sake of living, the fear of breathing too loud, of coughing, of needing a doctor, no! Not at my age, it is not worth the effort. You are younger and for you the risk may be worth taking. You must all do as you think right.' Father was not yet fifty when he decided that it was no longer 'worth the effort' to live in fear.

That spring was a testing time for Warsaw Jewry. More than twenty thousand Jews had died during the winter but the spark of hope was still glowing.

The Gestapo was busy transporting Jews from around Poland to Warsaw, for a fee. From the tightly sealed ghetto of Łódź, some two thousand Jews arrived at the Warsaw ghetto, having each paid the Gestapo and their Jewish middle-men between three and five hundred marks. It was a lucrative business for the Germans. For the price of an open army truck used for one and a half hours they collected between ten and fifteen thousand marks. In one week some members of that elite group, the German *Geheime Staats Polizei*, or Secret State Police, were able to earn more illegally than they might ever have been able to earn honestly throughout their entire lives.

After the harsh winter, the warmth of the late spring and early summer lightened the depression and despair. The general feeling in the ghetto was that, although many people would succumb, the majority would survive. This optimism was particularly noticeable in the youth organisations and other socially active circles. These groups undertook, illegally, more and more activities that before the war would have been handled by the state. The young, gifted Jewish historian, Dr Emmanuel Ringelblum, founded one such organisation with his friends, called *Oneg Shabbat*, the 'Joy of the Sabbath'.

To traditional Jews, *'Oneg Shabbat'* was a household expression. It was a most suitable name to use to avoid drawing attention to the group and its real activities. The uninitiated assumed that Dr Ringelblum's organisation met on Friday nights or Saturdays for religious study.

The *Oneg Shabbat* institution, however, was anything but the Joy of Shabbat. Dr Ringelblum had managed to create a network of individuals who documented items of historical interest and collected them under the innocent name that he had suggested. Not all of those who gave material knew where it would be stored, and only trusted members were told who the main collectors and evaluators were. The main collectors were members of Ringelblum's circle. Each of them was expert in a particular literary or musical field. They sorted the diaries, poetry, statistics and other scraps of information relevant to their own field, deciding what materials were to be hidden from the evil eye of destruction. By the spring of 1941, *Oneg Sabbath* had become a password among individuals who were involved in social activities of all kinds.

Dr Ringelblum was well known in the ghetto but the Germans did not take any particular interest in him. It was known that before the war he had belonged to left-wing organisations, but so had thousands of Jews in Warsaw. Gestapo informers did not consider him dangerous or outstanding in any way.

I knew Dr Ringelblum reasonably well. Although his interest lay more with the Zionist organisations of the left, the war years had weakened the hold of the ideologies which separated us and strengthened those which united, namely the need to fight our deadly enemy, the Germans. Being acquainted with Dr Ringelblum had once caused me some hours of anxiety.

It was a summer's day in May or June. I had left the ghetto with a group of workers to dismantle a building. As was customary, we had finished around four o'clock and were returning to the ghetto. Our intention, as on all other work days, was to march through a gate as a working group in columns of four, walk at least half a kilometre, then turn into a side street, before disbanding and each going in different directions.

On that day we entered through a gate near a building which, before the war, had housed the Jewish Polish-language newspaper, *Nasz Przegląd*. Ringelblum had been a contributor to the paper. The building was supposed to be empty now, except for one tenant, an obscure officer from the office of the *Judenrat*.

As we entered the ghetto and turned right, three men, including someone who looked like Ringelblum, ran out of the building straight into a German motorcycle patrol. They halted and called on the men to stop. We marched on as if the incident hadn't happened. As the others were taken away, the man who looked like Ringelblum had held onto a lamp-post. A shot was fired and to this day I can see, in my memory, the man slowly buckling under, leaving a stripe of blood on the lamp-post as he slid down.

My father's building at 17 Muranowska Street still held many tenants. And one of the ground-floor shops was rented to an Orthodox Jew, a quiet man known as Reb Chaim Joachimowicz. Reb Chaim was an old-fashioned milkman and his shop was considered strictly kosher. As well as the standard dairy products, he also sold *parve* goods — those which, according to Jewish dietary laws, are neither dairy or meat — such as herrings and pickled cabbage. He mixed little with our family, which was totally secular to the point of being considered anti-religious.

Reb Chaim rented a cellar, too, where he stored perishable foods and kept the milk cool. He also filled it with empty milk cans. There were so many that my brother Eliezer had once joked, 'Reb Chaim must have male and female milk cans, they seem to multiply in such great numbers.'

When the war started, Reb Chaim's business shrank, but he had enough smuggled products to keep his head above water and the collection of milk cans was as large as ever.

Another tenant in the building was Chaim Przygoda, one of our poorest tenants. Our mother used to help his family from time to time. Chaim Przygoda was always involved in what we used to call 'politics'. With little formal education, he was nevertheless a well-informed man who expressed himself clearly.

I had come home on that day shocked and distressed, and I sat down to calm myself. The bell rang. I opened the door and saw Chaim Przygoda. He greeted me warmly and I invited him in. He sat down and came right to the point. 'You know that if I come to you I need something. I believe you can help me.' I assumed he needed food or medication. What else could a man need in the ghetto? He continued, 'David, I know what you think, and you are wrong. I have not come for food or something like that. I need to use your good standing with Reb Chaim. Will you speak to him?'

'Have you two quarrelled?' I asked in surprise, knowing that they were both very peaceful people.

Przygoda smiled, embarrassed. 'No, David, we two would never quarrel. We live in friendship. Before the war I often bought my goods from him on credit, until I could pay him back. No, I have come to you to ask a communal favour, one which he would not easily understand if I were to ask him myself.'

I pressed him to come to the point and he apologised. 'You're right, forgive me, you don't have a clue what I'm talking about. I have just returned from Dr Emmanuel Ringelblum's, the historian.'

I felt an electric current run through my spine. 'You've already heard what happened?'

Now Przygoda was surprised. 'Heard? Heard what?'

'When did you see Dr Ringelblum?'

'About fifteen or twenty minutes ago. Has anything happened since then?'

I had to make a real effort to keep my secret to myself. 'Please forgive me, I was mixing him up with somebody else. What do you want me to speak to Reb Chaim about?'

Przygoda hesitated. 'What I am going to tell you must be in confidence.'

I assured him and he continued. 'I work very closely with Dr Ringelblum in his *Oneg Shabbat* organisation. We are having difficulties storing the documents we collect and, the other day, Dr Ringelblum asked me to speak to you about the industrial chemical bottles used in your family's tannery. However, I don't believe they are really suitable for burying underground, which is what we are planning to do.

'But, on the way home it hit me that Reb Chaim has a basement full of heavy milk cans. I know they cost money and that we have none, but I am sure he would part with some of them if you were to ask him. Would you do that?'

'Would you mind if I speak first to Dr Ringelblum?' I said. 'I would like to talk to him first before approaching Reb Chaim.'

'Are you too tired to visit him now?' Przygoda asked. 'He's at home.'

These were like an angel's words to me, as they meant that Dr Ringelblum was alive and well. I hurried over to Miła 29, where he welcomed me warmly. We spoke about the tannery bottles first, but I, too, expressed my doubt that they would survive the pressure of underground burial. Then I mentioned the milk cans.

Ringelblum was delighted. 'Wonderful! The cans would be much better. You will be rewarded for this in the world to come! Ten cans would be ideal. Can you get that many?'

Reb Chaim would only part with two. It was no good trying to convince him to hand over even a single additional can.

Sadly, Dr Ringelblum was discovered and murdered by the Germans in the summer of 1944. But I was proud and elated years later when these two milk cans were found and the documents in them were still in good condition. To my knowledge, nineteen more metal boxes were also found, and the writings contained in them have been published.

12

The Kiercelak

OUTSIDE the ghetto there was an open market called the Kiercelak, which had existed since before the war. One could buy anything there, including goods not available elsewhere in Warsaw. During the war it became a symbol of resistance to the German occupation. It was probably the only place where the most dangerous actions of the Polish Socialist Party went on in the open.

The Gestapo and its treacherous collaborators tried to penetrate the Kiercelak and catch the Underground leaders, but neither bribes nor their frequent raids were of much use. Occasionally they succeeded in hauling away some minor player, but the leaders remained beyond their reach. Known collaborators or informants were always swiftly dealt with — executed — by the Underground. Some of the major dealers were even protected from persecution because the Polish police recognised them as being leading operators at the market. In a few cases individuals reappeared at the Kiercelak only days after being arrested. I never managed to find out if a bribe, a threat or both had gained their release.

At the Kiercelak one never asked unnecessary questions. A buyer seeking grenades (called 'potatoes') would approach a 'stranger' with whom he had dealt many times and say, 'You don't know me, but I am interested in potatoes. They must be of the highest quality, hard and without any blemishes.'

The 'stranger' would reply, 'I have no potatoes myself but can get you some. My friend has a few but they are imported. If you care to come with me you may have some.'

The experienced buyer would then reply, 'I would prefer the local variety, but I may be interested in your imported ones. However, you must bring them to me here.' A deal would be made, delivery arranged and the money would be paid in advance. Deals made at the Kiercelak were always honoured. This was not because of the honesty of the deal-makers but because anyone who tried to act otherwise, to 'make a quick killing', ended up being killed themselves.

Nobody used their real names at the Kiercelak. A man who had made a deal under the name of Stasiek would appear a week later calling himself Janek. If another dealer greeted him with the name Stasiek, he would be told, 'I am not Stasiek. You must be mistaken. But if you are interested in . . .' and the two dealers would introduce themselves to each other under new names.

The Kiercelak was neutral territory even for German soldiers, including SS officers. Some were on leave and wanted to have a good time, others wanted to deal. Nobody asked if the revolvers, grenades or even heavier arms offered in a dismantled state, were theirs or not. It was strictly cash and carry each time. Parties to such arms deals would leave the Kiercelak within seconds, but within an hour or two a new session would be going on, with 'new' people and new goods for sale.

I was known to most of the dealers. We sometimes met up in a *knajpa*, a pub, outside the Kiercelak, where we would drink illegally distilled vodka, called *bimber*. Whenever we met in the Kiercelak, however, it was always as strangers, as if we were meeting for the first time. The rules of the Kiercelak were strictly adhered to.

Once, while drinking in the *knajpa*, I asked what would happen if I were arrested. My companion became serious, although in a friendly way. 'Why do you want to know things that would be of no use to you? I can assure you that, as soon as it became known that you were in jail, the wheels would start turning very fast. Of course we do not always meet with full success. If we were successful, however, you would have to pay up.'

At the Kiercelak I often met a young Christian man who was closely connected with the Jewish Underground, the ŻZW. His name is Jan Kostański and we have remained friends for life. Kostański and his mother, Władysław Wierzbicka, saved many Jewish people, including his future wife and her family.

Jan Kostański and I first met in a coffee house in the ghetto. Zygmunt Zawadzki had to make *Kennkarten* (Aryan identity cards) for twenty members of our organisation and had sent Kostański to me to collect the necessary photos and details about height, hair colour, eye colour and so on. Although the names and addresses on these *Kennkarten* were false, the documents themselves were real, filled out and stamped by trusted people in the Warsaw Department for Registration. One of these *Kennkarten* was for Luba and it remains in her possession today.

We met at the arranged time and I handed Kostański the photos. He scrutinised each one for what seemed to me a long time, but I did not question him about it. The reason for his action was made clear when we met next. He gave me only nineteen documents, saying, 'One face was rejected as too Jewish. I thought so when you gave me the photos, but didn't want you to think I was anti-Semitic, so I said nothing.'

Nobody at the Kiercelak ever looked at me in a suspicious manner. If some had their doubts, they kept them to themselves, as I was one of the regular dealers. But in general we Jews were in less danger at the Kiercelak than anywhere else outside the ghetto. The Kiercelak worked to its own rules. In quieter moments two 'strangers' would exchange risky jokes. Each time another German 'victory' was reported, there would be a new joke. 'Once again the poor stupid krauts have let themselves be trapped further away from their beloved Führer.'

One joke was about a Polish prisoner who had been sentenced

to hang on Christmas Day. He is given three last wishes. For the first wish, he asks for strawberries. 'But strawberries won't be available till spring!' he is told. 'That's OK,' he says, 'I can wait.' His next wish is for fresh spring onions in sour cream. Again he is told they are not available and again he replies, 'I can wait.' For his third wish, he asks to be buried next to the Führer.

'But the Führer is still alive,' screams the German officer, slapping the condemned man's face.

'There was no need for that,' replies the man demurely. 'I have already told you, I can wait.'

Anything and everything went on under the noses of the Germans at the Kiercelak.

Smuggling goods in and out of the ghetto kept it alive, figuratively and literally. It was the secret channel by which we extended life beyond German patience. Without it, we would all have starved. May we remember those who paid for it with their lives.

To have goods to smuggle, the ghetto needed to produce items that were wanted on the Aryan side. Tailors, shoemakers, metal workers and even jewellers received raw materials (which were themselves smuggled in) and transformed them into finished goods. In conditions that could scarcely be imagined, in confined spaces and with the most primitive tools, Jewish skill and the desire to survive produced miracles.

The prices paid for these goods were a joke. They would have constituted slave wages even if the artisans had received the whole amount. But after the middle-men and smugglers had taken their substantial shares, they received barely a slice from an already meagre loaf.

The children in these artisan families were shown no leniency in terms of hours or productivity. All members of the family worked. In the more decent of these families, the parents gave their children extra food or at least allowed them their fair share. But in other families, parents betrayed all responsibility for the children they had brought into the world. Woe to these young people who bore the slave-like sufferings in the short span of their lives.

Children were also prominent among the beggars on the streets. Many were genuine orphans, who stood or sat outside buildings, apathetic with the hunger that precedes death, their thin arms stretched out for alms, as indifferent to their fate as the passers-by who ignored them. Others were the 'bread winners' for their parents, who hid in the nearest house and waited while their child begged. Sometimes their waiting was simply to protect the child from gangs of other children, who would terrorise the beggar and take away whatever donation they had received. These donations were small and infrequent, given only by those who were not yet stone-hearted and could still afford to give.

We would need a new language and a new poet to convey the heroism of those small children. They learned early that being young meant they had less right to life than their seniors, that they could not rely on others for their survival. They knew that they must make additional efforts to buy their right to life.

Unlike the adults who had money to bribe the German guards and be safe, the children moved in and out of the ghetto without security. In the mornings they scaled the wall hoping that they would not be caught. Throughout the day they wandered God knows where, in the streets of an alien Aryan world, collecting scraps. With a few vegetables or whatever they had picked up, they would once more risk their lives to bring their treasure back into the ghetto to share with older members of their families.

In the early days of the ghetto the young smugglers risked only losing the scraps they had collected and, sometimes, a beating. But soon the German thirst for Jewish blood was no longer satisfied with such a minor penalty for such a capital crime as disobeying the decree to die quietly. The order came to shoot young and old smugglers alike.

In dark, empty rooms, the furniture long since burned for fuel, despairing parents waited, fearing to mourn, for children who had left in the morning and not returned. Thousands and thousands of Jewish children paid with their young lives for keeping the ghetto alive.

There were some 'lucky' children, those who had belonged to a youth movement before the war or joined the illegal youth organisations that were active in the ghetto. They were able to enjoy at least the taste of a happy childhood, some singing together, the guidance of older people who fought for them to remain young, some additional soup or even just an extra carrot. There were also rich parents who could afford to give their children a better life. But most of these belonged to the new elite, the dubious aristocracy of ghetto police, the higher echelons of the bloated offices of the Eldest of the Jews and, above all, to our shame, the Jewish informers who co-operated with the Gestapo.

One of the tragedies of Betar was that, for reasons described earlier, it recruited so few youth in the ghetto. Before the war, it had as many young people as other Zionist youth movements, offering the familiar curriculum of sport, Judaism and love for the Jewish land of Eretz Israel. In addition, Betar trained its members from a young age to be ready to fight for the rebirth of our independence.

After Betar went underground in November 1939, affiliating with the ŻZW, it differed from other Zionist groups through its co-operation with the mainstream (Christian) Polish Resistance. We were disciplined according to rules dictated from the 'other' side. It would be as false to claim they trained us merely for their interests as to claim they did it merely for our own. Our benefit was mutual. Before, during and after the Uprising, our Polish friends stood by us. A few even entered the ghetto to fight, and some died fighting with us. But it was all on their terms, the terms of the Polish Underground. We were forbidden to accept individuals who had no connections with existing members and for security reasons we were forbidden to station a representative on the Aryan side. We felt handicapped by this. When the Jewish

Fighting Organisation ŻOB was set up in the last months of 1942, its representative, Antek Zuckerman, was stationed permanently outside the ghetto. Other Zionist movements had maintained such representatives from the moment the ghetto was closed within the wall. This made communication much easier.

It is hard to believe that, in the total separation between ghetto and the outside world, the Germans never cut off all the telephone lines. Organisations needed only to phone through the resolutions of their meetings to their representative on the Aryan side in a coded cipher and action could be taken immediately. We of Betar/ŻZW, however, had to get our messages across physically to the other side. Our leaders had their own reasons for not trusting the phone lines. Although we had an impressive organised smuggling apparatus, it sometimes took us days to make the required contact and just as long to receive the reply.

A special group of smugglers — who deserve not just a few lines, but a whole book — were the young Jewish women, mostly from the political organisations of the left, the Zionist or Bund movements. They travelled elbow to elbow with the Angel of Death to bring information, materials, encouragement and hope to the dying ghetto. It was nearly impossible for men to undertake these particular missions. Although Jewish men, too, had to live with the cold knife of fear at their hearts.

In October 1942, the ŻOB had an illegal representative on the Aryan side, a member of Hashomer, whose Jewish name was Aryeh Wilner, but the Polish side knew him as 'Jurek'. His Polish contact was Henryk Woliński, the official supplier of arms to the ŻOB on behalf of the Armia Krajowa (AK), the Polish Underground Home Army. Jurek had a typical Polish face, which did not betray any Jewish features, and he played the role of a real Pole to perfection. However, somebody on the other side betrayed him. One day when he returned home to his rented apartment on the Aryan side, the Gestapo was waiting for him. The large wooden box in which he had stored his purchases had been pulled out and was waiting as evidence of his crimes. His hands were immediately tied and he was taken to the Gestapo offices.

But something was wrong with the interrogation. While being beaten, Jurek was questioned about people and matters of which he knew nothing. It was a nightmare within a nightmare. After some days, it dawned on him that his German interrogators kept referring to him by his false name. He realised that he had been denounced to the Gestapo as a member of the Polish Underground and that they had no clue as to his real identity. He decided to end the torture and the charade, and to tell them who he really was. He knew that they would then take him out to the jail yard and shoot him.

When the interrogator called him once more into his office, Jurek began with the words, 'I have decided to tell you the truth.' He was given a chair. 'My name is Aryeh Wilner,' he said, 'and I am a Jew.' According to Wilner, who lived to tell the tale, the Germans were stunned into silence. 'For some moments they forgot all about me. They looked at each other as if asking what to do next. For the first time since my arrest I was left in sufficient peace to observe them. I thought nobody had told them what to do in a case such as mine.

'After a short interval the officer behind the desk lifted the telephone and spoke quietly into it. There was then total silence in the office until the door opened. The officer and the others in the room rose to attention. The man who entered was in civilian clothes. He looked at me and decided. "Get up!" he yelled. I rose from my chair. "Drop his pants!" he ordered one of the officers. I spread my arms and the officer untied the string which held up my pants. He lowered my underpants.'

Wilner finished his story: 'I was under the most severe stress but suddenly I felt completely relieved. This was going to be the end of my misery. I would be taken out at last and shot. Part of me stood outside myself and laughed, as they all looked at my private parts and, like an ancient Greek chorus, let out the same sigh, "Oh, dear God! He is a Jew!"'

Not once did they ask Aryeh Wilner who he was buying the arms for. The poisoned German mind could not imagine, even for a moment, that a Jew could buy arms for the purpose of killing Germans. To them, a Jew could only be a trader and nothing more.

There are two versions of what happened next. One is that he was taken to the Pawiak; the other that he was taken to Rembertów, a camp for Jews near Warsaw. Whatever the place, he was soon rescued.

13

Darkness and light

THE news spread like wildfire running through a dry forest: Germany had attacked the Soviet Union.

Few knew in the first hours of that fateful Sunday, 22 June 1941, if the rumours were true. By midday, though, the German loudspeakers had confirmed the news, blaring it forth from the street corners.

The change in our mood was euphoric. It felt as if the war might end in just a few hours, with the defeat of Germany. People said, 'The Russian Army will show them what a real blitzkrieg is', and 'The Soviets will smother them with their army hats alone.'

The general opinion was that the Soviet Army was fresh and had been preparing for just this possibility. The German Army, on the other hand, had fought for nearly two years and was tired.

People began to bring out maps and locate the names the loudspeakers announced. We did not believe the reports of German victory. 'It's propaganda,' we said. 'Within a week the Russians will be at the Wisła.'

But after ten days our hopes had turned to resignation and despair. A darker prophecy was heard in the ghetto. 'We are doomed. The war will last years and in the meantime we will all die.' (We meant that we would die from dysentery, typhoid, typhus and starvation. We never dreamed the Germans were even then planning more comprehensive means for our destruction.)

We heard names like Kharkov, Kiev, Brańsk, Smoleńsk . . . We looked on the maps and our hearts sank at the speed with which the German Army was advancing. The radio told not of thousands or tens of thousands of Russian prisoners, but of hundreds of thousands. Whole armies were encircled and fell into German hands.

The Christian Polish Underground also confirmed the German victories. 'Unfortunately, they don't need to exaggerate at all,' our Underground commentator informed us, 'but the fight will go on until we are either victorious or dead. We have not yet said our last word!'

The Christian Poles had one thing which we, the Jews, did not: time. For them, time meant the possibility of fighting on, if only on a small scale. We heard about partisan groups being organised behind German lines and remaining successful, even as German supply lines grew longer. We were told of sabotage actions which destroyed whole army trains of ammunition and killed many soldiers. But all this was a world away from the confined streets of our ghetto.

In the midst of this gloom I decided to propose to Luba. It was a crazy idea and it suited the times. If we had only a short time to live, let us live bound within marriage.

Luba had just passed her seventeenth year, but her childhood had long since evaporated into the atmosphere of war. When I said to her, 'I would like us to be together for the time we still have before us,' she accepted, not with elation, but with rational acknowledgement.

There was little difficulty in convincing our families. When we told my father of our decision, he said, 'In times such as these I believe you are both grown up enough to make up your own minds. My blessings go with you.' He was reluctant to disappoint me, following the death of Mother.

Luba's family was more reserved to begin with. Esther, her oldest sister, was the first to give us her blessing and support. Within a short time, we had made both families realise that our desire to marry was not as foolish as it might seem.

We contacted Rabbi Kahane, who had at one time been Chief Rabbi of Warsaw. At first he treated us as if we were childish and unable to understand the seriousness of marriage. He questioned Luba particularly. But when he realised how mature she was, and that she was aware of her responsibilities and the significance of marriage, he agreed to perform the ceremony, provided her mother would give her consent. He expressed the hope that my father would not be against it and added, 'I hope you are not abandoning your parents altogether.' I assured the venerable Rabbi that we were not abandoning them at all.

By autumn we were ready to stand together under the wedding canopy, but the ceremony was far from joyous. The latest news was that the German armies were approaching Moscow. We prayed for rain, which would bog them down in the muddy roads of Russia. We prayed for an early winter with heavy snow and frost which could decimate their ranks. And amongst those prayers, we also prayed for some joyous moments for ourselves.

The ceremony took place at Rabbi Kahane's house on Gęsia Street. Early in the afternoon of 21 October, the wedding canopy was put up in the last room of his apartment. It was a windowless room and the ceremony was conducted by electric light. Only our immediate family was there. The religious and traditional part of the Jewish wedding ceremony lasted just a few minutes. After I had placed the ring on my young bride's finger and stamped my heel on the traditional glass, Rabbi Kahane began his address, saying that once the decision to get married had been taken, we should look on it as an act of hope, an act of faith in the future, even though the present was dark. 'Dawn will come,' he said, 'the light of a new day will rise.'

At precisely the moment he said these words our windowless room was plunged into darkness and the Rabbi stopped speaking.

We waited for the light to come on again but it did not and the speech remained unfinished.

As we left the room I heard the Rabbi whisper, 'I don't believe in omens. Jews are forbidden to search for omens. The lights went out because the Germans cut off the power.'

The reception was at Luba's mother's house. It was small, only seventeen guests, including the Rabbi. We tried to be happy, to give each other support and hope, but our hearts were filled with dark forebodings. Unlike the Rabbi, we couldn't help considering the power failure as an ill omen.

When I visited Rabbi Kahane some months later, he remarked, 'I am not saying it was an omen, but I'm still waiting for the lights to come back on.'

A few weeks later a new trade began in our streets — selling candles.

The Polish late autumn can be depressing even in peaceful times. In late 1941, in the ghetto, I often felt that it was playing a silent dirge to lament our fate. Within days of our marriage, the heavy, cold fogs were covering the ghetto in a white shroud. The days shortened, together with our hopes, and the cold seeped into the emaciated bodies of the people around me.

In conversation with the older men from ŻZW, I learned that our ghetto was relatively comfortable compared with those outside the capital. I could not imagine how anyone could survive in worse conditions. Even though I sometimes went into the countryside to do business, I had no idea of what was going on in the other ghettos. I found it hard to understand the newcomers from Łódź who were willing to pay several hundred marks to be brought to us. Some admitted that it had not been worth it, but most were glad to be in Warsaw.

In the early days of October the first rains had begun across the Russian front. The German tanks, the *panzers*, which had been the spearhead of the blitzkrieg in the summer, were now useless, sunken above their heavy wheel chains in mud, and the Germans had to drag them out with teams of horses. With the rain the supply lines had been reduced to replenishment by rail only.

Messengers sent by the Polish Underground deep in the eastern front came back with eyewitness accounts of the misery that had begun to plague the German soldiers. They told us that the Germans had surrounded Leningrad, but all their efforts to take the city had failed. They were ill-equipped for the Russian winter.

During the first days of December, the same sources reported that the Soviets had opened a counter-offensive on the eastern front. In the ghetto, reliable informants shared details about the new armies of Russian soldiers, kept warm in white fur coats, confronting the Germans at the outskirts of Moscow and inflicting huge casualties. The Russian General, Źukov, a strong and faithful Russian had, it seemed, turned the war around on the eastern front.

This was of small comfort to us, however. Moscow might as well have been on the moon. While German soldiers were freezing in the east, collection commandos were removing the frozen bodies of the dead from the ghetto pavements each morning.

Of all the members of our families Luba and I felt closest to her oldest sister, Esther. She had been the first to give us her blessing and, with her husband, Maurycy, she guided us in our first steps of married life.

Esther had married soon after her father's death. Her husband had taken over the running of the fur business with Luba's older brothers. They had a six-year-old daughter, Noemi, who had been cared for by a nanny, Janina, a Christian. They had always treated Janina like a member of the family. When the war started and non-Jews were forbidden from working in Jewish households, she had to leave. This had been difficult for both her and Noemi as they had become attached to each other. But not long after the ghetto was established, Janina contacted the family and offered to care for Noemi on the Aryan side for the duration of the war.

Historians of the Holocaust write that Jewish children quickly learned the danger of their situation. Their mind was the mind of an adult, while their helplessness was that of a child. By the age of four, all Jewish children understood that they were more vulnerable because they were of no use to the Germans.

When Noemi was told about her nanny's offer, she reacted with enthusiasm, assuring her parents, 'I won't say that I am Jewish when I'm outside the ghetto. Nanny will teach me how to behave as a Polish girl. I'll wait for you to come and take me home.'

The financial side of the plan posed no problem and by late December all the arrangements had been made. The nanny had found a place outside Warsaw to take Noemi for a 'holiday' for a few weeks. Then she would bring her back as her niece whose parents had been taken on forced labour to Germany. Returning to Warsaw with a previous address was an important cover in case some curious individual should ask the child where she came from. Noemi knew that while she was on holidays she had to make friends with some Polish girls in the village. Back in Warsaw, she could name those girls and their parents as her old friends, with whom she had played 'before daddy and mummy had gone to work in Germany' and she had come to live with 'auntie'.

It became my responsibility to take Noemi out of the ghetto and hand her over to her nanny. The date had been set and the place arranged. I would hand the child over as quickly as possible and Janina was to disappear with her immediately into a nearby building, while I went on my way.

In theory, the arrangements seemed perfect, but every stage of their execution was a matter of life and death. We had to ensure that the appropriate German guard had been bribed in advance. I had to confer with the leader of a work-group to take me in his party and to march us along the right road. The group had to cover me somehow while the transfer was made. Above all, I had to work out a way to carry Noemi at least partially concealed through the ghetto gate and along the road to our meeting point.

The only Jewish policeman I felt I could trust with Noemi's life had fallen ill a week earlier. I spent two days at the central office of the *Judenrat*, where group leaders organised work-groups to be taken outside the ghetto. Here our luck changed for the better. I found a group leader willing to take me along and to bribe the guard. He would stop the group outside our meeting place and cause some commotion. The whole group would then surround me as the child was handed over to her nanny.

He would do all this for a price. I knew the man and felt I could rely on him. We agreed on the sum, which was to be paid in German marks or dollars, depending on the course of the previous day. I had only one condition. 'If I should be betrayed, make sure I don't have a chance to speak, as otherwise you'll be dead together with me. Oh, and by the way,' I added, 'if I or the child should die because of these arrangements, for whatever reason, a bullet will be waiting for you back in the ghetto.'

He asked, 'Wouldn't it be easier for you to arrange my bullet on the Aryan side?' With the threat of death if anything should go wrong, he said, 'I accept your conditions, but the price has just been doubled. You understand why?'

I did not bargain with him; not even when he said that his own fee would have to be paid in advance together with the bribe for the German guard.

I realised on the day how good he was.

I borrowed a coat more that twice my size and prepared a sling with a secure seat on it. On the evening before, we rehearsed at Esther's place. I put on the sling, Noemi was put inside it with her face to me and her arms around my neck. She had been told beforehand to place her head on my chest and to be as quiet as a mouse, not to speak no matter what anybody might say or ask her. This little six year old understood precisely what she was told. As she sat on the sling and put her head down with her arms around my neck, I felt uncomfortable. I said, 'Noemi, you must move more to the middle, you are pulling me too hard to one side.' She did not react. I repeated the order.

Her father said, 'You are at home now, you may speak and move. Only tomorrow you will have to be quiet. Do you understand?'

The little girl was silent. I put her down on the table and undid my sling. Noemi was proud of herself. 'You thought you could trick me. Didn't you? But you didn't win. I know you wanted to see if I would forget, well I didn't. I'll be as quiet as I am in my sleep.'

Next morning I remembered to give Noemi non-verbal instructions. 'If I touch you with a finger very lightly, please move slowly and carefully to the side I push. Nothing else. Because if you pull me too much on one side I won't be able to carry you. Do you understand?' She understood.

When we approached the gate the next day, the German guard made some very slight movement towards the Jewish policemen, turned and went demonstrably into his guard box. As we were passing, a Polish policeman noticed my heavy coat. I looked like a pregnant woman and he wanted to stop me. At that moment our leader came up between him and the guard box and whispered something. The Polish policeman looked to the Jewish one who moved his head slightly in the direction of the German guard, and I passed through untouched.

Our leader came back to me. 'It was close. Once bribed, no German guard wants to lose his customer. I am one of his regulars.'

He had arranged for one of the group to make a dash for the entrance to the marked building. As the man moved out of the row the leader screamed, 'Hey, stop!' The man kept running and we all ran after him. The group stood at the entrance, hiding the doorway, while Noemi jumped down from the sling, gave me a quick kiss and hopped into the arms of her nanny. Then together they disappeared. Within less than a minute, we were marching on.

14

Bandages

I have described my memories of Hitler's reign as a cage. There is no Jewish survivor who is not surrounded by such memories. Some feel their confinement daily, while others act as if they have forgotten those bitter experiences. But scratch the surface of their past and darkness flows up from hidden recesses.

I was in hospital in Australia in 1994. During the night, when I could not sleep, I found myself recalling the ghetto hospital. I had an urge to call the nurse and tell her what the ghetto hospital was like. I didn't do it. I knew it would be impossible for her to visit the Warsaw ghetto with me in her imagination. So I lay there in the dark, eyes open, listening to my neighbours, remembering.

I relived the day the combined special deportation command (made up of Ukrainian volunteers, Latvian murderers and Germans) came to empty the ghetto hospitals. Patients who could walk were taken from their beds to the horse-drawn carts waiting for them in the street. None were permitted to get dressed. Some went in pyjamas, others in hospital dressing gowns or whatever they had on. A thousand patients were murdered that day.

In the operating theatre, a young girl was having her appendix removed. Her father was an officer in the Jewish police. While he was leading his fellow Jews to the *Umschlagplatz* to be collected by the death carriages, his daughter's life was being saved by doctors who themselves would soon be taken. The uniformed German soldier who interrupted the operation did not know the identity of the patient, nor did he know the exalted position her father had in the ghetto hierarchy. And he would not have cared. When he pushed open the door to the operating theatre, he already had a hand on his gun holster. By the time the terrified eyes of the doctors and the theatre nurse had met his, he had his weapon in his hand. He motioned the staff to move back, went over to the anaesthetised patient and finished the operation with a bullet to the young girl's head.

This was just one story told to me by our neighbour, who had cleaned up the deserted hospital. Another was of a German, half drunk, who asked the hospital director how many patients were in the infectious diseases ward. When told the number, he said with a slight grin, 'Well, what am I to do with all that vodka?' He went on to boast that he had been promised a litre of vodka for every patient shot.

My neighbour and his team removed over four hundred bodies from their hospital beds and collected the bloody linen in bundles, under the supervision of the Jewish police. While doing their work the police paid close attention to anything of value the patients had left behind. Even the food left on some of the beds was collected under their alert eyes and given to the workers at the end of that bloody day.

By a rather black coincidence, on the same day I managed to buy some precious medical supplies for our group. They were sterilised and hygienically wrapped bandages, packed in a secure box and complete with instructions on how to use them. Stamped on top of the box in sharp black print was the warning, 'Attention! This product is the property of the Army. To be used only for the treatment of the military. Not to be sold to or used by civilians.'

I bought the box at the Kiercelak and, in the tradition of the place, paid for it sight unseen. I was told that it would be delivered to me wherever I wished, outside the ghetto or in. I never found out how the package came into the hands of the Pole who sold it to me. He was known to have contacts in lucrative but very dangerous places. He would appear from time to time with goods that were usually unobtainable even for large sums of money.

At first I kept away from him, suspecting him of being too dangerous to deal with. He was of average build, with a cold and murderous face, known only by the nickname 'Miotła', 'The broom'. After a few visits to the Kiercelak I found out some details about him and became one of his customers. He was a member of the People's Army, a fledgling group orientated towards the Soviet Union, in contrast to the Home Army, orientated towards the Polish Government-in-Exile in London.

By August 1942, the Home Army had a vast network, with Underground connections that could reach London. A delegate of the Polish Government in London ran the operations in Warsaw. In contrast, the People's Army was rather small and poor, but run by some extremely dedicated people. It received very little from Moscow in the way of arms or other help. Miotła was an important source of finance for this army.

When he offered to sell the box to me, he said, 'There is no price for this on any of the markets, as normally no one would touch these bandages, because they can be so easily identified. There is nothing to equal their quality in the whole of Poland, and maybe even in Germany. In the ghetto they would be worth twice their weight in gold. I was told to offer them to the Jews only and you, I know, are one of the buyers for the ghetto. We need the money urgently and you are one of the best sources for immediate money.'

We arranged to have the box delivered the same day to the wall of the graveyard which bordered the ghetto. It turned out to be much bigger than I had expected, but fate played its part and there were no guards cruising the area on that day. I tied a rope to the box and climbed up the wall. Then I pulled my treasure up after me.

I traversed Warsaw for more than two years, buying goods for the ghetto, and that was the only time I was made such an offer.

Medical goods were rarely sold at the Kiercelak. The other times they became available they were sold as soon as they appeared, not to individual dealers like myself but to organisations. Our own group, the ŻZW, received only two or three deliveries of bandages from the Polish Underground. And they were not of the same quality as the ones I bought the day they liquidated the hospitals in the ghetto.

During the war we became so used to danger that we lived with it somewhat in contempt. On the other hand, sometimes a miracle intervened to save one from one's own foolishness. In the ghetto, miracles happened often. They bought an additional slice of life: additional hours for some, days or months for others. Surviving as a Jew under Hitler during the Holocaust was a miracle in itself. Some miracles were so unbelievable that one would ask, 'Did it really happen? Was it really by such flimsy chance that I am still alive today?'

One such miracle happened to me. It came via a relative on my wife's side, Tola Lipszyc, who was a chemist. Tola had accumulated stock of a particular type of cream for cracked lips. Some of it was combined with traditional lipstick, for women, and some was colourless, for men.

At one stage I offered to sell her creams outside the ghetto. I can visualise the alternating rows of coloured and colourless sticks in their metal cases, four rows in a box, ten sticks in a row. But I never got round to selling them. Little did I think that my forgetfulness would one day pave the way for my own survival. But by such unimportant acts we lived and died.

It happened on a summer's day in July 1942. The previous day I had visited my father and found that his food supply was running low. He had given me some gold bars and I had promised to sell them as soon as possible on the Aryan side to buy food. There was no ŻZW duty the next day that would tie me to the ghetto or send me outside it.

It was one of those glorious mornings when I could afford to be selfish and indulge myself, and take no notice of reality. My young bride made breakfast and I told her about the gold I had received from my father. She suggested I take no more than two bars with me. 'Look,' she said, 'if you don't have any need for it why take it outside and have to risk bringing it back? We have to take risks when it's necessary but it is foolish to tempt fate for nothing.'

I listened to her. The whole morning is deeply engraved in my mind. Slowly I rose from the table, warmed some water for a shave and tried to tell myself that there was a real world in which I lived and not the one I saw in my dreams. But when I looked at the five bars and worked out that together they totalled one kilogram of verified gold I had to admit that I was better off than many others, even if I was still a Jew who had to risk his life daily.

I decided to leave the ghetto via the Leszno gate. The road there was near the courts and it could be dangerous. But I was going to take the first left-hand corner and turn away from the courts towards the money market, the trading post for dollars, pounds, gold and jewellery.

Outside our building I met the body collectors. They were lifting a skeleton of skin and bone from the pavement and throwing it into their cart. Not the right omen, I thought, although I was never one for omens.

The streets were crammed as usual and one of the young mob who made their living from passers-by greeted me as a friend. I felt a kind of relief and made a mental note to have something for him on my way home.

Near the gate it was quiet. Unlike other times, when I went out with a group as an unmarked man, I decided to have a word with the Jewish policeman and see if I could leave with a bribe. The policeman took the bribe, told me to take off my armband and went with me towards the German post. In under half a minute the German guard had turned towards his sentry box and I had gone straight out of the ghetto.

Some two hundred metres away on the Aryan side was a place known as 'The pit'. I had no intentions of walking anywhere near it. The pit was an execution point. It consisted of a narrow door in a building which was otherwise completely featureless, simply a blank wall one floor high. I had been told that the pit was a vertical shaft. One stepped through the narrow opening and fell down about three or four metres, or descended a ladder attached to the wall. The place had gained its name because people who were taken there finished up with a bullet in the back of the head and were thrown into the pit. Every few days the cleaners came. They went down by the ladder and carried the corpses up on their shoulders like sides of beef.

I had walked less than twenty metres and was about to turn into a side street when I heard the steps of boots behind me. Another few steps and I was tapped on the back. I turned around and found myself facing two German military policemen. '*Wohin*?' (Where to?) one of them asked. I noticed that his partner had black lips. It was no use pretending I wasn't Jewish, but instead of speaking, I made hand-signs and spoke in mime to show that I wanted food.

They could not have cared less. The one who had spoken indicated for me to turn round and begin walking. They followed, only a step behind.

My mind was working fast. Should I give them the two bars of gold? But what would be the point? They would bring me to the pit and shoot me anyhow. I must have something these soldiers need, I thought, something that will make them take me back to the ghetto.

By now we had walked some twenty metres. Then I remembered something. I stopped and turned around. They moved back, startled. Before they had time to respond, I pointed to the one with black lips and, half-speaking and half-gesticulating, said, 'Russia, cold, yes?'

I had hit the right nerve. The black-lipped one turned to his companion and asked for a translation. I realised that he moved his lips with difficulty. His companion asked in the same careless way as before, '*Was hast du gefragt?*' (What have you asked?)

It was my only chance. With mime and broken words, I explained that I had the most wonderful cream for frozen lips. 'Cold, Cold!' I kept repeating and indicating his lips, adding, 'Best cream.' The soldier pointed to my pocket, wanting me to show him the cream. I was afraid he would begin to search me. I pointed to the ghetto and repeated, 'Police, Jew!'

I had to say this a few times before it dawned on them that the cream was in the ghetto and they should take me back to the police. We turned around and walked back to the ghetto. From the conversation between the Germans and the Jewish policeman, I realised that the bribe I had given him, a substantial one, was for the three of them.

This policeman knew that they had been waiting in the entrance to the first house outside the ghetto, and had been prepared to send me to my death for a small part of the bribe. He spoke to me in Yiddish, 'What did you want to say to the officers?'

I made out I didn't understand Yiddish. I explained in Polish that at home I had a cream which had been made especially to give immediate relief to cracked lips. The policeman translated correctly. When they asked if I could be trusted, he said, 'Yes and no.'

After a short exchange of words the Germans told the policeman to take me to my home to collect the cream. They would be waiting for us at the gate. The policeman asked where I lived then told them that it would take some ten minutes before we could return.

I didn't want the policeman to know my address; I could not trust him after what had just happened. Our apartment was in one of three buildings that surrounded a large courtyard. I told him to wait at the gate of the courtyard, but he insisted I take him with me. When I refused he tried to take me back to the ghetto gate. I put up some resistance and after some minutes I told him, 'If you don't get back in time they will find you for sure, but they will not find me. You have to trust me. You have no other choice and I promise you I'll be back. I really have this cream but I don't want you to know where I live.'

I left him in the passage in one of the buildings while I ran up to the apartment and grabbed the cream. Within less that two minutes I was back.

The two military police were waiting for us. I handed the cream to the one with the cracked lips. He opened it and painted the cream on his lips. I was mortified. The other German had a fit of laughter. '*Hallo, Fraulein,*' he said, '*aber schoehne Lippen haben Sie.*' (Hello, miss, you have beautiful lips.)

In my rush I had grabbed a coloured stick. I turned quickly to the Jewish policeman and said in Polish, 'Tell him to rub the cream into his lips and not pay attention to the other's laughter.'

He translated. The German did as he was told and the miracle happened. The colour was absorbed into his black lips and the skin became immediately soft. He was elated. I could hardly believe my luck. He said to me and with a light grin, 'Good, very good.' Then he turned to leave.

The other one was not so willing to let it go at that and motioned to me, 'You come with us.'

I stopped dead and looked at the one with the cracked lips, without saying a word. Something must have moved him. 'Let him go this time,' he said, speaking for my life. 'If we catch him again we will take him.'

I often ask myself whether the murderous German who had been so generous with my life for a tube of lip cream would have done the same if he had known that, by this action, I would survive the war.

15

Escaping from death

THE Nazis not only isolated the Jews in Poland from the non-Jewish world, but also isolated one ghetto from the other. Each one was ruled by minor dictators, who derived their strength from German support and were overseen by a *Judenrat*, a Jewish Council, which had no real authority. Everything depended on the strength of the leader.

Any German, at any time, was of higher standing and authority than any Jew, even if the Jew had been authorised as the Eldest of the Jews by the Germans.

The Germans repeatedly promised that the Jewish leaders and their families would be spared. Not all leaders were that blind. There was a case in March 1942. If my memory doesn't play tricks, it was in Zduńska Wola, a township near the large city of Łódź. The ghetto there had reached its final days. There was no chance for an organised resistance. The Gestapo came to the leader of the community and asked him to nominate ten Jews to be hanged in the marketplace on the day of Purim. The Eldest of the Jews asked, 'What have they done? Why are they to be hanged?'

The German official replied, 'Because they are Jews, of course.'

Witnesses to that conversation, who were subsequently deported to the Łódź ghetto, reported that the Eldest of the Jews rose to his full height and with an outward expression of calmness and finality, replied, 'I can only supply you with four Jews to be hanged for being Jewish: myself, my wife and my children. I am not authorised to deliver any other Jews for your purpose.'

One of the deeply shameful chapters in the history of the Warsaw ghetto arose because Adam Czerniakow, the leader of the Jewish community in the ghetto, was too weak, too liberal and too naive to save the Jewish lives entrusted to him. The tragic end of the ghetto probably could not have been changed, but the road to it might have been different under a stronger leader. There can be no doubt that if the Uprising of the Warsaw ghetto had taken place in August–September 1942, when there were still three hundred thousand Jews, the Germans would have paid a much higher price and other Jewish communities that still existed at the time might have been encouraged to follow suit. Who knows, the Polish Resistance might even have joined in under such conditions.

That it was not so, is to our shame. Adam Czerniakow was an honest man and one should respect him for committing suicide the moment he realised the Germans' treacherous plans, rather than hand over a single Jew to the murderers. Unfortunately, this kind of heroism was too little under the circumstances, and too late. By the time he had made peace with his conscience, the real power in the ghetto had been usurped by the Jewish police, who had been progressively corrupted.

During this time and right up to the last moment before the Uprising in 1943, some of the Jewish leaders remained blind to the German plan for the total destruction of all Jews and clung to their irrational hope to survive the German death sentence.

Many of these leaders, whether through lack of courage or in the mistaken belief that they were protecting their families, actively assisted the German plan. They were protected by personal bodyguards and believed that as long as they served the Gestapo they were safe. It was a tragic necessity, but over time we had to clean them out — assassinate them — to be free to deal with our enemy.

The lower echelons of the hierarchy, the ordinary police and heads of departments, we could silence through fear. When the average policeman or manager eventually realised that the price of his co-operation with the German authorities had changed from providing security for his people to endangering it, he stopped co-operating.

The people in the Warsaw ghetto had lost all faith in their ability to resist. When the first high-ranking policeman, Firstenberg, was shot by the Jewish resistance ŻOB in February 1942, the rumour in the ghetto was that Polish Underground Army officers had carried out the execution. Few Jews believed a Jewish bullet could have silenced the traitor.

In July, the deportation of more than three hundred thousand Jews to the death camp Treblinka began. The Jewish police were overseen by a special Jewish task force, the infamous '13'. This was an open agency of the Gestapo, supposedly set up to combat criminals. When the order for the deportation came through, the Jewish police were, morally, no longer members of the suffering community, but rather the 'Chosen Jews' of the Germans. Like the non-Jewish assistants to the German death machine, the Lithuanians, Latvians, Estonians and the Ukrainian SS units, the Jewish police willingly helped their German masters. They played the role of guard dogs only, and carried no firearms. They had, however, big sticks and the supportive power of the few armed guards under whose control they worked.

On the first days of the deportation order, the task of the police was simple. They had sufficient volunteers who, not knowing that deportation meant death, were willing to leave the ghetto hell. The police needed only to supervise their orderly deportation. But within three or four days there were no more volunteers.

The first signal to ghetto dwellers that all was not as it seemed came with Czerniakow's suicide. Within four days the Jewish workers on the ghetto rail station, the *Umschlagplatz*, had noticed that the train which had left late in the afternoon was back already the next morning. For some reason the shortness of the journey puzzled them. Soon it was noticed that here and there food had been left in the wagon. It raised the alarm: how could food have been left behind?

Less than ten days after the beginning of the Action, the most horrible rumours began circulating that not far from Warsaw all the deported Jews were being killed in gas chambers within hours of leaving the ghetto. No one knew how or who brought this news back, but it was known somehow to be true.

The first recorded eyewitness to come back from Treblinka was David Nowodworski. He was a member of the left-wing Zionist youth movement of Hashomer. He had been rounded up by the police on the first day they went into action to take people by force. He landed in Treblinka and was put into one of four groups. After horrendous beatings, the groups were assigned to different tasks: to collect the bodies of the dead after gassing, to sort the clothing the victims had left behind, to bury the dead in a deep pit, and to load retrieved goods into the now empty wagons. (At that stage those who ran Treblinka had not established permanent teams to carry out these tasks, although these were set up soon after this.)

Nowodworski's group sorted the clothing, while being beaten constantly. In an unguarded minute he hid in one of the wagons in which the clothing of the murdered was being loaded. His co-workers covered him quickly with bundles. Hidden thus, he passed the German inspection before the train left Treblinka. Once outside the place he managed to jump from the train when it slowed down at a bend and make his way back to the ghetto.

The leadership of Hashomer, who saw Nowodworski within a few hours of his return, realised that he was in shock but he gave very lucid answers to the questions they put to him. His account, together with reports of the annihilation of Jews in the east and the ghettos in western Poland, and other reports about the existence of a similar place in Chełmno where Jews from the Łódź ghetto were being put to death, left no doubt in anyone's mind that the time had come to resist physically. But no plan had been prepared at that stage.

In the meantime, the Jewish police were being coerced to co-operate in delivering their daily quota of Jews for slaughter. They were coerced in two ways. One was the reward of a whole loaf of bread, two kilograms daily, together with sausage and other goods; the other was the threat that any policeman who failed to deliver his quota would forfeit the lives of his own family. (Families of Jewish policemen were still exempt from the deportation order and adequately secured in special reserves.)

I had been away from the ghetto buying provisions for my family and for Luba's mother when the deportation started. The day after my return I left home early to deliver the food. But before going out into the street I made sure that the human-catchers were not in our area. Everything seemed quiet. I dropped off my parcel at the Gutrajchts' house, and as I was leaving Luba's mother said, 'I'll come with you now, while it is quiet. I want to visit my family.'

I protested that it was too dangerous, but she would not have it otherwise and I gave in.

We made sure the path was clear and began to walk towards Muranowska Street. We turned a corner in what seemed to be a safe street and came face to face with three policemen and a Ukrainian guard pointing his rifle at us. 'Turn around and begin marching!' the Ukrainian ordered, and the Jewish policemen surrounded us. I had the urge to lose my life by taking one of them with me but for whatever reason, perhaps the presence of Gitele Gutrajcht, I kept the rage to myself. It was foolish, as we were going to our certain death, but I did not want to be the direct cause of her dying.

They delivered us to a mustering place, a square, where German officers, Ukrainian SS guards, Polish and Jewish police were already holding a considerable number of people. The houses around the square were closed and guarded to stop people escaping. In quick succession, other groups joined us, eventually totalling some ten thousand people. The whole width of the street was packed, only the footpaths were kept clear by the guards. We were made to face towards the *Umschlagplatz* and wait.

We were very close to the front, part of the street near us had been cleared and Gestapo officers stood in a group talking amongst themselves, waiting for something unknown.

In a short while, the officers moved to make room for more people. Then, walking towards us, I recognised one of the most famous faces in the ghetto. Janusz Korczak was walking stiffly, with a young child in his arms. At his side, assistants were keeping pace, holding youngsters by their hands. It looked quite unreal. The children were dressed as if they were going to a picnic. Some carried rag dolls, others had paper flags and a boy of about thirteen carried the flag of the orphanage which Korczak had created in the ghetto.

In silence the Gestapo watched the march. As the group approached us, one of the assistants gently turned the first row around, another did the same with the next row and then the children took over and turned around and filed into place by themselves. The assistants placed themselves at intervals and Korczak, with the child still in his arms, walked up to the front, on the fatal day of 6 August 1942.

Mrs Gutrajcht drew my attention to an officer who had walked over and was speaking to Korczak. It seemed to me that the tall man shook his head, as if to say no. After a while he repeated the same head movement. The officer went back to the footpath, nodded, and everyone in the square started to march, with the children leading the way. The children, in turn, were led by Korczak with his assistant teacher, Stefania Wilczyńska.

I looked behind me. As far as I could see there was nothing but people. At every few rows a guard stood with a rifle or a light automatic held on the ready. Thousands of thoughts ran through my head as we came closer and closer to the point of no escape. I recall the silence of the mass of the people, the sound of their footsteps marching, and the screaming of the guards and, over them, the voice of Mrs Gutrajcht, 'Save yourself, my child! Do you hear me, save yourself!'

We were only two blocks away from the entrance to the *Umschlagplatz* when an army truck came towards us. The guards stepped down from the footpath and began pushing the people to one side of the street to clear the way for it.

The truck had slowed down. As it approached us, I heard Mrs Gutrajcht say once more, 'Save yourself, my child!' Before I realised what I was doing, I had jumped up into the rear of the truck, pressing against the floor of the wagon, hidden from the eyes of the guards by the high sides. I could hear a German shouting, but felt the engine accelerating beneath me.

I had managed to escape from the *Umschlagplatz* by jumping into a German army truck, going I knew not where.

I dared not lift my head. The driver and whoever may have been with him had not noticed me. I turned on my side to make sure I was below the rear window of the cabin. I was aware that we were still in the ghetto, because it was completely quiet in the street. This could have meant either that we were going through the empty part of the ghetto, or that the street had been surrounded by Ukrainian and Latvian guards. I felt chilled with fear. I began to think about my next step. The only thing to do was to jump down and be careful not to be noticed by the driver. But by the time I had collected my wits it was too late. The truck made a sharp right-hand turn and sounded its horn. From above us somebody screamed some words and I knew I could not jump out. A heavy iron gate opened and slowly the truck drove through, then the gates closed behind us.

I stood up and looked through the split in the rear black curtains; my worst fears were confirmed. I was in the infamous Pawiak, the dreaded jail built by Russian slave labour for the Czar in the 1860s. It had been planned to hold the most dangerous political prisoners. The prison served the Russians until the First World War; during the war years the Germans used it; after the First World War, the

Poles; and now it was once more in the hands of the Germans. The Pawiak was within the ghetto but was not under Jewish jurisdiction. The Germans used it almost exclusively for 'dangerous' Poles and a small number of Jews. I had escaped death in Treblinka and had instead sent myself to die at the Pawiak. I knew that people had jumped from the cattle trucks on the way to Treblinka and had returned to the ghetto, but I could not recall a single case where Jews taken to the Pawiak had ever returned.

I heard the sound of people jumping down from the cabin of the truck. After a few seconds somebody came around to the back and pulled open the curtain. I was facing a very surprised, big German in a black uniform. In a quiet voice, as if speaking to somebody he knew, he asked, 'Who are you? What are you doing in the truck?' His friendliness almost struck me dumb.

'I am a Jew,' I said, glued to the spot.

'Would you please get out of the truck and come down?' he asked in the same surreal, well-mannered voice. I was flooded with relief. As I jumped down, his fist came down hard on my neck. My eyes blurred, my head spun and I felt my balance failing. This man was twice my size. I had no intention of testing his strength. He waited patiently until I oriented myself; I lifted my head, opened my eyes, and he gave me a flat chop with the edge of his hand under my stomach. I bent forward as he stood in front of me. I braced myself for a third blow but he did not hit me. Instead, he grabbed me by the neck and started to push me to walk. He twisted his grip and I had to move.

We walked up some steps, went through a passage and then walked down some more steps. He had his hand firmly on my neck all the way. He stopped in front of a door and a jailer came running. 'Open the door for my friend here,' my polite guide called. Keys turned, the door opened and the last remark of my guide was: 'You won't have long to wait, in the meantime . . .' and with that he literally lifted me by my neck and threw me. I flew through the air into the cell.

It was sufficiently bright for me to see where I was. People pushed me away from the door deeper into the room. The place smelled badly at first, but that quickly became the least of my worries. I found myself in a small cell which was meant probably for twenty prisoners but was holding around ninety Jews at the time. Nobody took any particular notice of me as a new arrival. Here and there some groups of two or three went on with their quiet conversations, while most stood or sat around aimlessly. I began to talk to the man next to me. He listened to my story and laughed painfully, using a Polish proverb, 'So you came from the rain to hide under the spouting.'

I had met the right man. He had been in the cell for nearly two weeks. 'They come, like you came, from anywhere and everywhere and go just as quickly,' he said. 'This is like a railway station. It is not meant for long-term prisoners. In fact,' he added knowingly, 'we should not be here at all. This building is called Serbia and it belongs to the women's wing of the Pawiak. They have taken it over for the Jews temporarily.'

'How do you know all this?' I asked.

'Because before I was brought here I was in one of the Gestapo cells at the Szucha. I was caught in a raid on the Aryan side. I recognised one of the guards who took us away as the son of our Ukrainian neighbours before the war. I gave him my wallet while we were travelling and he managed to arrange for me to stay in the cell at Szucha without being interrogated for three or four days. He was not bad. He brought me food and told me that he was trying to get me transferred to here. Of course, he did not tell me that from here the way is up.' My new friend pointed towards the ceiling.

'How do you know that?'

'You are a funny man with your questions. You will find out soon enough. If they don't take you out tomorrow morning. You see, I am sitting in the middle. I want to remain unnoticed. My Ukrainian friend has said he will arrange for me not to be called out, but he won't be able to help me if I'm taken at random. So I sit here and hide from the eyes of the German dogs. I think that I am one of those who has been here for the longest. They come in the mornings, or at midday, or in the afternoon; they come at any time they like. They either call out names or point to this one or that one. Those who are taken out don't come back. I don't think they are taken to recuperate.' My friend smiled wryly.

'And when is the food distributed?' I asked.

'When they feel like it. Usually every second day. You just missed out. We just finished what they call soup and bread before you came in.'

I moved away, found a place near the wall and tried to sleep. When I became aware of my surroundings once more, the cell was lit by the small central lamp high above us, protected by a net of steel. From then on it was one of the longest nights I can remember.

'To the toilet!' I heard the voice of the jailer call in Polish. There was a rush to the door. A few people were taken out and the door was closed again. Some minutes later the door opened and the performance was repeated. Those who had gone came back and a few others went. After seeing that the others had all returned I moved up and went to the toilet. It was an important lesson. The washroom attendant, a Polish man, spoke to himself, but loud enough for us to hear: 'The Pawiak is in the hands of the Huns, the Latvian dogs and the Ukrainian mongrels, but our Polish guards work for Poland. If anybody has any message to leave you can do it here and now. I don't look at you and you don't look at me. So I don't know who you are and you don't have to be afraid that I'll betray you.' Nobody in my group had a message but I made a mental note to try to check whether what the attendant had said was true. Moments later I realised how silly the thought was.

The day of sitting in the cell and waiting had begun. I was leaning crouched against the wall when the door opened and a

German stood in the doorway: 'I need five strong fellows to clean out a truck in ten minutes. Volunteers!'

As I had the day before I acted before I realised it. I jumped over the heads of others and was at the front like thunder. The guard was no older than I, maybe even younger. He looked at me and at the other volunteers and selected five of us. We walked up the steps and into the yard. A truck, like the one I had come in, was parked in the middle of the courtyard. The German pointed to some buckets, to a tap and brooms and said in the same calm voice as my 'friend' had spoken the day before: 'You have ten minutes to get the thing cleaned up. After that there is a bullet for every five seconds. Half a minute over the time and the job may not be finished but you will be.'

We started our work. I went up on the truck and nearly vomited. The back was full of blood and human excrement, mingled with rags and clothing. The guard gave us his instruction: 'Undo the side tarpaulins and open the flap. Sweep the dirt down and wash it in to the drains. This is the quickest way.' He didn't have to say it twice. Somebody had already jumped up into the truck after me and without saying a word we untied the side tarpaulin towards the drain, lowered the back flap of the tray and began sweeping. Two green-uniformed guards passed by. The German stopped them. 'Stay here with them, both of you. They have just under nine minutes to get the truck clean and ready to leave. I'll be back in time.' The German left. A foreign guard came on the scene and within minutes they were taking little notice of us. When we had finished and were ready to wash the blood and dirt into the gutter, one of our group reported that the truck was ready for inspection. Two of the guards jumped up, had a quick look around and came back: 'You have not finished yet, sweep the dirt to the drains, put back the flaps and tie the tarpaulin in place. You have four minutes to do it.'

This was my chance. During the few minutes I had thought things over and come to a decision. If I stayed there I could consider myself already dead. If I took a chance I might be caught and shot on the spot but . . . I dared not think anymore for fear that I would weaken. I jumped up on the truck once more and called the others to lift the side flap. As they locked it in position I told them to forget about me. 'I never came out of the cell with you.' An elderly driver in a military uniform came over to the truck and addressed the Latvian guards. 'Who was supposed to check out the cleaning of the truck?' Two foreigners reported that they had inspected the truck and it was clean. 'Take the prisoners back to the Jew cell,' he said off-handedly and climbed into the cabin. I was afraid that, at the last minute, one of the prisoners would say something, but nobody did. My heartbeat seemed so loud I felt sure it would betray me. I sat in the corner near the curtains and felt quite faint when the truck came to the gate and a hand pulled away the curtain next to me.

'Everything is all right,' I heard the man report.

The heavy gates opened and seconds later I knew I had used up the greatest part of my share of luck. I had come out of the Pawiak alive. When the truck turned the corner away from the jail, I jumped out. I must have become invisible for a moment because there were two Jewish policemen walking towards me who should have seen me jumping off the truck. But they took no notice of me. I turned around and went back in to Dzielna, the street of the Pawiak. I reasoned that no one would dream that a Jew or Pole would walk towards the jail! I went from there through ruined houses and cellars to Schultze's workshops, where I knew I would find some of my friends from the ŻZW. In their care, I related the extraordinary misadventure of my previous forty-eight hours.

16

Deportations

THE dimensions of the Holocaust are too vast to be understood in a general frame of knowledge. It is meaningless to say, 'Within thirty days the German death machine had taken out of the Warsaw ghetto some two hundred thousand Jews and murdered them in Treblinka' or to say, 'Between 6 and 12 September 1942, they removed a further one hundred thousand Jews.' It would be the same as saying, 'The distance from our sun to the nearest star in our galaxy is six light years.' The figures would be right but would convey nothing.

To understand the extent of the human tragedy of the deportation of the Warsaw Jews during July and August 1942 to Treblinka, one would have to frame the drama in single images and study the details; the faces of the victims. One would need the story behind each picture. For only in the individual stories could one begin to grasp the depth of the tragedy.

I do not mean tragedy in terms of the destruction of life itself; that part of the German crime has superficially healed. Grass has grown over the unknown graves of the murdered. Except for the few camps that have been left standing completely or partially, there is little evidence to describe the suffering of those who were the victims of the German madness. But the sin of Germany that will remain unforgivable lies in the destruction of the culture and way of life which had nurtured Jews for a thousand years in Eastern

Europe. Nothing can bring that culture back and nothing can atone for that sin.

The dawn of Polish history in the times of Mieszko the First in the tenth century is also the dawn of Jewish history in Poland. Step by step, Jewish and Polish history grew in the same soil. At the beginning of the sixteenth century, Polish Jewry started to blossom, and by the end of the eighteenth century, more than eighty percent of world Jewry lived in Poland. On 1 September 1939, when Germany attacked Poland, three and a half million Jews lived on Polish soil; on 6 August 1942, the Polish Jewish educator Korczak walked together with his two hundred orphan children, perhaps the final generation of Polish Jews, to their deaths in Treblinka.

Individual stories? In the summer days of July 1942, Hillel Kajtlin went to his death dressed in his tallit and tefilin, surrounded by a congregation of many thousands. He walked in their midst through the streets of the ghetto speaking aloud to his God. Before the destruction of Polish Jews began, the mention of his name was enough to make one silent with respect. Hillel Kajtlin. The poet, philosopher, writer, the Talmudist, the Cabbalist, the humanist, the man with the golden soul who lived a humble life for himself and a most illustrious one for his fellow Jews and others. The man who had in his philosophical essays about good and evil asked if God has already found the full truth and goodness, or was our world and all it contains one of the many experiments of the Creator along the way to seeking truth and goodness? When the Orthodox Jews attacked him for teaching what they considered atheism, he was not afraid to reply that in his honesty he was closer to the spirit of God than they were. He said, 'At least I am still seeking, while they believe they have already found the truth which the Creator may still not have found.' Hillel Kajtlin — snuffed in the flames of Treblinka.

When the great Hassidic Rabbi of Alexandrów was marching to the *Umschlagplatz* he was also surrounded by thousands of Jews. I was told that at the beginning of the war he was offered, like the

Hassidic Rabbi of Gur, Góra Kalwaria, to be shuttled out of Poland by the Gestapo for a fee of fifty thousand German marks. The followers of the Gur dynasty paid the money and their Rabbi left occupied Poland for Palestine to continue his 'court'. Two followers of the Rabbi of Alexandrów, Efraim Fishel Milrad and Benjamin Russ, wanted to pay the same fee for their Rabbi, but he forbade them, saying, 'When the field goes up in fire a shepherd should not leave his flock.' The Rabbi of Alexandrów finished his days in the Warsaw ghetto working as a shoemaker. People who knew him remembered him saying, 'I tell you, God will regret this ghetto. He regretted the flood He brought on the world and He will regret what is happening now to His Jews.' Reaching the *Umschlagplatz*, he took his followers to one side and together they sang Hassidic melodies. As they were driven to the cattle wagons they began to sing a well-known prayer, '*Vetaher Libenu*', asking God to cleanse their hearts to serve Him in truth. One of the Ukrainian guards lifted his whip and hit the Rabbi over the face. The Rabbi managed to turn around and say to his tormentor, 'Thank you.' He was whipped a second time over the face and called out, 'Louder! Sing louder, we are sanctifying the Holy name!'

While the deportations were swallowing more and more lives each day, individuals and organisations continued to function. The Underground organisations were discussing if, when and how they should as one body begin to resist the deportation. The futile differences of opinion between them were debated long and often. Some argued that every day of waiting meant a day of lost opportunity, while others preached patience and believed that the right time to go out in an uprising was yet to come.

For shrewd Germans, the time of the deportations was the best time to become millionaires. They offered their protection in the form of jobs. Working for the German war industry had been declared 'essential', and 'essential' Jews had been promised protection from deportation. Germans with the right connections, like Többens and Schultz, arrived from Germany empty handed. With the help of the Gestapo, they confiscated buildings at the fringe of the ghetto, ordered the Jewish police to throw out the people who lived there and set up factories in them. Jews seeking protection had to provide the machines for their jobs. Often they had to bribe somebody to be given the life-guaranteeing work. My young bride Luba handed over a diamond of more than a carat, framed in a gold earring, and received for it a treadle sewing machine and a job in a German factory sewing army uniforms. Her wages consisted of a daily soup, a portion of bread and 'security'. The overseers, the *Werkschutz*, were Jews, while the running of the factories remained in German hands. Within weeks, the 'protectors' became rich beyond their dreams. The German employers regularly asked for and were given small gifts; those who had money or jewellery paid up willingly, not thinking of what may happen the next day: gold watches, bracelets, earrings, brooches set with precious stones. The rush of events was too traumatic to let one realise that nothing was going to extend one's life long enough to survive. Survival was only for the day; for the hour. All organisations in the ghetto had but one aim: to get their own people into the German factories, and to place them in the 'safe' houses which German employers had appropriated.

After I carried Luba's sewing machine to her new work place and saw her safely settled, I felt less worried. But it took only a few weeks for the Germans to make a laughing stock of the 'security' these employers had been promised. When the streets of the ghetto could no longer supply the required daily quota for deportation, they took the families of the employees while the employed were at work. When that failed to fulfil the quota, the Gestapo and the Germans came to the 'secure' work places and made their own selection. Luba had the good fortune to be considered worthy of further service to the German war effort and was, for the time being, spared the final journey in a cattle truck.

If I had known on 21 October 1941, what was to happen in the months of July, August and September 1942, I would have warned my new bride that she would be marrying a man who would only partly belong to her. I would have told her that a time would come when I'd have to weigh my loyalty to her and my loyalty to the organisation. I would have asked her if she were willing to take second place to my Underground loyalty. With hindsight I might have postponed the wedding for better days. But I am grateful that we did not know what was in store for us.

The great deportation caused us to grow apart. I was forced to fend for myself without working papers, while I knew that Luba was secure in her job. My affinity for those who went to the *Umschlagplatz* grew, and swallowed bit by bit the loyalty I owed my wife of only a few months. The daily fight for survival overwhelmed everything else; not only in me but in everyone. The only desire that was stronger than the desire of individuals to survive was the desire to become part of a group. This had been seen with Korczak and his orphanage, in the youth movements, and in my own case with the ŻZW.

A day or two before the deportations were interrupted, the Jewish Chief of Police, Szeryński, was shot by an Underground agent, Israel Kanal. The two bullets he received from the ŻOB failed to kill him but he was seriously wounded. Szeryński had been the mastermind who organised the Jewish police to assist the Germans and their cohorts in the deportation. He had done his work well. The Jewish police behaved not as unwilling assistants to the murderers but as if they were a loyal paid service.

From the first day of the deportations, a routine was established, and Szeryński had trained his Jewish forces to perform their part. A block of streets would be closed off in the morning; the Jewish police would call out that the street had been surrounded and no one was to leave their dwelling; the caretakers of the buildings would immediately close the building gates and anybody found in the street would be either shot on the spot or handed over to the police. The Germans and their assistants would then go from building to building and the Jewish police would call to the trapped inhabitants: '*Alles herunter!*' (All to come down.) Pressure was applied to hurry: '*Schnell, schnell!*' It was the duty of the Jewish police to go in first to check the apartments in case anybody had disobeyed the order. Walls would be tapped, wardrobes opened; they would look under the beds. The cellars and attics were searched for anyone who failed to obey the German order. The police would drag out those found hiding to be dealt with by the Germans or their helpers. Often the Germans would not trust the Jewish police and would follow them after they had made their inspection. More than one policeman lost his life on the spot, or was forced to go with the deportees for having let a Jew hide in a moment of weakness.

When all tenants were assembled in the yard the selection started. In theory, those who had valid working cards (*Arbeits Karte*), were to be released unharmed to return to their apartments. But the fate of those people who were trapped in the closed-off yard was more a matter of luck. It depended on the whim of the selector. He decided who went and who stayed. Those selected for deportation were handed over to the Jewish police. Together with their Aryan colleagues the police led the victims to the *Umschlagplatz* on foot or in carts. For this they received a loaf of bread daily and additional rations. While the deportation went on, their families were secured in special dwellings. Szeryński had not been known to take part in the operations directly. It was known only that he received daily reports about the operation. The few times when a Jewish policeman fell victim because of his failure to be vigilant in his work, Szeryński called a special 'after work' parade at which he spoke to his force. He told them that if he were there when a Jewish policeman failed in his duties, he would immediately order that all the policeman's protected family be deported with him.

Various rumours spread in the ghetto about who shot the Chief of Police. He was taken out of active service and replaced by his second-in-command, who was also his relative; a man by the name Jacób Lajkin — the personification of evil itself. A small, short man, he tried to compensate for his physical shortcomings by inflicting his evil authority over others. He ran berserk in his desire to be cruel. With a whip in one hand he was everywhere chasing, beating and screaming. The Germans sometimes even smiled, seeing how eagerly he performed his duties. Lajkin was proud of his reputation. People told of how he had once scolded a policeman for being slack in his duty by telling him, 'If I were told to bring the mother who bore me, I would have performed my duty with more devotion than you have shown to yours.'

The deportations took their toll on our marriage. It was not that I felt any less for Luba; simply that the organisation needed me more. When the deportations ceased, Luba and I rejoined each other in a somewhat calmer state of mind.

17

The Kettle

In the Łódź ghetto in September 1942 the word '*Spere*', meaning 'closed off', was coined. To this day the Spere is known as the period between 5 and 12 September, when some twenty thousand Jews, mostly children and elderly, were sent to their deaths in the gas-trucks at Chełmno (Kulmhof). At the same time, on 8 September 1942, the word '*Kettle*' became part of the Holocaust lexicon in the Warsaw ghetto. In less than five days, the Kettle devoured over one hundred thousand Jews of the already decimated ghetto population.

The main deportation had stopped as suddenly as it had begun. On 24 August, after the daily quota for the transport to Treblinka had been filled, rumours began to spread that the deportation was over. Nobody could know who started the story, but the next morning it was confirmed. No SS, no Gestapo, no Ukrainian, Lithuanians, Estonians or Latvians were to be seen. The Jewish police who had a day earlier roamed the streets like dog catchers were suddenly more human. The Jewish administration began sending workers to the emptied houses to bring the apartments 'into order'.

Those of us remaining tried to focus on our new situation and debate the possibilities. The optimists were sure that now, after the ghetto had been 'cleansed' of the unproductive elements, we would be left in peace. The Germans, they argued, needed Jewish war production and Warsaw was saving them thousands of men who would have to be taken off the front if all Jews were to be destroyed. The pessimists were just as sure that no Jew would be permitted to survive the war. They argued that it would matter little how the war finished, one thing was certain, no Jew under Hitler would be allowed to live and see the end. According to the pessimists, the reasons for halting the deportation could be the lack of killing facilities; a switch of attention to other ghettos; or some reason known only to the barbaric nation itself.

By the beginning of September, things began to look hopeful. When the remission extended into a week most people began to reorganise their lives. I was called to the headquarters of the ŻZW and told that if any new deportation should start I was to report immediately to the administration. They would decide the steps to be taken under the circumstances. I felt a surge of pessimism, having just repaired the damage which the deportations had caused to my relationship with Luba.

My intuition was correct. On 6 September, the deportation went back into full swing. This time the Germans and their helpers seemed to be in a much more vicious mood. The suddenness of their return caught the ghetto once again unprepared. But the system had been altered during the few quiet days. At the conclusion of the second day of the new Action, the Jewish police toured the streets announcing that in the morning, all work in the ghetto would come to a stop. No factory was to open. 'Everyone,' they announced, 'will leave their dwelling at dawn, taking only food and drink for two days, and, leaving the doors unlocked, they will come to Miła, Lubecka, Smocza, Niska and Zamenhoff streets by ten in the morning. Whoever is found outside this area after the stated hour will be shot on the spot.'

Some of those who had working cards still clung to the illusion that they were protected; but not all. Before dawn a messenger from the ŻZW came to our home to tell me to go into hiding at a place prepared for active members. I asked if my wife, her two brothers, and her sister and family could come with me. No. Only I was to come to the hiding place. I said I was unable to do this, and the messenger did not argue with me. As a family, we all went to the appointed place — together, for whatever our fate was to be.

Nobody knows who first called it the 'Kettle' but the name caught on. Within hours this was the name given to the place and the Action, and so it remained in the pages of history. People waited in the designated area. Some stood in the street, others in entrances to houses, some joined friends who lived in the area and others walked around restlessly. At ten o'clock the whole area was quickly surrounded with a heavy rope and a chain of German guards. Within this area, officials of the German factories handed out new round badges to their employees which proclaimed the work place of the person who had received them. The number of badges, however, was less than one third of the number of people who were entitled to them. The rest were left to imagine their own fate.

I turned to the ŻZW leaders who were urgently trying to get their members into hiding. Again I refused to leave my family but asked for a saving badge to put on my left lapel. I was given a false one which could pass for being real if not inspected too closely. The German authorities had set up a single passage through which everyone had to pass. In rows of six the long columns had to approach the Germans, who sometimes took notice of the badges and sometimes ignored them. With the now notorious move of the hand the selection took place. Those to the right had been given a reprieve; those who went to the left were surrounded by another group of guards and with the help of Jewish policemen were driven away to the slaughter.

Nothing less than having been there physically can conjure the atmosphere of the place. The very air smelled of fear and resignation; of the despair of those who had failed to receive the life-giving worker badge; of the enormous effort to appear composed and dignified — not to show fear to the Angels of Death before they decided to move their hand one way or another. An unknown darkness hovered in the sunshine. The long rows moved slowly. Here and there the columns halted, as the Germans stopped to take counsel about a particular Jew, or to ask a question of this man or that woman.

Luba had been given a badge which she pinned to her left side just below the shoulder, as ordered. I had some hope that she would pass and be sent to the right. In all this turmoil something reminded me to be grateful that little Noemi was already outside the ghetto.

I had placed myself three or four rows behind Luba and observed as she came closer and closer to the point of inspection. In front of the rows, guards kept some semblance of order. They observed if everything was as it should be and if it was not, they intervened according to their whim; from a quiet order, to shooting. I watched the columns as Luba's row approached the front. For dreadful seconds I felt an icy wind of fear. She was shown to the right. My sweat was cold, and I shivered with relief.

I still had some rows to go before facing the German gods. I decided to move back and watch the fate of Luba's older sister and husband, and her two brothers. I had no plan of action if they were sent to the left; it was just an illogical curiosity of the moment. A guard noticed my move. He didn't like it. With a wave of his hand he stopped our row, came over and inspected my badge. He called me out of the row, tore the badge from my breast and pointed me to the wall of a building where those commanded to turn left were waiting. I saw bodies spread out in the middle of the road, with pools of blood around them. Two other men were already at the wall. A Ukrainian guard was standing nearby with his submachine-gun on the ready, pointing to the men at the wall. I joined them. As if I was standing outside myself, I realised that the fear I had when Luba was passing the selection and the fear I had felt when the German had called me out had evaporated. My head was clear and I felt indifferent to the thought that soon these men and I would join those who were already lying in the middle of the road.

After that there would be nothing. I tried to visualise my own dead body. Strangely, I could no longer hear the noise from the Kettle.

The man next to me said quietly that when five people were collected, the German came over and shot them. I wanted to ask him why he was waiting patiently for his death without making some move but realised then that I, too, was simply standing and waiting. I felt relieved that nobody else had joined us yet to make up five. From my position I could see a military car coming from the direction opposite the ghetto columns. It pulled up just before the street crossing where I was standing, and two civilians in leather coats got out and walked towards us. They stopped, looking somewhat puzzled, in front of us. I stared into their eyes as they looked at me and one of them went over to the Ukrainian who was guarding us. In a voice which has stayed with me to this day, he asked, 'Why are these men standing at the wall?' As if the laws of nature momentarily changed, the guard became as frightened as a ghetto Jew. Pointing anxiously to the guard who had sent me to the wall he repeated, '*Deutsche, deutsche!*' and turning his hand towards us he again screamed with fear in his voice, '*Jude, Jude!*' Panic-stricken, he kept repeating these words and pointing in one direction, then another. The civilian Germans quickly tired of him. The one who had spoken, asked, 'Don't you speak proper German?' Receiving once more the finger pointing and the reply, '*Deutsche, deutsche, Jude, Jude,*' he called me over, looked at me for a second and, pointing to the right side, barked, '*Mach das du fortcomst*' (See that you get lost). With a kick to my behind with his jackboot, I was once more among the living. All I can imagine is that the German, seeing a strong young man, wanted me working for the war effort.

Luba's sister passed the selection. So did her two brothers. But her brother-in-law, the one who had been the family protector, was shot on the spot. I was unable to believe that this wonderful and astute man had really gone.

The Kettle lasted another three days. When the deportations and the killings were over, the ghetto had been reduced from around four hundred thousand people to some sixty-five thousand. Around a thousand had been shot when discovered in hiding and some four hundred had lost their lives in the Kettle itself.

The epilogue of the deportation came some days later. On 21 September, the Germans came to repay the Jewish police for their help in the Action. They surrounded the buildings of the police families and ordered those who were not on duty to come out in their clean uniforms for inspection. An officer of the German guards thanked them sincerely for the help they had given to make the deportation Action a great success. When he finished his speech, he called them to attention. They obeyed, then he ordered them to turn right. Surrounded by the same guards who had been their colleagues a few days earlier, the police were marched off to the *Umschlagplatz*, where cattle wagons were waiting for them. It would be a lie to say that those of us left in the ghetto mourned their deaths.

The Warsaw ghetto, which had been established by the decree of 12 October 1940, died a slow death between 22 July and the beginning of September 1942. The place which existed after that date was no longer the same ghetto; the people who lived there were no longer the same people. No dying children sat on the pavements begging for food and waiting for their death. No health inspectors ran around disinfecting the overcrowded houses and stealing whatever they could lay their hands on. No elderly leaned against walls, staring vacantly.

The ghetto began with two parts, connected by a wooden bridge which crossed over a main thoroughfare left outside the ghetto. With minor changes this was the body of the ghetto until the start of the great deportation. When the deportation started the disintegration of the ghetto began, although it happened so naturally that it was not immediately noticeable.

Every few days after the deportation the German authorities

declared new areas of the ghetto forbidden territory for Jews. Slowly, parts of the ghetto became separated from each other until the remaining inhabitants lived in four separate islands. The deserted streets were declared 'wild', no-man's land. Whole rows of houses stood empty, with open doors and windows, and bedding feathers all over the place. The German heirs to the goods left in these buildings were in no hurry to give the streets back to the Poles. They needed time for those whose lives they had spared to sort the valuables. A fortune was there to be made out of the stock of dead Jews, using the labour of those still living.

Often Poles from outside the ghetto would come in to collect whatever useful goods they could lay their hands on.

The majority of survivors had moved out of these homes to find accommodation in 'secure' houses, which their German employers had claimed for them for as long as they worked for the German war industry. In these houses, thirty-five thousand Jews lived in semi-barrack conditions under the supervision of their protectors, the Többens, the Helmans, and other Germans who had become major industrialists during the deportations. They used Jewish machinery, Jewish capital and Jewish slaves, who worked for nothing but the right to live another day.

It has been estimated that close to thirty thousand Jews had survived in hiding without passing the selection in the Kettle. The Germans allocated rations for the ghetto after the deportation according to the numbers they had registered at the time of the selections. The others were considered dead. They had no work and no rations. Yet, ironically, it was now easier to find food and accommodation for the illegal thirty thousand who came out of hiding than it had been for the Jews who had lived legally in the ghetto before the deportations began.

We no longer lived with the hope of survival. There dawned among us the awful realisation that allowing three hundred thousand Jews to be taken out of the ghetto without resistance had been a most horrendous error. On the other hand, those of us who remained wanted to consume the few days or weeks left to us. Materially, this became easy to achieve: the groups who worked outside the ghetto began a blossoming exchange of goods which were needed for the Aryan side but had become useless in the ghetto. In return, we obtained food, alcohol and cigarettes. It had been forbidden, under threat of immediate death, for the 'Central ghetto' to have contact with any of the islands separated from each other by about four streets. But as we had managed to survive so far, the prohibition meant nothing. There was no longer any need to use the streets. No longer would a living soul be seen walking out in the open, except for the cursed and despised Jewish police and workers of the Jewish administration. The rest of us walked through the upper levels of buildings which were connected one to the other. One could cross a whole block of buildings without losing the roof over their head. When it was no longer possible to walk through the houses, one could often use the tunnels which joined one side of the street with the other. There was seldom the need to risk walking through the desolation from one ghetto island to make contact with another.

The only people who had not completely disintegrated socially were those with some political affiliations, in particular the Zionist groups, the Bund and the communists. The latter two were relatively small. It was known that the left Zionist groupings had been the most successful in preserving their numbers during the deportations. The Bund had been reduced from many hundreds of members before the deportation to less than sixty afterwards. The communists, although supported from the outside by the People's Army, were of little significance, as they were just starting to be noticed on the Polish streets. Their arms were meagre and they could give no more than a few small-calibre revolvers for which they had too little ammunition to spare for the ghetto.

The greatest despair was among the youth. They had been taught to prepare for the fight for life or death when the time was right. And what had happened when the enemy came into the ghetto daily and removed thousands of Jews and sent them to their death? Nothing. Some of the leaders had themselves gone to the *Umschlagplatz* without as much as trying to knife their guards. Jewish police had helped to keep the rows moving faster and faster. And among these police one could find some of the youth leaders who had preached resistance. But when the time came for resistance, they had sold their souls.

A silence then descended on the ghetto. A silence after death, after hope. A silence beyond despair, beyond self-pity; the silence which comes with knowing and waiting.

18

Jan Karski

When I look back to the late summer of 1942, I keep asking myself the same painful question. The Germans on Polish soil were the deadly enemies of the Poles as well; why did some Poles denounce fellow Poles and hand them over to the Germans as criminals for giving assistance to Jews? The stories of betrayal arise again and again. Every second Pole who became a recipient of the Medal of a Righteous Gentile for having helped Jews told the same story: 'We had to be careful that the neighbours didn't find out that we were hiding a Jew.' Maybe I am unjust towards the Poles in singling them out. Historians have found over a million letters to the Gestapo in France documenting the same attitude. The French Government of Marshal Petain began to prepare lists of French people who were hiding Jews, before the German occupiers asked the government to remove Jews from the French population. The head of the 'independent' Slovakian Government, which Hitler created after having destroyed the Czechoslovakian Republic, was a priest who fulfilled the German orders by denouncing Jews and sending them to the death camps.

There were, of course, outstanding exceptions. I had the great privilege to be of some assistance to one of the most dedicated, most noble and gentle Poles. He tried — sadly, in vain — to make the leaders of the free world take notice and do something to stop the slaughter of European Jewry. At the time I served him he was known to the Polish Underground, and the Jews who maintained thin ties with it, by the pseudonym of 'Witold'. He has, since that time, found his honourable place in the pages of history as Professor Jan Karski. He was the first man to tell the English War Cabinet that the Jews in Europe were being annihilated in a well-planned campaign with the most modern techniques. And he was received with a terrible and deafening silence. Karski also met with President Roosevelt and the Chief Judge of the High Court of the United States.

I was the man who led 'Witold' through the narrow underground tunnel that divided the world of occupied Poland from the nightmare of our Warsaw ghetto. It was late 1942. A handful of Jewish activists had managed to keep their prewar contacts with the Polish organisations that were now functioning illegally in the occupied capital and all over Poland. In the days of the deportation some had managed to find shelter outside the ghetto while others lived permanently as Aryans under false names on false papers, working hand in hand with the Polish Underground. They were well informed and well connected with the Polish activists who represented the Government-in-Exile in the Delegatura in Warsaw. Each of these activists represented a political section of the Jewish community but none represented them all. Jan Karski, an officer of the ex-Polish Army, who had started his diplomatic career in 1938, had become a courier for the Delegatura and had accomplished some difficult missions between occupied Poland and the Allies. He had once been caught by the Gestapo and had cut his veins to avoid giving away secrets under torture. The Gestapo had obviously known enough about the importance of this particular courier not to let him die too quickly, at least until they could obtain some information from him. They saved him and had him hospitalised. The Delegatura considered Witold to be of the highest importance and organised a daring and successful rescue.

Some time in the summer of 1942, Witold was asked by the

Delegatura to once more undertake a mission to the Allies. The Jewish activists who were in contact with the Polish Underground found out that he was about to depart for England. Seizing the opportunity, they requested permission from the Delegatura to brief Witold about the annihilation of the Polish Jews, which was being carried out intensively at that time. The Underground 'delegate' was ready to allow the briefing but only if Witold agreed to accept the mission. Witold turned out to be willing to do much more than was expected of him by the Jewish representatives. He knew, of course, about the deportation of the Jews from the Warsaw ghetto. He knew, as did the majority of Polish people, about the existence of the death camps where thousands of Jews were being slaughtered daily. And he was willing to tell the world about them. He felt, however, that to be fully acquainted with the Jewish situation he would have to see it himself. Therefore, he decided to visit the ghetto and one of the death camps.

It was not a simple task to organise such visits. In the higher ranks of the Jewish and Polish leadership it was decided to bring Witold to the ghetto first. It was, however, considered too risky to bring him in while the deportation was going on. Hundreds upon hundreds of important Jews had been caught in the net of deportation without anybody being able to rescue them. Witold, it was feared, could fall victim to such a situation. There was also the question of who would take him through the ghetto during his short visit. It was decided that he would be guided by a leader of the Bund, Dr Feiner, who lived on the Aryan side, as a fully fledged member of the Underground leadership, and Mr Kirszenbaum, a leader of the Zionists.

The most secure entrance to the ghetto was chosen; the tunnel leading from the Aryan side of Muranowska 6 to the Jewish side of Muranowska 7-9, where the ŻZW had its quarters. I did not belong to the inner circle of the ŻZW and was not privy to their planning. But on 26 August 1942, on the second day without deportation, I received the order to present myself immediately to the administration of ŻZW. I was not told why I had been called up. I was only told to wait and was introduced to a man who had also been called to Muranowska. He must have belonged to an Underground group but I did not know him and he was introduced to me only by his first name, Marek. I never met him again. I do not recall if it was Rodal, or one of the Łopata brothers who told us to be patient and make ourselves comfortable. He warned us that we may be waiting many hours for nothing. There was an unusual coming and going of people who I did not know. Every quarter of an hour someone would go into the small office of our leader Frenkel. The door would be closed, some minutes later it would open, the messenger would leave, and after a short interval another messenger would arrive. We sat and waited.

Some time in the early afternoon, after a messenger had been closeted with Frenkel for more than the usual amount of time, Frenkel called us over. 'Do either of you have a personal weapon?' he asked. I had a Belgian revolver which was my personal property. I do not recall if my companion had a weapon or not. 'Give them each a light automatic and two grenades,' Frenkel ordered the storeman, 'and send them out to me.' With these words he locked up his office and went outside. We received a light automatic pistol each with loaded magazines, a spare magazine for each and two hand grenades. Frenkel was waiting for us in the passage of the building.

'You'll take up positions across the road on the Aryan side, in the streets of both sides of number six.' Pointing to me he continued, 'You'll take up your position on the corner of Muranowska and Sierakowska streets, and you,' he turned to my companion, 'will take the Przebieg and Muranowska corner. At those corners you'll wait for two people. One of them will look like an aristocrat with a newspaper in his hand and a pipe, the other will be dressed rather poorly. Whoever sees them coming will signal to the other. From that moment on, the one who sees the two men will pay attention only to his visitors, while the other will guard the area to make sure that it is safe to lead them to the bunker entrance and watch out for any unexpected danger. If anything should look suspicious you'll go towards your guests and in passing give them a sign to ignore you and go on. If the area is clear it will be the duty of the one on whose side they come to bring them through the tunnel to the ghetto. That's all.' Frenkel did not repeat his instructions, and without even asking if we had understood, he turned and left us.

We went back inside Muranowska 7-9, down into a cellar, opened the trapdoor to the tunnel and began to make our way towards the Aryan side. After the first few steps, my companion called back to me to bend down. The tunnel became a narrow passage not much more that a metre high and not wide enough for two people to crawl side by side. Our torches were of little use as the tunnel turned this way and that way, avoiding pipes and cables. We had to crawl on all fours. The tunnel was supposed to be less than forty metres long but it seemed to us more like forty kilometres, as we crawled through narrow passages which closed in on us. It had been built out of desperation for some safe passage, and its construction had involved a number of the city engineers who knew what lay under the surface of the roads. Unfortunately, one of the larger sewerage pipes ran right along the street and the tunnel had to be dug under it. To make it easier to crawl through, the tunnel had to be elongated as it twisted. At the higher sides the road began to collapse and the roof required strengthening. At one stage, the engineers had been ready to abandon the work, but on the insistence of the Jewish side and the help of children aged twelve to fourteen years, who became human moles, the tunnel was finished. Now we were supposed to bring our guests through it into the ghetto and, obviously, back out again.

I felt a great relief when I heard the friendly voice of my Polish Underground friend, Kazik. We came out into a cellar with a sliver of daylight coming from somewhere high above us. We were in the yard of Muranowska 6. 'What took you so long?' he asked.

'Whoever planned that tunnel should have been sent to a lunatic asylum,' Marek complained. 'How is one supposed to come out alive from such a place?'

Kazik had been waiting for us since before midday. He had an automatic revolver similar to ours hanging from his shoulder. He offered us a warm drink, then we left the building separately. I went first and took up my position. Within a minute or two Marek followed and stood at his post; we signalled to each other and waited. It was not the safest place to wait: the streets were empty and I was concerned that somebody would notice us from a window in one of the buildings. But the order had been given and we waited. They came from the street I was observing. I recognised the face of Dr Feiner, whom I had seen once before. I wondered why he had decided to dress so elegantly as to draw attention to himself. When he came closer I understood: he looked like a real Polish aristocrat and being so noticeable was a good disguise. The *szmalcowniks*, who made their miserable living by blackmailing Jews who lived outside the ghetto, had developed a sixth sense for detecting Jewish fear. They could not suspect that this very Polish-looking aristocrat was, in fact, a Jew and a leader of the Jewish Underground, working with the Polish Underground. Dr Feiner was aged in his mid-forties. His companion was a tall, slim young man, not much older than I. He was walking at Dr Feiner's side as if he was his employee. Even from a distance I could tell that the younger man had learned how to appear close to invisible. Dr Feiner had drawn any attention to himself, making his companion seem insignificant, and therefore safer. I took off my cap and the thin man made the tiniest nod. I turned the corner, gave my companion a signal that the visitors were coming from my side, and began to walk very slowly towards Muranowska 6. They followed a few steps behind. I, of course, could not see anything and was relying on my companion leading them behind me. I entered the gate and walked on a few steps. Kazik was waiting inside the building. He greeted the two guests and assured them that everything was in order. He asked them to follow me and he walked behind them to the opening of the cellar. Marek arrived as we started to descend the steps. Kazik left and went back to have a last look to reassure himself that everything was all right. When Marek and I entered the cellar we both lit our torches. I told our visitors that I would go first and they would have to follow me. 'It is not a long way,' I tried to assure them, and Dr Feiner said he had been warned. Nobody spoke throughout the whole time we were making our way through the tunnel, except when I called back instructions. The younger man fired a solitary curse when he hit his head on a pipe, but otherwise the two men made no comment. When we reached the ghetto side, the difficulty of the journey showed on their faces. Marek took over and opened the doors of the cellar at Muranowska 7-9. I had not been told who would be waiting for us and was sure that Frenkel and others of our leadership would be there. Not one of them was at the post. A stranger was standing there with a revolver in his hand, and to my great surprise I heard my companion reporting to him that everything had gone off smoothly.

'Where to now?' Marek asked.

'Follow me.'

'First, tell us the password.'

'*Chmura*,' he replied, and we followed.

He entered one of the buildings in Plac Muranowski, only five or six buildings up from the cellar. I knew that it had been deserted for some weeks; it was in one of the 'wild' areas in the ghetto. The leader walked up to the first floor and stopped at one of the doors, opened it for us and invited us to enter, while he waited at the door. The room was typical of the deserted area. A table and some chairs had been brought in for the meeting. Two people were already there. I knew one of them; a Zionist leader of one of the more religious organisations, Mr Kirszenbaum, and beside him, a woman, who seemed out of place. Dr Feiner introduced the guest and for the first time I heard the name 'Witold'. My companions and I were introduced simply as 'trusted security'. The woman was introduced as 'a ghetto friend who has volunteered to offer you our humble ghetto hospitality'.

At that moment we heard two or three revolver shots. We trembled and Witold became very concerned. He could not have been blamed for thinking that the whole scene was a trap. He looked at us and must have concluded that we were just as worried as he. In an unusual act for a man of his position he went over to the window, although very carefully, and moved a piece of the curtain. 'Don't,' the woman called out. 'They'll shoot at you!' Witold moved back and crossed to the other side of the window. This time he made sure that he could not be seen from the outside. Two German teenagers, in the uniform of the Hitler Youth, were standing in the middle of the road with revolvers in their hands. One was calling to the other and pointing to some window, and the other lifted his revolver and fired. We could faintly hear their shouts of joy and the splintering of glass.

In a whisper Witold asked, 'Does that go on all the time?'

The woman spoke hysterically, 'Please, go away. Leave and go. You can get away; we cannot. Please go away.' I can't remember if it was Feiner or Kirszenbaum who spoke next.

'They will be gone soon. They call it a hunt. As far as we know they never dare to enter a building. Since the deportations began they have started coming more often. It would be safer to wait until they have gone than try to leave right now.'

One of my two companions had silently left the room. He was obviously concerned for the safety of the visitors and had taken up his position outside. As if nothing unusual had happened, Dr Feiner asked the woman to prepare 'something for our visitor'. I joined her in the kitchen to try to pacify her. There were two slices of bread on a plate and next to it our famous marmalade made of carrots or beetroot. The woman lit a primus to make coffee and I went back to the sitting room and posted myself next to the door.

Snippets of conversation remain in my mind as if they were burned into my brain. To this day I can visualise the calmness of Dr Feiner and the painful face of Kirszenbaum as they spoke about the ongoing annihilation; about the helplessness of the Underground to save a significant part of Polish Jewry. My companion whispered to me, 'The Pole looks more distressed than either of the two Jews.' I had to agree. Witold asked very few questions but was riveted by what his hosts had to say. The woman brought in the bread and marmalade, then returned with coffee made from burned grain.

Listening intently, Witold lifted his coffee while gently moving aside the plate with the bread. The way he did this has never left me. It was a gesture which said: you cannot afford to share your bread with me.

I did not see this brave Pole again until nearly fifty years later. By that time, his story was known the world over. Professor Jan Karski's efforts to meet with Allied leaders and release details to the Western world of Nazi atrocities are well documented. When we next met we were old men with memories overflowing and haunted. He, too, remembered moving the plate and refusing to eat the bread. He also remembered me, and knew that I was his guard. Since then we have found in each other a bond which can never be destroyed.

19

Preparing for the Aryan side

AFTER the Kettle, only fools and those who could believe their own lies were able to think that any Jew might be left alive under German control to see the war's end. Among those were the members of the *Judenrat* and the police. Even though a great number of police and their families had been sent to Treblinka, those who were left could not resign totally from their hope that some Jews would remain alive at the end of the war. Each one of those 'privileged' clung to the hope that he and his family might be spared. It has never been established why the German murder squads did not complete the liquidation in the Warsaw ghetto while they were at it. In most of the larger towns in Poland the system had been the same: an initial major deportation, followed by a second one. Warsaw, Łódź, Białystok, Vilno, Sosnowiec, Będzin and Kraków — in some ghettos it meant total liquidation, while in others, some Jews were left to wait a little longer for their final journey.

The Warsaw ghetto after the great Action was already certain of its fate; all that remained to be seen was when it would happen. During the deportation, German orders had made it appear that those employed in German industries would not be taken. Many Jews in the ghetto had bought working places in the factories. People offered machinery, raw materials and money for the security of being employed. One of the conditions of that security was to have a roof over their heads, under German patronage. People left their own homes as soon as they were accepted into the slave labour, and moved to the houses which the new industrialists had confiscated from others for their use. After the Action, the German industrialists did their utmost to continue their role as our 'protectors'. Some were cunning enough to pretend that those who remained would be more secure than they had been before the deportation began, because they were now all the more necessary for the German war effort. Schultz and Többens assured the thousands of slaves that because the deportation had taken place, the Gestapo would show some understanding for the families of the Jewish workers, who they needed. Rumours spread that a cinema and schools would be opened in the ghetto and there would be no more disruptions such as there had been before, when the ghetto had too many idle mouths to feed.

Luba and her family began to make plans to leave for the Aryan side. Many had done it successfully but others had lost their lives. To get out and establish a survival net on the other side was like trying to climb through electrified fencing; the chances were slim. But the alternative was to remain in the ghetto and wait for the end. The first step one had to take when deciding to leave the ghetto for good, was a financial one. It meant much more than having enough money to live on for months or even years. Some of those who had left the ghetto earlier had returned to its misery, happy to have escaped with their lives. Some of them had gone away with money and jewellery and come back with nothing. Some had entrusted their fortunes to old Polish friends who promised to look after them and attend to all their needs. Others fell into the hands of the *szmalcowniks*. If one was able to bribe a *szmalcownik*, the next step was to establish an address. This was easier said than done. Usually, by this stage, a Jew had little left in hand with which to organise a new residence. Living on the Aryan side meant living from day to day, as best as one could, with insecurity and fear as companions.

We had no financial problems to consider. Luba's family had managed to keep their stock of pelts intact. Even at rock-bottom prices the stock was still worth a fortune. Inside the ghetto the furs had no value but on the Aryan side they were worth their weight in food. Jews were not allowed to wear fur coats by decree. Poles were only allowed to wear furs inside their clothing, but the Germans could wear them on the outside. I had often wrapped a fur around myself as I went to work outside the ghetto and come back with food and money sufficient to live on for a month or more in reasonable comfort. We also had close friends who had settled quite securely on the Aryan side. Some had to stay in permanent hiding, while others with Aryan looks and good papers could afford to take chances and get work to earn their living. In addition, those who had good connections from before the war could call on their Polish friends in moments of need. Nevertheless, the final arrangements could be difficult. Often one had to consider the need to split up husband from wife, or parents from children. This was known as 'farming out'. Our connections were better than average; we had only to organise the details and ensure that we would be not only financially secure ourselves but also able to help those who were willing to risk their lives for us.

Corruption and greed had eaten through the German guards at the ghetto gates no less than it had eaten through the Jewish and Polish police. I arranged a deal with the leader of a working group which involved paying him a bribe that he would share with the German guard who would be on duty. Once I was given the date when this guard would be at the gate, I left the ghetto and arranged matters through my friends. When everything else had been organised, the group that was to go out on that morning was told about the plan. Each of them would have to walk out with a fur around his waist. In return, they would be rewarded for it handsomely. At a designated place we would stop and the furs would be taken off them. The evening before the group was to go out, the leader asked me if I wanted an additional ten men in the working group. We quickly collected another ten furs and in the morning fifty people left for work each carrying a costly fur through the ghetto gate.

We had to detour from our course to meet with the Polish fellow who was to take the goods from us. The meeting point was at a tall building which had stood empty since it had been bombed in September 1939. The windows and the doors had long since been removed and the facade had partly fallen down. But in the yard behind it was a smaller brick building in which two people were living. The Gestapo could hardly have imagined that the two tenants were employed by the German Air Force in Warsaw. The tenants had agreed to let a horse and cart park in the yard for the morning while we smuggled out our furs. The whole group marched through the gate into the yard. One by one they divested themselves of the furs. which were counted and thrown on the cart. We helped the driver to cover them with sacks and loaded the cart with timber and bricks taken from the building. The whole action was over in less than ten minutes. After the cart left with the goods I went over and slid an envelope under one of the doors in the small building. It was payment for the service. A few days later I was informed that the money had reached its destination. The first step towards setting up financial security for Luba had been taken.

It must seem hard to imagine but life in Warsaw outside of the ghetto continued in a normal way. Of course, it was not the same as it had been in peaceful times, but normal in so far as there was the rhythm of a daily routine in which babies were born, children grew and played, lovers were married, people fell ill and died. Many young people died in too many tragic ways, but that was also part of the routine of the occupied capital. People went to work; there were morning and afternoon peak hours; the tramways functioned, the shops were open; people followed funeral processions, celebrated Christmas, and in spite of tough rationing by the Germans, did not go hungry.

Despite this superficial appearance of normality, the Nazis ruled the city with an iron fist. They considered themselves the deserving owners of all that Warsaw had to offer. Whatever they took, destroyed or plundered, they believed was their own. They tolerated the Polish population out of necessity, out of being busy with other things for the moment and most of all, because they needed the slaves to do their bidding. The signs *Nur für Deutsche* (only for Germans), were everywhere. The front sections of trams were *Nur für Deutsche*, as were the food shops where rations were sold. The nightclubs were *Nur für Deutsche*, because the Polish population had to follow a strict curfew or risk being arrested or shot.

The centre of Warsaw, which had not been destroyed completely during the September 1939 siege, was taken over by the Third Reich. It began with the army, which settled in the buildings and offices of the former Polish Government. Close on its heels came the dark, macabre, German Secret Police, the Gestapo. They brought with them their wives and children, who were accompanied by school teachers from Germany. Considering themselves the superior race, they expropriated the best apartments by the simple act of throwing out the owners and forbidding them to take anything that their new masters liked. Within a few months of the occupation of Warsaw, the Aryan society became heavily Germanised. The Polish people had to get used to the new ways. Poles had become second-class citizens in their own capital, physically subjugated.

Two worlds existed: one belonged to the new order, which was now in the hands of the conquerors; the other belonged to the Polish Underground, which had begun to build a new Poland practically from the first day that the old Poland had ceased to exist. While there were signs of moral decay among the general Polish population, the Underground was full of courage and fighting spirit. But in all this there was no time to consider the fate of the Jews. Most inhabitants of the capital were disinterested in the plight of the ghetto. To that majority the brick wall that had appeared in the heart of the city had become a closed-off world in which people had to live their own lives and fight in their own way. Those who had any kind of political inclination towards the Jews acted according to their own attitudes to anti-Semitism. Some political activists who before the war had been rabid anti-Semites showed unusual understanding for the Jewish tragedy. The best-known institution in Warsaw which tried to help the Jews, the Żegota, answered the call of a woman named Zofia Kossak-Szczucka. Before the war, she had been an anti-Semite, but she expressed disgust for the way the Jews were being treated and demanded that the Poles help them on moral grounds. On the other hand, masses of Poles became devoted anti-Semites out of greed. Some became convinced that Jews were paying for the old sin of not having accepted Jesus as their saviour.

The Polish population was not allowed to forget their place in the German plans. People's sleep was often disturbed by the familiar sounds of Gestapo vehicles stopping outside a building. Heavy boots, shouting, then anxiety would spread throughout the building. Somewhere a door was pounded on; the fear would rise in the stillness until the heavy footsteps receded and with them the shouting and the banging. The vehicle would leave and in the morning the residents would discover who had been taken away in the night. It was better not to get too involved in such situations. At times, whole blocks would be surrounded. The heavy boots of the Gestapo would tramp from dwelling to dwelling, from apartment to apartment, checking documents, looking for suspects or acting on specific information. During such raids it was normal for the Germans to take away most of the men. Sometimes the families were able to trace their loved ones, but just as often that would be the last they ever saw or heard of them. Fortunate families would, many months later, receive a letter from somewhere in Germany telling them where their fathers, husbands or sons had been taken. Others found their loved ones' names in the official Polish paper the Germans published in Warsaw, among those who had been shot or hanged for illegal activities.

No one was ever completely safe in Warsaw. The safest area was probably the Kiercelak. But outside this unusual place in the heart of the capital there was no fully protected sanctuary where one could escape from the cursed war and its effects. In the middle of a meal in some restaurant a man or a woman could be approached and asked to leave the table. The person would be frisked for illegal arms, asked for documents, or simply taken away. Nobody would react; it was part of the norm. During the day, a street would be closed off, a Gestapo vehicle would come along, and some luckless creature with his hands tied would be sitting in the back. The vehicle would stop near a lamp-post over which a rope was thrown, and the man would be hanged on the spot. The German officers would wait to make sure the dangling body was dead before they climbed back into their vehicles. Sometimes they would leave one of their servants, a collaborator, to make sure the victim wasn't taken down too quickly.

But it wasn't all one-sided. It happened sometimes that a pair of street musicians would walk along peacefully, one with an accordion, the other with a violin case. They would stop near the entrance to an elegant restaurant, frequented by known German agents. The accordionist would start up a popular German tune, the violinist would bend down, open his case and take out his instrument. While the accordionist would play as loudly as possible the violinist would turn his instrument in the direction of the entrance and spray the interior with the music of bullets. Within seconds the musicians would be gone. The people nearby would run in all directions to get away before the Gestapo arrived. Innocent people would be taken hostage and on the next day, an announcement would be made through the official German mouthpiece or plastered on placards or printed in the Polish daily, about how many had been shot or hanged in retaliation. On the other side of the walls of Warsaw or sometimes as an illegal insert in the same daily, a notice would appear which stated that for the crime against the Polish people the soldiers of Poland had executed such and such a person, and 'The German henchmen should know that they will pay with their own blood for the blood of the innocent.'

Fear lived together with courage; the illegal became enmeshed with the legal; hatred went hand in hand with self-sacrifice; and the desire for peace embraced an understanding for acts of war. Within this kind of life the greatest sacrifice of all was to try to shelter a Jew. The price for such an act was often the lives of whole families, sometimes executed on the spot. Yet in Warsaw, unlike any other place in prewar Poland, thousands of Jews were given shelter and help; sometimes on an individual basis and often in an organised way. They often had to be moved on very short notice from one place to another. Those involved in this work lived in constant danger of being caught or being denounced by their own neighbours. I would be remiss if I failed to remember the many Polish people who paid for their noble work with their own lives and sometimes also with the lives of their families. My wife and I and a handful of our friends survived these times to record the great nobleness of a number of Polish citizens in Warsaw. For some Poles, the protection and rescue of Jews was part of the normal rhythm of their difficult lives. We are grateful and indebted.

20

The revolver

I began to spend more and more time on the Aryan side. I had a 'good face' and 'good papers', and had learned not to show signs of fear in critical moments. The only risk I ever took was alway to carry my security companion, a Belgian revolver, tucked in the front of my trousers over my stomach.

Like most of the Warsaw population I used the tramway as the main means of transport around the city. In the early days of the war I had worked out that the safest place to stand on a tram in case it was stopped by the police or the Gestapo was on the rear platform of the motor wagon. The front platform and the front part of the tram were *Nur für Deutsche*, but the rear part was usually occupied by Poles. Germans avoided that part of the tram, feeling safer among their own kind in the front. To avoid close contact with others, who were often curious about their fellow passengers, I had developed a method to discourage them. I would wash my mouth with alcohol and sometimes pour a little over my clothes before catching a tram. I would step up onto the platform acting like a drunk. Noisily, and swearing loudly, I would begin to tell everyone around me what the German swines had done to our beloved Warsaw. I would remind those around me that Hitler had ruined our capital; that the Germans were our eternal enemies and that for a real Polish patriot there was only one thing to do: to fight them before they killed all of us. This always worked. The other riders would consider that I was either a provocateur working for the Gestapo, or a real drunk who had gone so far that he no longer knew what danger meant. Either way, they would try to move as far away from me as possible. I often had the whole rear platform to myself and felt reasonably safe; as safe as one could feel in the streets of Warsaw.

The Gestapo would sometimes stop the tram in the middle of the street. Suddenly a vehicle would drive out in front of it and the Gestapo would close the tram off at the rear. The passengers were prevented from escaping by a cordon of Polish police and German SS. They would fall over the passengers, demanding to see documents, or asking which of the passengers carried the official daily newspaper and check it for the illegal inserts which may have appeared that day. Very often, unlucky passengers were taken away for one reason or another. For Jews, the trams were the greatest danger and very seldom did they use them. Only in moments of immediate need would a Jew risk taking a tram, but I had become so used to riding them that I no longer considered them to be any worse that the other dangers that surrounded me. I carried on my skin the death sentence for being a Jew. I carried another death sentence for having left the ghetto and for being illegally on the Aryan side. I also carried a death sentence for not wearing the armband with the Star of David which every Jew was ordered to wear when leaving their house. I carried a death sentence for having an illegal weapon on my body. I carried a death sentence for smuggling food into the ghetto. I carried a death sentence for dealing illegally with Gentiles. So, what the hell? If I carried one additional death sentence for riding the tram reserved for Aryans, how many times could I die? In any case, it was a question of being caught first.

The only times I did not act the drunk was when I was riding with somebody on a particular mission. During such times I had to show myself as calm and collected, so as not to scare the person who was with me. Even then I insisted that we stay on the rear platform. It was during one such ride that I was thankful for having a companion with me. At that time, Luba was already on the Aryan side. She knew my companion well — a young woman named Zosia, whom everybody called Zocha. She was an active member of the Underground and knew that I always carried my gun on me. We had caught the tram together before and had not met with any difficulty.

We were standing on the rear platform with other people around us; the tram was not very crowded but the place where we stood was rather confined. The tram had reached the middle of the long iron bridge, Kierbedzia, when it was stopped right over the Wisła. A heavy truck was parked across the road in front of us. By the time the tram came to a halt with a screech of the iron brakes, two heavy black Gestapo vehicles had closed off the other side. The only escape would have been to jump over the bridge some twenty metres or more down to the river and wait to be fished out or shot in the water. I had no intention of doing this. Within a moment I felt Zocha's body against mine, pressing on me. 'Give it to me,' she said. Her hand was moving towards the place she knew held my gun. Instinctively I pushed her away.

'Leave it, Zocha, and get away from me!'

Instead of listening to me, she pressed herself closer to my body and spoke in a louder voice for others to hear, 'Darling, give it to me!' It sounded to those close by like a request for something other than a gun.

I can still hear the half-whisper of one man: 'Give it to her. Go on, give it to her.'

By the time I pushed her away she had managed to get hold of the revolver and was gone in a flash.

Four men entered the rear carriage while guards took up positions at the entrance. There was just enough room between the tram and the footpath of the bridge for one person. We had to wait for our queue to move. In the meantime we noticed that the passengers from the rear carriage were standing single file along the bridge. Nobody was being frisked or identified in any way. Zocha returned from inside the carriage to the platform just as the guards ordered us to leave the wagon. We stepped outside and, like the others before us, we stood in single file while four Germans in civilian clothes entered the tram. We could see them looking along the carriage and under the seats. But nothing was found so they let us board the tram again. The truck in front reversed all the way back to the end of the bridge and we moved off. The conductor told us that they were looking for the daily paper. A very seditious insert had been placed in it and nearly three quarters of the edition had been confiscated from the stands. They were looking for parcels of the paper that were usually thrown on the tram platforms to be delivered to addresses at various points along the route.

I began to demand quietly but persistently for the return of my gun. But to my great surprise Zocha said, 'I haven't got it,' and it dawned on me what she had done. She had managed somehow to throw it into the Wisła. I was furious. 'I told you to leave it with me. Why have you thrown it away?' I whispered fiercely.

'Don't worry. It's safe. Just wait. I haven't got it on me but it's safe. Just have patience and wait.' We travelled a few stops. An elderly woman with a basket over her arm came out from the interior and pushed against us to get off. Zocha nodded at me. 'When she gets off, we get off too.' I did not ask for an explanation. We descended with the elderly woman and Zocha went over to her, asking in a very friendly way, 'Could you spare us some of the eggs you are carrying? Of course we will pay for them.' Zocha already had her hand on the basket. The woman became very protective of her treasure. Moving her arm away from Zocha she said decisively, 'I don't sell any eggs. My daughter is sick and I have risked the eggs in my basket all the way from Pruszków. I don't sell them. Good day!'

Zocha moved back and whispered, 'She had the gun in her basket, but doesn't know it. I put it there. What do we do now?' We followed her for a while and the woman began to grow suspicious. We had to do something. Zocha had a plan. 'You go away. I'll start talking to her and you call out suddenly, "Stop! Police, here!"' I understood. Zocha went over and began to talk to the woman who was still adamant. As they approached a building I jumped on them.

'Police! Halt! What are you two women smuggling? Into the entrance. Quick!' Without asking for identification both women stepped into the entrance. Zocha didn't waste a single moment. She pulled away the eggs and retrieved the gun. I acted bewildered. 'Are you carrying a gun?' I asked the frightened woman.

'Oh God! No, sir, I don't know how the gun came into my basket. I don't know how the gun came into my basket!' I interrogated Zocha for the record, and she played the indignant one.

'All I wanted from this woman was to buy some eggs. You don't think I would carry a gun only to give it to this old lady to keep for me? Do you?' I could see the little old lady was close to collapse. I calmed her. I took the gun saying I was confiscating it. I told the woman to remain in the gate for some time, warning her that I was arresting Zocha. I told her that if she in any way interfered in my duties I would arrest her too. We left the trembling woman and went on. We turned the nearest corner and walked as quickly as we could without running. I kept my own counsel about the incident but Zocha could not keep quiet. 'That poor old woman,' she kept muttering, half laughing, half in shock. 'That poor old woman!'

Since the beginning of the war I had led a busy life, but never before had I been as busy as I was at that time. Never before had I so many things to attend to at the same time and never before were so many things a priority. First and foremost I had to find a secure place for Luba on the Aryan side. We had many friends among the Gentile population and many contacts. Also, some of our relatives were already accommodated with Polish families. But for permanent accommodation with people who could have us and whom we could trust, we still had to make our own arrangements.

I also had an urgent priority to get the huge stock of furs over to the other side. We had to store them somewhere secure and accessible as we would have to live off the proceeds we got for them at least for as long as the war lasted or the Germans were in Warsaw. I had to be pessimistic and consider the possibility of living under the Germans for at least another two or three years. In a normal market, the value of the stock would have provided for us for at least ten years. But this was neither the time nor the place for a normal market. I needed help storing and selling the huge stock. For both of these, I had to find a trusted person. It was no secret that many Jews had trusted their good Polish friends with all they possessed and were betrayed out of greed or cowardice.

I was also busy, more than ever before, buying and smuggling arms and ammunition for the ŻZW. There was seldom a day I went to work outside the ghetto when I did not carry a roll of banknotes for the organisation's needs. Often I had specific orders with regard to the ammunition we needed for the arms we had in stock. The arrangements were that I bought whatever arms I could lay my hands on with a small number of bullets. Later, we would order the calibre of bullets we needed. After the great deportation, armament had become essential and I had established myself as one of the key buyers on the outside.

Luba was still working for the German industrialists. We talked things over and she was very practical. 'First of all we must get the furs out of the ghetto. We can leave any day, even tomorrow morning if need be. But the furs will take time,' she said, 'and I am not sure how much of the stock we will manage to get out.'

I listened to her but had no real plan and said so. 'You remember how many days it took me to arrange the first transport. I had to sell it first, before organising the people to carry the furs out of the ghetto. Where am I going to put the furs I take out?'

Like lightning, my brother-in-law Abraham had it all solved: I'd go and talk to Feliks. He would be our best bet. In a single sentence he had solved a problem that had dogged my mind for days. Feliks had been employed by the Gutrajcht family for many years while Luba's father was alive. Later he worked under Abraham. He was a reliable and conscientious worker. We had kept up our contact with him on a more or less social level. Sometimes over the last three years he did us minor favours and each time he offered to be of whatever further help he could be. I hadn't called on him because I knew little of his family and these were times when a mistake in trust could cost us our lives. But I went to see him.

I met his wife and their baby. They lived in one of the poorer districts but quite comfortably. I had left the visit until after I had finished work, which was not long before the curfew began. Luba knew not to expect me home, but I had made no arrangements for the night. Although I had two or three places where, in times of need, I could stay, unannounced, for a night.

Feliks showed genuine friendship. The first two questions he asked after inquiring how I was and how Luba was, were: 'Will you have a bite with us?' and, 'It is close to the curfew. If we are going to talk you'll have to stay with us overnight. Does Luba expect you?' He put some *bimber* on the table but cautioned me against drinking too much. His wife was obviously going out of her way to make the meal better than usual.

After dinner she went into the kitchen and we sat on the sofa. I began by asking him if he was still in the fur trade. His answer was encouraging. 'I am in the fur trade. Rabbits. They make very interesting hats out of them; quite nice. They are about ten dollars on the black market. On the open market one could starve waiting for a rabbit.'

'What about high quality fur?' I ventured.

'Only second hand. From private sales. I could sell any good fur tomorrow if,' he hesitated, 'if I could get it. Have you anything for sale?'

I had a whole night in front of me and was not going to hurry.

David Landau at around sixteen years of age. This photo was taken at approximately the time when David ran away from home to try to join the International Brigade fighting in the Spanish Civil War. The recruitment office rejected him because of his age and lack of military experience.

Mrs Miriam Landau holding David's brother Mietek.

Itzhak and Lutek Landau, David's father and brother, on winter holidays before the war. The Landaus were keen skiers and tobogganists.

David (centre) holding a flag, standing with his brothers and friends on holiday in Miedzeszyn, near Warsaw. Perhaps this is a prophetic photo, with David carrying the white flag.

The Landau brothers. Left to right: Joziek, David, Mietek and Lutek.

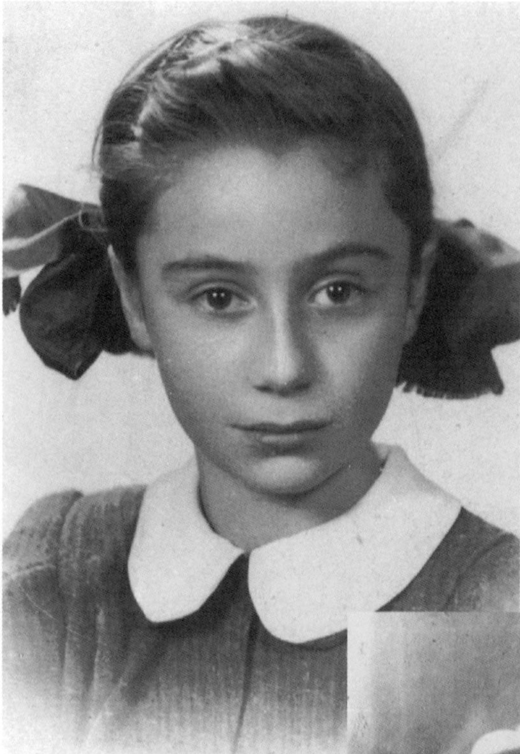

Noemi, the daughter of Luba's sister Esther and her husband Maurycy Nickin. David smuggled Noemi through the ghetto gates to her nanny who protected her on the Aryan side. This photo was taken in about 1946, before she left for Mexico. Noemi's parents perished in the Holocaust.

Luba's parents, Gitele Deborah and Alexander Zisha Gutrajcht. Gitele was taken to Treblinka during the first deportation from the ghetto and Alexander died before the war.

David on holiday in Druskieniki in 1939 ~ his last holiday before the war.

Luba's sister Esther (top centre) and her friends before the war.

Helen Gutrajcht, Luba's sister. David last saw Helen at Kolejow 3, a collection camp in Warsaw, days before she was sent to the death camp at Treblinka.

Jakubek, Luba's brother, photographed before the war. He lived in hiding with Noemi but returned to the ghetto after being severely beaten by thugs.

Luba's brothers. Below, Meir, a fighter in the ZZW. He was killed in the first days of the Uprising. Yechiel (standing), her older brother, joined the Anders army in the Middle East and went to Palestine. Photographed in Srodborow near Otwock, Poland, in approximately 1937.

David in the uniform of a SS guard, Warsaw, 1943. Before the ghetto Uprising, Luba and other women had been working in a German uniform factory. They made a few extra SS jackets for the Jewish fighters to wear as disguise as they fought the Nazis in the ghetto streets.

Minutes after this photograph was taken, a German plane flew low over David and his comrades-in-arms, dropping bombs and grenades. David managed to jump into the opening seen behind him in this photo and was saved. The man standing in the background was killed.

rechter Zeigefinger
palec wskazujący prawej ręki

linker Zeigefinger
palec wskazujący lewej ręki

Stanisława Borkowska
Unterschrift des Kennkarteninhabers
Podpis posiadacza karty rozpoznawczej

Warschau, den 15. April 1943
dnia kwietnia

Der Stadthauptmann
Ausstellungsbehörde
Władza wystawiająca

I.A.

Unterschrift des ausfertigenden Beamten
Podpis sporządzającego urzędnika

Luba's *Kennkarte*, her Aryan identity card. When she lived on the Aryan side during the war, Luba was generally called Zosia, but on this *Kennkarte* she goes under the name of Stanislawa Borkowska.

General Jürgen Stroop's men shooting down Jewish fighters during the Warsaw ghetto Uprising, April 1943.

Luba and David in Erding, Germany, after the war, 1946.

Home in a new land, Australia. Rear left to right: David, Luba, Yechiel and Abraham, Luba's brothers. Front left to right: Miriam Landau, Allan, Ronald and Lodzia, Abraham's wife.

'Never Again', 1983.

The postwar Pawiak. David escaped from the original Pawiak Prison by hiding in the back of a German Army truck.

The farm house in Bartosze, outside of Warsaw, where David hid from German soldiers in a storks' nest made in the thatch on the roof.

A meeting with Ania Cielnik in 1993. Ania, David and Luba shared a bunker under the streets of Warsaw with seventeen others for over three months until the Red Army finally marched into the city.

Eddy Jagodzinski and David reunited in Warsaw in 1993. In 1944, David pulled Eddy out of the ruins of his home and carried him on his back to the bunker where they lived until the end of the war.

Jan Kostanski, Melbourne, 1998. Jan is a Christian who, during the war, was closely connected to the Jewish Underground. He and his mother saved many Jewish people including Jan's future wife and her family.

David, 1992.

David in Warsaw, 1993, standing in front of the building where the Jewish Committee, appointed by the American Joint, sat after the war. The Committee gave aid to Jewish survivors.

Professor Jan Karski reminiscing with David during his visit to Melbourne in 1994. Professor Karski was the first person to tell the English War Cabinet that the Jews in Europe were being annihilated. He was met with a deafening silence.

Jack Eisner and David at the Jewish Holocaust Centre, Melbourne, 1993. They are standing in front of photos of Germans shooting in the Warsaw ghetto and David as a young man.

David and Luba Landau, 1995.
Reprinted with the kind permission of the photographer, Elizabeth Gilliam, and La Trobe Picture Collection, State Library of Victoria.

'I came actually to find some reasonably secure place for Luba. You know the ghetto. Maybe a week, a month, but we have to get out or be murdered. I was wondering . . .'

He looked at me with a smile. 'If you can wait a few days, I think I may have something for you. It would not be the best but it would be a full apartment to yourself.'

'It would be ideal. When can we have it?'

'Actually, no, I don't think so.' Feliks cut me off. 'You would be exposed to all the tenants in the building. You would have to do your own shopping and leave every morning as if you were going to work. Too much exposure for a Jew even with a "good face". Do you need it?' I had to admit he was right. 'I haven't told you,' he continued, 'because you haven't asked until tonight, but I am involved with finding places for people in the ghetto. If you can wait a few days, let us say no longer than a week, I'll arrange something for you. It may have to be only temporary but it will be somewhere where you'll be well looked after and it won't be too dear. Can you wait?'

I assured him that I could and changed the subject back. 'Tell me, Feliks, and don't be embarrassed by my question because here I may be of considerable help to you: how are you managing financially?'

For the first time he showed some sign of stress. 'We could do with some improvement. In fact, I would be willing to give you both shelter right away with us, to make some additional income, but I cannot. Don't ask for details but I am not allowed to do it. It has to do with my work.'

I came to the point. 'Could you handle large quantities of fur for us? I mean really large quantities?'

He sighed. 'The quantities would not be a problem. The problem would be the finance. I told you my business is only giving very small profits. Sometimes I cannot even pay the rent. But if you can hold on, I am sure I can find somebody in the trade within a day or two.'

My heart skipped a beat. 'I don't want you to find anybody for us. The money is not the most immediate concern. You know the stock we had when the war broke out. What would you say if I told you that the major part of it is still available?' He became very animated. The stock of the Gutrajcht family had been very large. We often wondered ourselves how we had managed to keep so much of it, for so long, from the hands of the Germans. Now Feliks was sitting opposite me with his eyes wide open as he visualised it in his mind.

'Is it in the ghetto or here?' he asked.

I was not going to answer fully, not yet. 'You will get it on this side. Can you handle it?' He made no comment so I went on. 'I can let you have between forty and fifty pieces of our original stock daily, for as long as we can move it. And we will not ask you for any money; we don't need much of it. But when we have to leave the ghetto we will need money to live on. We don't know for how long but we will have to rely on the stock we give you. Are you willing to do it? I don't know what the risk of suddenly handling such big stocks may be though, so think it over.'

He asked me to excuse him for a moment, and he came back with his wife. Only then did I learn that she was a qualified accountant and it was she who kept the business afloat. She sat down and I let Feliks repeat my proposal to her. She had only two or three questions to Feliks and none to me. When she was satisfied that she knew the details she turned to me. 'Mr Landau, tell me, do you realise what you are offering?' I assured her that I knew precisely what I was offering and that Feliks had understood it correctly. She was not satisfied. 'But this sounds so fantastic that I can hardly ask my husband to accept your generosity. Why do you do it?'

'Your husband, obviously with your knowledge, risks his life to help others. I can see for myself that he does not do it for the financial reward only but out of decency. It is the same here. I can help you to live more comfortably, not only you and your husband

and baby, but also those in both your families who could do with financial help and who can also be trusted. Does that sound more realistic?'

'Yes, it does,' she said as she bent over and kissed me lightly. 'I'll leave the details to Feliks but even for the price of wanting to survive it is still generous.'

'Does survival have a price?' I asked in astonishment.

'Of course it has!' she retorted strongly. 'If there was no limit to the price of survival we would not risk doing what we do. I can assure you we will trust you not one dot less than you are willing to trust us. Now I'll go to wash up and prepare your bed. Excuse me, Mr Landau.'

She left it to us to arrange the details. The smuggling was organised and began within three days. It involved the German guard and the Polish and Jewish policemen at the gate of the ghetto, the leader of our work-group, the members of the group, two receivers on the Polish side, and myself. The morning after I had spoken with Feliks, I went from his home directly to the place where I knew the group would be working on that day. The leader, through whom I had organised my first fur delivery, asked for only one day to prepare the security at the gate. By next morning he had arranged all the bribes needed and he had the price for the operation. It was to cost one thousand złotys a day, to cover the German, Polish and Jewish guards, and whatever he kept for himself. The group leader suggested that I also give one kilo of bread to each of the members in the group present on the day. I changed it to a whole loaf of two kilos each for everyone present. Neither the German guard nor the Polish or Jewish police would know what we were taking out. The group would wrap the furs around their bodies in one of the rooms in an empty house near the ghetto administration. I would have to be there with the goods by seven o'clock in the morning or the night before. I went back to Feliks the next day, to tell him where to come for the fur.

When we met I felt, for a moment, that he had not fulfilled our agreement. He had taken a partner, explaining that because he would not be able to come personally to collect the fur every day, someone else was needed. I was worried and said so. But Feliks made light of it. 'Believe me, you can trust us both.'

'You mean, I cannot trust you, either,' I said angrily.

'The man is a brother of Noemi's nanny. His name is Paweł,' Feliks explained. 'He is a policeman, which means that he can move around during the day at will. I decided there would be enough in it for two families to live on.'

He was right but I was still not appeased. 'You should have told me before you made the arrangements.'

This time Feliks showed signs of impatience. 'You said yourself that every day counts. Would you like it if somebody was in danger and I went according to the book? Every day may be the last day. Having Paweł in it means we may know what the Germans have in mind for the ghetto a day or two before it takes place. Tomorrow we start. I will bring him with me so that you can get to know him.'

'Bring him in his civilian clothes.'

'He never wears his uniform outside duty hours.'

I met Paweł and we became friends immediately. He knew my name as David. Of his own volition he repeated to me the assurance that I would receive a monthly payment for as long as we needed it. 'After all, this will be over by this time next year,' he said encouragingly, 'and we will come to some new agreement. There is no need to make too great a promise in advance.'

For weeks on end we delivered between forty and fifty furs daily to Feliks and Paweł. We worked out a routine where each member of the group would hide somewhere for a few minutes, divest himself of the fur and pack it into a sack. This was done first thing in the morning, as soon as we reached our work area. Usually Feliks but sometimes Paweł would come to the arranged place in a horse-drawn *dorożka*, which they would pull up somewhere nearby. We would be ready, looking out for the *dorożka* and on its approach, we would place the sack close by on the footpath. Feliks or Paweł would grab the sack, jump on the *dorożka* and be off like lightning. They failed us once only, on a most unfortunate day.

We had brought out fifty-five furs, worth a fortune on the black market. I was working in front of a demolished building stacking cleaned bricks. I was waiting for Feliks, hoping he would come early as I wanted to attend the Kiercelak. Usually he was not later than about ten o'clock. On this particular day, the time passed and he did not arrive. I became impatient. By two o'clock I began to worry. I wondered if something had happened to Feliks or to Paweł, or both of them. I also wondered what to do with the furs. There was no way of taking them back to the ghetto. It was also dangerous to try to move them from the place by ourselves. I could have hired a *dorożka* and taken the furs to my friends but then the driver of the *dorożka* might denounce my friends or blackmail them.

I waited restlessly. Half an hour before we had to leave, the leader of the group decided for me. We had to bury the furs somehow and hope for the best. But we could not leave them packed overnight; they would be ruined. We had to straighten them then hide them in a improvised box we made of bricks. I asked some men in the group to remove their shirts, paying them three or four times the shirts' value. We placed the shirts on top of the fur, and collected some boards which we put across the box and then began to pile the cleaned bricks on top of them. I wanted to stop after two rows but was advised to stack them much higher.

When we returned the next morning without new stock my heart fell. As we approached we could see that the bricks had gone. All was lost and I had no furs if they should come to collect them. But miracles, especially small ones, happen sometimes. The thieves who stole the cleaned bricks had left just one row untouched. One more row and they would have found the furs.

Feliks came at the usual time. I was going to scold him, but held back and just asked what had happened. He was obviously distressed. He had been called up for work on very short notice and he had no way of letting Paweł know. From then on we collected empty boxes and planks to hide the furs in a safer way.

By this time we had four of the family on the Aryan side: Luba's sister, her brother, his wife and Noemi. Now what was to become of Luba?

During the first week of smuggling out the furs I became aware that at the rate we were going most of the furs would remain in the ghetto. Something had to be done very quickly about moving the stock and getting Luba out as well, permanently. Feliks and I had further arrangements to discuss so I stayed overnight at his apartment.

I could see the changes that had taken place in their household in the few weeks that Feliks had been receiving the furs. His wife had cooked a nice dinner, and we ate and spoke about life in general; about politics; about the difficulties of knowing whom one could trust these days. Feliks was more open with me than he had been on my last visit. It was a very interesting meeting. I was given some important information which Paweł had asked Feliks to pass on to me. Although not officially confirmed, Paweł believed that the deportation of the ghetto was to be renewed soon after the beginning of the New Year, 1943. I knew that men were drawn from the ranks of the police force and elsewhere to check that everyone was obeying German orders. They would 'fly' in when no one was expecting them. Now Feliks told me that these 'flying inspectors' had received orders to strengthen their duty in the ghetto, particularly within the area of the 'wild' parts; the streets that had been emptied and were now dividing the ghetto into separate islands. Any unauthorised person found in those 'wild' streets was to be identified and asked to show their Gestapo permit. The document had to be of valid date. Any Jew without a permit was to be shot on the spot and the Jewish police were to be informed and ordered to remove the body. Listening to Feliks I realised that he had made a very important and valuable choice in taking Paweł on as his partner. As soon as I could I would advise our heads of ŻZW of Paweł's news.

'We have some two months to get out as much of the stock as we can,' Feliks said, 'because we can only assume that two months is the maximum time left for the ghetto. If it should change it would be only for the worse.'

I had a most important question which I thought Feliks probably could not answer, but as Paweł was not with us I asked him anyway.

'Does Paweł think it will be the final liquidation of the whole ghetto, or will the factories working for the armament remain as islands?'

To my surprise he knew the answer. 'It will make no difference what the ghetto produces and who the owners of the factories are; that much I know. I made it my business to get the information I thought would be useful to you and the ghetto, and so did Paweł.' Feliks knew that some firm named Ost-Industries, or Osti for short, had been established further east in the vicinity of Lublin. The Chief of Police in the area, an SS General named Globocnik, had been put in charge of Osti and of the concentration camp Majdanek, which had been active for some time on the border of Lublin. 'The whole of Lublin knows and sees what goes on there and Globocnik doesn't care.' Osti had built two huge camps in Poniatów and Trawniki, not far from Lublin, where Jews from other places had been brought to work as inmates of Majdanek. 'But Majdanek is a death camp for Jews,' Feliks told me. 'They have built gas chambers there and crematoria.' I had known about Treblinka, Sobibór and Bełżec and was not surprised to hear about Majdanek.

Feliks' wife served up a late supper of huge proportions, but I was very upset and couldn't eat. The interval helped to bring our conversation back to the matter at hand — smuggling out the furs.

Feliks said he could pick up parcels from more than one place, if we could organise it. Paweł would have to be involved and he was ready to stand by at any time.

It took no more than a day to make the necessary arrangements. We began to throw bags filled with furs over the fence of the ghetto at designated points and times. One and sometimes two bags would be smuggled into the cemetery under the dead bodies. The bags would be hidden in the death chambers where the rabbis had their room and the lime which was daily spread over the pile of fresh corpses in the open grave was kept. Those two rooms were safe. The German patrols that often came on their motor bicycles on sudden inspections and shot on sight any Jewish suspect who was not working around the corpses, never ventured into those rooms. They were afraid of becoming infected with typhoid or typhus, or some other 'Jewish disease'. During the night a voice would call over from the other side of the cemetery, giving the arranged signal. The bags would be thrown over and whoever picked them up on the other side would look after them from there. In less than two months we managed to transfer around six thousand furs; nearly the entire stock we had managed to hide from the Germans since the war began.

21

Luba leaves

On my insistence, Luba left her job with the German industrialists and joined our group working outside the ghetto. Winter was approaching, the days were short and our spirits were very low. I felt we should be together as much as possible. We needed each other for moral support. Only people who have suffered from prolonged stress, fear and depression might understand how much the need to care for somebody near and dear can often be the most important reason to carry on. I needed to see Luba close to me to stop my spirits falling into total resignation. When I explained why I wanted her to give up work in the secure factory my young wife immediately agreed. The only condition she put forward was that I make sure we would be working together. This was not difficult to arrange. Our leader had become more friendly since I started giving him his daily bribe. We had organised for our group to have some warm soup or at least a hot drink during the day, and we now had a daily exchange of goods with Poles who we knew we could trust. Members of the work group would bring out underwear, clothing, jewellery and other goods that were no longer needed and exchange them for food and other necessities. We had become the reservoir of goods for the Aryan side.

The Germans had closed off the 'wild' streets in the ghetto and had established a new industry which they named *Werterfassung* —

'Collecting of Valuables'. *Werterfassung* employed more than a thousand Jews, working under the strictest German supervision, collecting everything that had been left by those who were now in mass graves in Treblinka. A fortune had been left behind, and while the Germans professed that nothing good could come from Jews, they didn't mind robbing the heritage of those they were murdering. The German supervisors grew greedier each day. The goods from the *Werterfassung* were intended for the suffering Germans whose homes had been hit by bombs. However, the greatest part didn't reach its destination. Furniture, antiques, kitchenwares and other valuables became the property of those who could lay their hands on them. Thousands upon thousands of sets of tableware, the majority in silver, were collected, sorted and packed as the property of the Germans. Tens of thousands of new suits, bed linen and woollen clothes were found in the empty houses; many had been collected by the owners and stored for better times.

Jews working in the *Werterfassung* would risk their lives to conceal valuables. A silver brooch with small sapphires or other semiprecious stones, which had once been a family heirloom, would be exchanged for less than a sausage or a pound of butter, to be smuggled back into the ghetto. The buyers, black-market speculators, would sell it for a hundred or thousandfold the price they had paid for it. Often the punishment for trying to smuggle such items from the empty houses, now considered to be German property, was death. One day when we were smuggling out the fur, a young man came with us in our work-group. For some deal which he had made on his own account, he had received forty złotys. Being afraid that a guard might ask us to turn out our pockets, he rolled up his shirt sleeves and hid the money inside the folds. Jews were not supposed to have such large sums when leaving the ghetto.

It was as if the devil was waiting to find a victim that day. In the morning we had met up with the 'flying' inspection of the two most murderous SS men, Klostermeir and Josef Blosche. They were known as the 'death riders' because they rode into the ghetto on bicycles and made a sport of shooting Jews. We had started to cross the ghetto gate as they appeared from a side street where they must have been waiting for us. As if someone had told them about the man, they asked him to step out. It was a cold, late October morning. One of them asked the man sarcastically, 'You are not cold at all? For your health's sake roll down your sleeves.' The man tried to say something but the order was repeated. He obeyed and the forty złotys fell to the ground. The SS man picked up the money and turned to the guard on duty at the gate: 'Put him down!'

We stood frozen in our rows as the German guard aimed his rifle and from a distance of no more that two or three metres, fired on the young man. The 'flying inspectors' ordered our leader to get two Jews to take the body back into the ghetto. They mounted their bicycles and rode off. The guard turned and went into his guard box. The Polish policeman tried to make sure that we didn't see his face, and the Jewish policeman said in a matter-of-fact way, 'Get on with it. Quick.' Had they decided to search all of us, it would have been a total disaster. Not a single person would have been left alive; we were all bundled up with fur.

I had to support Luba physically to keep her from collapsing from shock. She was cold and trembling as I had never seen her before. Her eyes were wide open when she saw me eating my lunch of bread and jam. I had to force her to swallow a hot drink of coffee. This was the last time Luba left the ghetto. She never stepped inside its walls again.

I was alone. I had not imagined what it would be like to come back to our dwelling in the evening and find nobody and nothing waiting for me. I felt empty inside, even though I knew where Luba was. I knew the woman in whose house Luba was sitting, probably talking or having a meal. Her name was Jadwiga; we had known her before the war and she had been checked out by Feliks. I kept recalling that I had once asked Feliks about a certain man, wanting to know how safe one could consider him. The answer was typical of Feliks. 'Who can be considered safe in Warsaw? Nobody. I don't know what kinds of torture the Germans would have for me if I ever fell in their hands. I would be safe for as long as my mind worked clearly. Would you call this safe? In our days we can only work on "reliable". I am reliable; you are reliable. Nobody is infallible.'

Was Luba safe? It was a curious thought and a curious feeling. For the last two years I had been roaming outside the ghetto, not only in Warsaw but going to all sorts of places and doing the most dangerous things. I always carried a revolver on me, a death sentence if it was discovered. Yet never had the thought of danger meant anything real to me. Now that Luba was on the Aryan side, I had started to feel the strange force of fear; my sense of danger for my young wife overwhelmed me. I warmed up some soup which Luba had prepared and ate without tasting it. I was thinking of going over to see my father but decided against it. During the year that I had been married I had rarely visited my family. My father had remarried and I resented it, which I realise now was not fair. I felt more responsible for Luba and the members of her family than I did for my own. At some deep level I could not let go of the fact that I was with Luba's mother when we were caught. I managed to hang on to a miracle while she went where fate pushed her, together with the other ten thousand Jews who went on that day to their monstrous death in Treblinka. I did not feel like going to see anybody.

But I had a visitor. The man who helped us to smuggle the furs knocked on my door. He asked me if I felt like listening to a proposal for which I might be the most suitable person. The lead-in to his proposal was an eye-opener to me. It made me realise that I had not seen the forest for the trees. Over the last two months, while I was smuggling furs and arms, a revolution of spirit had taken hold of the ghetto. I did not notice the small announcements which had begun to appear on the walls signed by ŻOB — the Jewish Fighting Organisation. My own organisation, the ŻZW, had been pasting up similar notices since the beginning of the occupation. The first illegal notice had been written before the ghetto was constructed. In August 1940 we had announced on a wall poster the death of the founder of Betar, Vladimir Zev Jabotinsky. Notices on the wall had little significance to me so I seldom paid any attention to them. But obviously they had moved the ghetto out of its resignation and fear. Like everybody else I had been aware that the ŻOB had reorganised itself and was now embracing many different political affiliations under a unified military command. I knew also that because of basic differences about the way we would eventually have to fight the Germans, not for survival but for the honour of our people, our organisation had decided not to join the ŻOB. Its rules, demands and discipline would have interfered with our own system. But we co-operated with each other wherever possible.

I had not noticed how much the ŻOB had managed to change the mood of the ghetto in such a short time. Now the leader from the working group was sitting in front of me telling me about it in detail as if to soften me for his proposal. I listened and learned that the Jewish police in the ghetto no longer dared to wear their insignia outside of duty hours, out of fear of reprisals. The leaders of the treacherous police who had co-operated with the Germans during the great deportation had been either killed or wounded by bullets from the Underground. At first nobody believed that a Jewish hand had executed these traitors. But when the ŻOB announced that its leadership had found someone guilty of betraying the Jews of the ghetto and the guilty one had, for his crimes, been sentenced to death and the verdict carried out by the ŻOB, the spirit of the population began to change. The passive resignation towards death had given way to an active spirit of resistance in whatever form was possible. This resistance would come into action when the Germans decided that they could repeat their performance and take the remaining Jews out of the ghetto to the slaughter unhindered.

'No longer do the people fear the Jewish police,' my visitor was telling me. 'The police are now afraid of the Underground forces in the ghetto. They work in groups of three or more and outside of the working hours they lock themselves away in their special houses. If they have to go out for reasons other than duty, they wear civilian clothes. People have taken to buying guns and building bunkers,' the foreman went on. 'Guns and bunkers have replaced everything else. You have not been out in the night-time, so you don't know what goes on. The empty buildings are being dismantled during the night to provide building material for bunkers. Kitchens, toilets, water pipes, bedding and furniture are being taken from them and installed in the bunkers. Even the simplest ones have a sofa and a bench and somewhere to make a warm meal.' I listened, registering what I was hearing without emotion, and yet I could hardly believe it.

During the day one could feel the change in the people. I noticed that the traders on the black market had lately lost interest in dollars and marks, and were buying revolvers and even larger arms. But I never knew how widespread the matter had become; as for the bunkers — I had no idea. Now my visitor turned his talk to the proposal: I was invited to become a supplier of arms for individual sales. The man who had never given me any sign of being anything other than the head of a group of workers going on assignments outside the ghetto, was offering to put up a considerable sum of money to establish a private business of arms sales. He was willing to take over the arms as soon as they came into the ghetto. He would take the risk of being denounced and he was willing to sell whatever I could buy. Was I dreaming? My mind became more and more hazy as he went on. In the same breath as talking about the new fighting spirit and unity in the ghetto, was he interested in making a profit from arms sale? Was he crazy? What for? His reply was telling: 'I can get any guard at the gate on my side for the right sum. They won't even ask what we are smuggling. We could push in a cart with a row of bread on top and full of guns underneath. If not for the profit alone at least we can help the people defend themselves.'

Nothing came of his proposal. But I was glad he had come. He made me forget my loneliness and my fear. Seeing my reluctance he tried a new approach. He invited me to come out and see the change in the ghetto spirit for myself. I went with him. For the first time I saw the bunkers being built, not by organisations but by individuals. We walked together until late in the night and I witnessed something I would not have believed possible. In pitch darkness, during hours when moving in the ghetto was forbidden under the threat of death, people were working. Dressed in black, with blackened faces, some wearing soft shoes to deaden the noise of footsteps, shadows were busy in the desolate, silent houses, dismantling taps and pipes, removing washbasins, even telephones. At one place, a handcart with rubber wheels, loaded to the brim, stood outside a ruined building. As we came nearer I noticed a most elaborate light fitting which had obviously been dismantled from some wealthy household. Two women were handing out the goods to two men who kept disappearing into the ruined house. They had seen us approaching but were not frightened. It did not take us long to find out why: in the shadow of the building stood a younger woman with an automatic pistol.

They knew my guide well. He told them why he had brought me. We went down into the basement of the ruin and my guide asked me to find the entrance to the bunker. I tried to find it, guessed once or twice, but could not find the opening. I gave up. He went over to a broken piece of bath, moved it some ninety degrees and asked me to walk down the steps. I had to bend my head but it was not too difficult. I stepped down and could not believe my eyes: in the dugout, some four metres below street level, I found a large, brightly lit room with white walls. Some building work was going on in the next room, while furniture was being brought in from an opening which I had not noticed before. 'We came in from a side entrance,' my guide informed me. 'The main entrance has been established around the corner.'

By the time I went home it was long after midnight. My guide and group leader tried once more to persuade me. 'You see what effort these people are putting in to defend themselves and make a stand? They would pay any price asked to lay their hands on a good gun. If not for the profit, we should do it for them.' I did not react. I returned to my room stunned and perplexed, yet somewhat more relaxed and calm. I felt much more certain of myself than before. This man knew of course that I bought arms outside the ghetto; I had used his group a few times to help me smuggle in parts of automatics and bullets. But now I knew that he thought of me simply as a private buyer, not connected to an organisation. If by chance he had to give me away, at least he would not know who was receiving the arms I bought. I suddenly felt less lonely and less frightened about the future.

22

The meeting

THE tall buildings of Muranowska 7-9 and number 6 opposite it had been neighbours across the street before the war. Jews and Gentiles lived in both buildings. Since the end of 1940, a three-metre high wall separated the two buildings. The wall had been built on the footpath of the Jewish side. The thoroughfare on Muranowska belonged to the Gentiles. To them the brick wall marked the end of their world. The life hidden behind the wall was largely unknown to them and they cared little about what was going on there. The same was true for those of us who lived entombed behind the wall; bleak existence did not leave much time for the luxury of curiosity.

In Jewish folklore there is a legend about the ten Jewish tribes that were lost before the destruction of the first temple in Jerusalem some two-and-a-half thousand years ago. The legend also told of the ten tribes of Red Jews who had their own kingdom somewhere in the Far East, behind the river of Sambation. The Sambation was the natural border between our world and the world of the Jewish kingdom of the ten tribes. According to the law no one could cross the river during the six days of the week, because the river was constantly throwing up huge, hot boulders. At sunset on Friday and on the beginning of the Jewish holiday, the Sambation quietened down. But the width of the river was more than any Jews would be permitted to cross on the Sabbath. Therefore no Jew of the Diaspora had ever managed to meet with the Red Jews who lived in peace and freedom across the Sambation.

The red brick wall in Muranowska Street was our Sambation River. It was, however, much more dangerous. A guard with a machine pistol was stationed at the wall outside the ghetto, not six but seven days a week. The penalty for trying to cross that barrier was instant death. According to the decree of the German authorities, each side of Muranowska was to treat the other side as if it didn't exist. Only those whose business it was to rule both worlds were entitled to enter both worlds. But the German rulers had never got around to ordering the Jews to brick up the windows which looked over the wall across to the Gentile side. Jew and Gentile in Muranowska could and did look into each other's world. Although it was no more than visual contact at first it was enough to start a lifeline between the ghetto and the Aryan side.

By the end of 1942 there was no longer a question of whether the ghetto would be liquidated — simply when. On my forays into the world outside I constantly heard of new towns and villages that had been made *Judenrein* (cleansed of Jews). Each time I visited Luba she implored me not to return to the ghetto. She constantly reminded me that I had a 'good face', many acquaintances and financial means to remain outside. But we would not have been able to live together. It would have been too dangerous for a single woman, as Luba was known to be on the Aryan side, to have a lover living with her. Anything that was out of the norm could become the trigger for danger. But it was quite safe to visit her occasionally, and I had many addresses where I could live in similar conditions to Luba. I listened to her, tried to feel the same way as she did, but could not. Over the last three years I had changed. I could no longer live in the cocoon of personal security. I had become restless to the point of challenging the very danger that looked me in the face each day. I had become addicted to struggling — the last thing on my mind was to hide from the dangers that threatened me and my fellow Jews.

As the winter at the end of 1942 set in I kept a busy schedule inside and outside the ghetto. The trade in arms was growing in leaps and bounds, despite the ever-increasing danger to the dealers. There was hardly a day without notices of people being shot or hanged for some crime against the Germans. There was hardly a day in which one section or another of Warsaw was not closed off and the people living there sent to work in Germany. Usually during such raids Jews were uncovered; some because the documents they had were not good enough to escape the notice of the German eye; others gave themselves away in fear. There was hardly a day without a hanging, without shooting. In the midst of it all I felt adrenaline in my veins pushing me to taste the danger. On a snowy Christmas Eve I returned from the outside and was told that an important meeting was to take place at Muranowska 7-9, which had become the headquarters of the ŻZW. The meeting had been called for that date because it was safe to assume that the Germans would not spoil their own festive season to chase after Jews. Some sixty members turned up that evening. Looking at the faces of friends I realised how much I must have changed outwardly. Most of us were in our twenties, those in their thirties were already considered old, and we looked as if we were in deep middle age. While waiting for the leadership to arrive I met my friend Geller. We drank grain coffee and ate dry biscuits. The conversation was mostly centred on who was still alive and who had died, who had been shot, or had been deported from the ghetto.

Someone brought the news that in the 'wild' section the Germans overseeing the removal of goods from the empty houses had begun to work with their Jews against other German supervisors. Each of them had become a buyer of goods. They no longer took what they liked as they had done in the beginning, but had begun instead to order particular goods from the Jewish workers. They paid for them with food and by looking the other way when goods were traded with those Jews who lived in the area illegally. I had known for a long while that the discipline of the German Army was very much exaggerated. More than once I had bought military equipment which had been traded on the Kiercelak minutes earlier. I had never dealt in arms directly with the Germans. This was strictly prohibited by the leaders of our organisation. I knew that some underhand deals were going on in the *Werterfassung*, in the collecting of Jewish goods, but I had not realised that it had become an undertaking of such proportions that the Germans now competed with each other for these goods and were paying for them.

After some time, Frenkel, Rodal and the Łopata brothers arrived. We settled on long benches in the largest room and without any formal introduction Frenkel began a speech which has remained with me to this day.

'Comrades! You have been called on such short notice because we have good reason to believe that the next Action against the remnant of the ghetto will take place immediately. It may even be that our murderers will not wait until after the New Year. We have not been informed so far about the return of the special detachments, the *Einsatz* group, but the Germans are receiving their greatest hiding from the Russians at Stalingrad, and they may turn even nastier than they have been so far and vent their anger on us. Last year, they failed at the gates of Moscow. This year they are being decimated in their tens of thousands around Stalingrad. They have been cut off for some months, nearly a quarter of a million men. It is only a matter of time before the armies there disintegrate. The winter, the lack of supplies, the new Russian armies will all contribute to the German fall. One cannot say if this is the beginning of the end of Germany or only the end of the beginning, but one thing is sure: the remnant of the ghetto will pay the price for it. In Africa their armies are finished. The British together with the Americans are cleaning out the dregs of Hitler's and Mussolini's armies. Yes, comrades, the end of Hitler's Germany has already begun. But we as a group will not live to see the end of that barbaric Germany. We have been sentenced to die before their heads are decapitated. This may turn out to be the last time we gather for a meeting and there is much we have to organise before the final battle for our honour takes place.

'Let me tell you, friends, the Allies know by now precisely what our fate is. They know in detail about Treblinka, about Majdanek, and the other places. Why they have not bombed those places we don't know. But we know that only days ago the British War Cabinet decided not to let the Jewish population in Palestine raise a Jewish army under a Jewish flag. These are our friends. We are on our own. Our friends of the ŻOB still believe in miracles. They still send appeals to London calling for help. I need not tell you that we wish them all the luck in the world but we, the Betar, here and over there no longer rely on any rescue from London, or from Washington or even from the Soviet Union, which is close enough to bomb the railways to Treblinka as they bombed Warsaw some months ago. The way we see it, we have to fight alone if we want to die with honour and for the honour of all Jews around the world. The leaders of the free world were briefed about our plight by a representative of Poland, Witold, who witnessed for himself the situation in the Warsaw ghetto as well as in the death camps. We have to organise ourselves to die with the greatest of dignity and to inflict on the Germans as many deaths as we are able. Those who by chance survive will have the duty to remember us to the world and to tell the younger generations about how deaf the Allies have been to the cries of the Jews when they were slaughtered. So let us attend to those things that we have to attend to and can attend to.

'As you know, both the ŻOB and the ŻZW have been collecting large sums of money from the rich Jews in the ghetto and from the departments of the Eldest to pay for the arms some of you are buying. Up to a few weeks ago we had mutually agreed to report to each other where collections had been made, in order not to duplicate our work. Of course, here and there, we used force, but in general even those who were approached knew that once they had paid up and the collectors gave them their receipts they would be in the clear. However, in the last few days it appears that some clever individuals have been going around making collections for their own pockets in our name or in the name of the ŻOB. At first the ŻOB turned on us, claiming that we were collecting large sums and not reporting to them. When we came across a similar incident we began to put our heads together, and I can tell you we have confiscated the collected money from the individuals who believed they were clever and have warned them that their game is very dangerous. If any of you are sent out from now on to collect donations, make sure that the receipt you sign has the required secret sign for the ŻOB. They promise to do the same for us.'

Frenkel turned to Rodal who handed him a note. He read it and went on. 'We have also managed to get hold of more SS uniforms and helmets. We plan, starting from tomorrow, to fit out some members with these uniforms. However, those who are selected should not think that they can take the uniform to their homes. They will be trained for their disguise and will keep their personal uniforms here. When the time comes to put on that cursed uniform, they will be ready; they will know how to act and what their specific job will be. I mention this only because some of you may not want to put on the German uniform even for the sake of our lives. Those who are ready to put on the uniform of the SS when the time comes will be able to register with one of the Łopata brothers at the end of this meeting.'

Once more Rodal handed him a note, which he read and continued. 'As you well know, there are very few old people or children left in the ghetto, and they are mostly the children of those who have worked with the Germans. A child of a policeman was beaten up by somebody who told the young boy that he was being beaten for his father's sin and his father will soon be shot by the Underground. We have not been able to find the perpetrator of this despicable deed. But in the name of the ŻZW, I am telling you that mistreating a Jewish child for the sin of his father will be treated with the harshest punishment. Every Jewish child has to be treated like the pupil of the eye. We do not want to be the assistants of the *Einsatz*, helping them to destroy Jewish children. The traitors already know that they are marked men but only the traitors will die by our hand and not their children. A man we sent to execute a Jew who was an informer to the Gestapo, did his duty; he killed the traitor, but he came back crying. When I asked him why he was crying, he said, "The woman had to die for what she did, and I am proud to have liquidated a Jewish traitor from our midst. But I cannot help thinking that some German in the Gestapo is laughing and thinking, 'Hey, we have succeeded in getting Jews to kill Jews. It's even better than us having to kill them.'" So you see, my friends, that killing even a traitor, if he or she is Jewish, is a duty but not a joy. The woman was Anna Milewicz, who previously belonged to the Hashomer Hatsair. She was removed from it. The Hashomer Hatsair was in full agreement with what we did, because it was proved that she worked for the Gestapo.

'Finally, as you all know, we do not have our own man on the other side as the ŻOB does. Those of you who go out of the ghetto are the only messengers we have apart from the contact with the AK, the Home Army. We know that the ŻOB has a formal representative, Arie Wilner, who goes under the name of Jurek and he deals with the representative of the AK in the Department for Jewish matters, a man named Henryk Woliński, who goes by the name of Wacław. I am telling you all this and give you their right names and their code names to show you that although we do not work under the same command we trust each other completely. We, the ŻZW, believe that the time has come when we can and should accept every Jew who has a gun and comes and says he wants to join us. We should take him or her in and train them as part of ourselves, but checking and re-checking that we have the right person. The ŻOB believes that such a policy may endanger everything in advance. This is the basic and most important reason why we are and will remain a separate fighting body. In the end it will make no difference — we do not believe that in either way we can win the final battle physically. The question that divides us is: which way can we inflict the greatest damage on the Germans and their helpers? Only time will show who was right and who was wrong.'

The debate after Frenkel's speech was long and exhausting. It became heated when somebody asked him, 'When they come next time to continue the Action, will we fight, or what?'

'It will depend,' he said.

His answer irritated many. 'Depend on what?' came a chorus of voices.

Frenkel looked at Rodal before he answered. 'It will depend on more than one thing. First of all, it has been agreed that our fight will be co-ordinated with the general Uprising. We will have to be sure that the general Uprising has really begun and the others have taken up arms with us.'

'Why do we have to depend on them? And if the ŻOB will not give the order to their people does it mean that we will finish up with talk like this tonight? Is that it?' The atmosphere grew tense. Frenkel felt the beginning of a challenge and let a few moments of talk between ourselves pass. When the question was turned back to him he was ready. He lowered his voice and spoke calmly. 'We, the ŻZW, are independent as far as the order to take up arms against the Germans is concerned. If we should find it right to begin the Uprising tomorrow, or even tonight, this would be our own decision and nobody will tell us what we can or cannot do. Let this be clear. It means that what you have heard tonight was precisely what I have said: this gathering was meant to be an information and organising meeting. The leadership of ŻZW together with our people from the other side have talked the matter over and we came to the decision that time is very short. It may be days or at best weeks, but neither we nor our friends on the other side believe that the Germans will wait too long before coming back to finish off what they started. But we also made other decisions which have to do with the moment when the revolt will begin.' Again he paused. This time everybody remained silent and let him continue.

'As far as we know, the ŻZW is better equipped to resist any German attempt to renew the deportation than the ŻOB is. But let us not fool ourselves, the ŻOB has managed to organise many different groups under one command, which we could not, as I have already explained. There is no question and no doubt about the Uprising taking place; it will happen. Three months ago we might have been right to think otherwise, but not anymore. The question which remains open is not "if" there will be some resistance but under what conditions it will take place. At the latest meetings we had with them it was decided that the full strength we have, although it is not much, should not be wasted. What this means is simple: if the SS come to test whether the ghetto is ready to make their job difficult, we should not open up with full strength. To do so would only give the Germans the opportunity to prepare themselves for the final assault with all the power at their disposal. It would, in the end, minimise our field of action and their losses. The final decision to say if the next Action means the liquidation of the ghetto and therefore the right time to open up with fire has been left to the command of ŻOB. When the time comes we may not agree with their decision but for the moment ŻOB represents many political streams. They have the communists, the Bund, the strength of the Zionist movement and the Jewish representatives on the Aryan side. It is therefore imperative that we leave the decision to them for the sake of co-ordination. Only if we conclude that they have failed to start fighting at the right moment will we be morally free to act on our own. Not before.'

I was not satisfied with this answer; nor were others. One of the fighters sitting behind me stood up and said, 'Let us say that tomorrow or in three days time a German unit enters the ghetto together with their helpers and calls "*Alles herunter!*" What are we supposed to do?'

'We are very close to each other,' Frenkel said. 'If the decision will be to fight we will hear quite clearly the guns of the ŻOB and the exploding Molotov cocktails and hand grenades. In theory at least we should quickly get a message. You all know that this does not mean a runner will come down the street. But it is not difficult to get out from Miła Street to Muranowska through the houses and the attics.'

We were not satisfied. 'And what do we do in the meantime, while the messenger is running through the attics?' someone asked.

'Do we go into hiding?' another added with sarcasm.

'Yes. We do go into hiding!' Frenkel replied, with authority. It was hard to believe what we had just heard. The situation became very tense, on the brink of exploding. But Rodal was already at Frenkel's side.

'The first duty of each of you and each of us is discipline!' His voice was resolute. 'Every one of us here is now a soldier and soldiers may sometimes dislike the command of their officers, but unless they decide to stage an uprising of their own, soldiers obey orders. They ask questions and wait for answers. What is going on here is deteriorating into a debating group. We have no others left to replace you. You will, in the end, be the ones who will take up arms or fail to do so, if you continue to demand personal satisfaction and personal opinions contrary to those that have been expressed. Believe me, all the questions you have been asking and those you still want to ask have already been put on the table between our own leadership, and between us and the ŻOB. We did not leave the last meeting with them in complete agreement. But we knew that we are now the last soldiers of the Warsaw ghetto. Our name, Betar, should tell you the whole history of the Uprising of Bar Kochba two thousand years ago. We are the sons of that final battle of Betar, and we must remain so. We have all been tested to the end of our nerves and beyond. Not one of us can say any longer that he is out to protect his family. We have no longer any family of our own, we are the only family we have and we must decide how we will make the last stand for that family! Let anyone here who has not lost a part of his family, or all of them, raise his hand.'

Rodal stopped and looked around. No hand went up. He lowered his voice.

'This is the saddest moment of this evening. Not one of us here has a full family left. Only we, the last soldiers of Betar, are left. There will be a living Betar when our deadly enemy is defeated. But those of us who have been commanded by fate to remain here must accept that they are soldiers. We must act like soldiers and must accept the discipline of soldiers, who, like the Roman gladiators, must know how to fight to the death, for honour! Our honour is the Jewish honour and therefore we must, for as long as we believe it is right, accept the decision to co-ordinate our action with the action of the others. It has been decided that everybody should, in the first place, not obey the call of the Germans, and go down to the bunkers. Therefore, going into hiding is not shameful but a matter of discipline. If that is still not clear to anyone, I want to know why not.'

He waited for some reaction. When nobody raised a hand he spoke once more. 'I will now ask the younger Łopata to come in. You are in for a surprise. But it is important that we get used to what you are about to see, otherwise the confusion we intend to cause the SS may cause confusion to ourselves. Is everybody ready?' Nobody answered and Rodal nodded to someone out of sight. From the corner Łopata appeared and a sigh went up from all. He was dressed in the full uniform of an SS soldier, complete with the dreaded light machine-gun in his hand. It took some seconds before the electricity which accompanied his appearance was discharged.

'How many of these uniforms do we have?' somebody asked.

For the first time in the evening Rodal permitted himself a faint smile.

'Not many for the moment. But let us say enough to cause

confusion to our enemies and inflict additional losses. But we have to work out a system by which we can recognise the Jewish SS from the German one. It has to be done in a split second or even less.' Suggestions came from all sides but it was obvious that they had not been thought through. In the end Rodal spoke up once more.

'Friends! You are the first and only ones so far to have seen the SS uniform on our soldier. The ŻOB has no such uniforms, or at least we were left with the impression that they don't. Nobody will leave tonight without giving the undertaking that this knowledge will not go outside these walls. Until we have worked out a safe system of recognition, the SS uniform does not exist. It may even be that we have to abandon the idea of using them; I hope not. But . . .' he stopped in the middle of his sentence. He looked around and remarked, 'I think this concludes what the command of ŻZW has to inform you. I'll ask our Commander if he has anything to add before we close this gathering.' He turned to Frenkel who stood up while Rodal moved off the podium.

'Yes,' Frenkel responded, 'I have something to add. First of all, I want to thank my deputy-in-command for so expertly turning your attention back to the important matters at hand. Secondly, I'll finish what he has left out: the younger Łopata whom you have just seen in the black uniform, has been put in charge of registering those who are ready to sign up to join his unit. It does not mean that everyone who registers will be given a German uniform, it will mean that we know who and how many we have at our disposal if we should decide to make good use of them. And finally, I want to thank everyone here tonight and invite you all to a small late evening bite together. My deputy said a few minutes ago that we are the only family we have, so let us share at least one meal together. The official meeting is now closed.'

I was first to approach Łopata to register for the uniform. He was very pleased and even smiled. 'I have already put you on the top of the list; Frenkel asked me to do it. He would love to see you in the German uniform on the Kiercelak, with a German automatic in hand. I will give you a high-ranking uniform, because of your height and looks, even though you don't speak any German.' Months later this quip turned out a sad prophecy. Frenkel saw me in the German uniform, not on the Kiercelak but in the ghetto. It was close to his last hour.

23

Twilight

THE daily routines we followed during this twilight time could not have fitted into the life of any other society. It is doubtful whether even in the many German ghettos, concentration camps or death camps, were they as twisted and bizarre as the routines in the Warsaw ghetto in that time of waiting for the end.

The huge industrial complexes which the Germans had built up in the last year, had, after the great blood-letting, once more regained their feverish, killing speed. The slave workers once more believed wishfully the words of their German protectors, that the Third Reich would grant them special recognition for their effort and reward them by letting them survive the war. The many commissions that came to visit the gigantic factories spoke kindly about some new approach to the Jewish workers. Again they promised to provide kindergartens and schools for those children who by some miracle were still alive. Better food and medication were to be provided in the near future for those in need of medical care. While making these promises the Germans never forgot to underline that these improvements depended on the production results which the employers could report to Berlin. The German employers kept telling their Jewish slaves that they should never forget their privileged position and not let themselves be misled by the propaganda that had begun to take roots in the other parts of the ghetto.

When the news that the Chief of Police in the ghetto had been shot reached the three largest factories — the brush works, the military uniform makers and the textile complexes — the Germans emphasised to their workers that they were looked after better than the Jewish administration looked after the rest of the ghetto. For the Christmas festivities, work had been reduced in some places to only half a day and additional soup and half a portion of bread were awarded to each worker. One employer promised the Jews in his factory that when the year was over the German employers would remember that it was the work of the Jews of the Warsaw ghetto that helped Germany to its victory.

But nothing could stop the Jewish Underground from penetrating the closed sanctum of the German industries in the isolated parts of the ghetto. In spite of the strict internal supervision by the *Werkschutz* — the task masters who were hired to keep the workers under strict discipline — wall notices kept appearing daily, calling on the workers not to believe any of the German promises. 'Where is your family? Where are your fathers, your mothers? Your husbands and wives? Where have your sons and daughters gone?' screamed an illegal poster in large capital letters. 'The Germans have not kept any of their promises in the past and they will not keep any of the promises they are making now! Fellow Jews! Do not go to the slaughter quietly any more. Three hundred thousand Jews have been murdered by the Germans in the gas chambers of Treblinka. They will not let you survive the war to be living witnesses to their heinous crime!'

The *Werkschutz* were there to stop such propaganda reaching the slaves. The posters were undermining their safe status. When the workers started receiving the Underground leaflets the German employers demanded more vigilance from the supervisors. The *Werkschutz* listened and obeyed. They tore down posters and whenever they could, they punished the perpetrators. Their self-confidence did not last very long, however. Delegates of the Underground from outside the workforce came to the factories when they were least expected. Well armed and fierce, they took some of the *Werkschutz* aside and whispered well-chosen words in their ears. They told the supervisors that if they wanted to breathe without interruption, they should look the other way when notices were posted on the walls. Hints were dropped that very soon the Jewish *Werkschutz* would come to understand that not only the slave workers but they too had no future. They were told that soon they would have to come to the Underground seeking protection for themselves in the same way as the Underground protected the workers. Ultimately, the strict message at the end of a loaded revolver fell on more receptive ears than the command of the employers.

While this fight for the souls of the Jewish slaves in the German industries went on, other routines in the ghetto continued. Groups went to work outside the ghetto; the smuggling of food and other goods flourished; the preparation of bunkers continued; the authorities delivered their daily rations as before and the Jewish administration functioned, with little authority. Officially, nobody was allowed to be on the ghetto streets during working hours without special permission. The penalty was the same as for all other crimes — a bullet. But there was an unwritten agreement, that Germans in uniform or civilians who came into the ghetto were not interested in the walking Jews. As long as the Jewish man took off his head covering and bowed and the Jewish woman bowed before the passing German the little sin of being illegally in the street was overlooked.

On a sunny day early in January 1943 I was working in the storeroom at the headquarters of ŻZW dismantling and cleaning arms. Someone had just made a warm drink when one of the fighters came in. He was offered a mug and while drinking he asked off-handedly, 'Would anyone by any chance know where I could get hold of some *Czarodziejek* cream? [*Czarodziejek* cream helped to mask any changes in one's complexion. If someone was going on a dangerous mission they would wear it so that others would not notice if they went pale or flushed with fright.] David, one of your friends, Kolniczański, asked for it.' Nobody had any to offer. I remembered that I had bought some only a few weeks earlier at the last chemist shop in the ghetto, on the corner of Miła, so I suggested he go there. 'Would you come with me?' he asked.

'You are not a child,' I said. 'You don't need me to lead you. Besides, one man walking is not as noticeable as two.'

He took off his overcoat and began to make himself useful in the storeroom. After an hour other people arrived. From the office somebody came out and handed me a letter to be delivered immediately to an address in Miła Street. This gave me an opportunity to go out with my friend to the chemist. Strangely enough we met Kolniczański, who was out looking for the cream. It was a fateful walk. My friend left with the letter we had to deliver. I stayed with Kolniczański to look for the cream.

We took our short walk through the ruins, avoiding the open streets as much as possible. The footpaths were covered in ice and snow throughout the winter. Also, we were glad to walk through backyards as our footmarks had been quite noticeable in the freshly fallen snow. But when we came to an open place we had to look both ways to make sure it was safe. We made our run and were seconds away from safety when a Ukrainian called out to us to stop, '*Stehn bleiben!*' We managed to turn the corner and as quick as our feet would carry us we ran into a building on Miła 2. It was empty. The doors of the apartments were open, some were missing. Neither of us thought of hiding in one of the apartments. Instead we made our way up to the fourth floor then into the attic. It was one large room with two entrances, one opposite the other. There were no places to hide except behind the two chimney stacks which penetrated from the lower floors. We could hear the cursing Ukrainian coming towards us. In desperation we hid behind the chimneys. I took the first one near the entrance while Kolniczański hid behind the other. We heard slow footsteps coming up towards us. At the edge of the stairs leading from the fourth floor to the attic they stopped. In a calm voice the Ukrainian said, 'I know you are up there. Come down and I'll let you go. If I have to come up to get you I'll shoot you.' We did not make a move. The Ukrainian didn't move either. He waited, and after some minutes he repeated, 'If I have to come up to get you, you'll be dead.' Again, we didn't move.

Time passed and we heard him climbing the stairs, slowly, hesitating, until he reached the top. It was now only a matter of seconds before he discovered us. With his submachine-gun directed towards us he stopped at the entrance and looked around sharply, not saying anything. I dared not look in his direction but, turning very slightly towards Kolniczański, I noticed in horror that his body was casting a shadow towards the middle of the attic. I could only hope for a miracle, that he would not move. All three of us were frozen in our positions. Kolniczański had not looked towards me. He made some move to cover himself deeper behind his chimney and his shadow moved imperceptibly. It was enough for the Ukrainian. Slowly he walked in. The tiny movement cost Kolniczański his life. The guard in his field-green police uniform was now fully focused on his victim. A single turn of his head would have given me away but he did not turn in my direction. Slowly, he walked in front of me and, coming close to the other chimney, made a dash and fired on Kolniczański point blank. To this day I ask myself what alerted me to switch around at the moment when he fired his weapon. As Kolniczański fell he murmured something. The guard pushed him aside with his jack-boots and walked out through the other opening in front of him. I waited in a cold sweat, listening to him walking down the steps, before I went over to Kolniczański's body. I was furious with myself for not having the revolver I usually carried tucked in behind my belt. There was nothing I could do for my friend.

When I returned to the headquarters and told those present what had happened it was taken with outward calmness. But the silence which fell on the place showed of our feelings. Only the storeman spoke as he busied himself in the storeroom: 'He will no longer need his *Czarodziejek* cream.' No one made any other comment.

A teacher of arithmetic is giving the fifth graders a lesson in fractions. She holds up a bread roll and says, 'Children, I want you to imagine that I break the roll in two. What would I have?' A small hand goes up and a boy answers, 'Two halves.' The teacher is pleased. 'If I now break each of the halves again what would I have?' 'Four quarters,' a chorus answers. 'I don't want you all to answer at once, I want to find out if each one understands fractions,' the teacher says and calls one pupil after the other. After the roll has been broken into sixty-four pieces, she calls on Michael: 'Michael, if I now break each of the sixty-four parts in two, what will I have?' 'Crumbs,' comes the answer.

It was a joke which best illustrated the reality of the Warsaw ghetto in its dying days. Only the outer skin of the carcass, the brick fence, built by Jews with Jewish money, was still intact. Inside, the ghetto was already physically destroyed before the Uprising.

Each of us was living on a little island of isolated groups. We were forbidden to have any contact with each other except for authorised purposes. Jews caught in no-man's land were shot on the spot. But the contact between the islands was not completely lost. We could walk through the passages made between the buildings. Where this was impossible people took chances and walked outside when they believed it to be safe. Often they made it from one island to the next. Here and there a life was lost, but it was not enough to stop the traffic completely. We had a unique proverb: 'If you want to stay alive in the ghetto, you have to risk it sometimes.'

Paradoxically, there was a lust for consuming as much of the short time left as possible. Smuggling grew to great proportions. Restaurants opened in which food and alcohol were plentiful and of good quality. Those who had money, not even great amounts of it, could afford to visit the restaurants and enjoy a good meal. One restaurant was known to the organisers of the ŻOB. Their Commander, Mordecai Anielewicz, was taken there by his friends from time to time to enjoy a fish meal, which he loved.

It is hard to reconstruct the ghetto in words — the contradictions of daily life were too many to make sense to an outsider. The Poles of Warsaw lived life close to death; for the remaining Jews, death was the rule around which life centred.

On Monday 18 January 1943, the ghetto found itself surrounded. No one was permitted to leave. The work-groups that usually left in the morning were stopped at the gates. The whole Action was so sudden that nothing had been organised and no decision had been taken as to how the groups should respond in such an event. The only thing that had changed this time was the attitude of the sixty thousand Jews still left in the ghetto. Nobody responded to the German command of 'All down!' The Germans had to enter the houses to remove the people they wanted for deportation yet they were still assisted by the Jewish police. I often ask myself what evil force made the Jewish police co-operate in January 1943, when they themselves had been decimated after the great deportation?

It was on this day that the first Germans were killed in the ghetto. They fell to Jewish bullets, their uniforms and their rifles were the first spoils of the ŻOB. The small battles which took place that day had not been organised. It was just that the luck of the Jewish fighters had turned and each group decided for itself to resist. On that day, the ŻOB commander was grabbed from the arms of death by one of the fighters who was with him. In the heat of the battle, a group being led to the *Umschlagplatz*, for transfer to the wagons, included Mordecai Anielewicz, together with some members of his organisation. They had dispersed and each one was to select his own guard to disarm. The signal was to be a hand grenade thrown by one of the women in the group. As soon as the grenade went off the Commander fired his revolver and it failed him. He threw himself on his German victim and began to choke him. An alert friend pulled him away and grabbed the soldier's rifle, pulling Anielewicz into the next house.

Our group held its fire. The leadership insisted that this was only a testing Action. If the murderers had come for the final liquidation, the argument went, the ghetto would have been overwhelmed by a much larger contingent. Also, the Action never came close to our part of the ghetto. It did not take long for our leadership to be proven right. The Action lasted about four days and was carried out in a way which made us believe that the Germans had no enthusiasm or their usual lust for their work. Some five to six thousand people were rounded up throughout the four days. Those deported were mostly elderly, the sick and those who had decided they would be better off dead than continuing a hopeless fight.

On the last day of the Action those of us at the ŻZW headquarters were given a lesson in courage. It was one of the most inspiring talks we ever heard from our leaders. It was given by Frenkel.

'Comrades! From time to time the leadership calls you to give you some inspiration for the fight which awaits us against the most bitter foe Jews have ever experienced. We keep telling you that the Germans will not win the war and our people will in the end prevail, although we are doomed. Today I want to apologise to you for my pessimism. I was wrong. We are not doomed.

'Comrades! Dying is not something new or something that happens only to the Jews in the Warsaw ghetto. There is also nothing new in the ways of dying. Death has lived, if you will forgive my paradox, since life was born. Even death in gas chambers was already practised by these barbaric German people before the war started. The only thing that is unique to our situation is that we, having been born Jews, have the death sentence already pronounced on us. There is no need for the non-Jew to receive permission to kill a Jew; it is being done under the general verdict. The opposite is true; murdering a Jew is something people are being rewarded for. But is that reason enough for us to go into the fight with the feeling of doom? Of course not. The pessimism we, the leaders of the ŻZW, carried in our heart was that we might be an insignificant few whose fight would be lost amongst the millions of Jews who have already been murdered. Our murderers will finish miserably and will have to pay for every crime they are committing. But we will not see it. Here and there one or two of our organisation, or some other, may still be alive to see the Germans' defeat. Our pessimism arose because we did not believe that we would ever present to the future the real spirit of the Jews. Our pessimism arose because we believed that even our final fight, which will now come very soon, would never be noticed, or if noticed, soon forgotten.

'Well, comrades, I was wrong and I apologise in my own name and on behalf of the whole leadership for having been so pessimistic. In the last weeks a lot has changed in the world which for us is completely closed off. Germany has been thoroughly defeated in North Africa. At the time of the great deportation here, we did not pay attention to the outside world. Hitler's armies had reached very close to the Suez. The British had begun to make emergency arrangements in case the Germans reached Cairo. I need not tell you what would have happened, God forbid, if Hitler's army would have entered Tel-Aviv and Jerusalem. Now the Germans have been liquidated in North Africa. The same is now going on at the Russian front. It is only a matter of days before the Hitler hordes at Stalingrad, which according to the English radio are hundreds of thousands, fall into the hands of the Soviet Army. They are totally encircled and cut off from any supply. Tens of thousands have already frozen to death. They have no winter clothing; no food; no medication; and — forgive me for what I am about to say — like us, they are doomed. I am now sure that we will live long enough to hear about the German defeat at Stalingrad.

'The last four days here have shown us that we will not be forgotten! Our fight, when it comes and no matter how short it is, will not be forgotten. We will live in the pages of Jewish history. Children in the future Jewish Land of Israel will learn about us and we will be the model for the courage they will need. You see, it may be late, but the Jews in the ghetto have decided to resist the deportation to death. Even those with no guns and no organisation are no longer afraid to resist. The murderers have already noticed it. The Germans are dispirited. Today they will leave us in peace while they prepare themselves better, to finish us off. Of course we will fight with guns in our hands and most of us will fall. But we will live on in the lives and hearts of future generations and in the pages of their history.

'Comrades! We will die before our time but we are not doomed. We will be alive for as long as Jewish history lives!'

It was an electrifying speech. Frenkel was usually a dry speaker even when he had to say something of great importance, but the speech he gave on that day made us eager for the final battle to begin, although we had no illusion about its outcome. On the same afternoon, the deportation command left the ghetto and did not return for its murderous task until 19 April.

24

It begins

If I should be asked what happened between the end of the January Action and the week before the ghetto Uprising, I would have to be honest and say nothing that is worth recording, as far as my personal life was concerned. I bought ammunition for the armament we had accumulated. I had lazy days when I risked visiting Luba for a few hours. Sometimes I volunteered to do duty at the headquarters; it was mostly of secondary importance. I was not counted among those who had key duties there. When I was outside the ghetto I never lost contact with my organisation. If I went out through the gate with a working group I could be contacted through the foreman; when I went over the wall of the cemetery the headquarters knew where I was going, and I visited my allocated group daily to make sure that everything was normal. Very seldom did I stay out of the ghetto overnight. When this was necessary I made sure not to stay with Luba. If I should be betrayed or accidentally caught I did not want her to be caught with me. Luba accepted this, although she often missed me and could not hide it.

Each time I left her I said the same words like a mantra: 'I'll be back when I come.' Sometimes I told her where I was going to and sometimes I didn't mention it. Luba never asked questions.

'Janek,' she said once, 'remember, my love goes with you whatever happens and wherever you go.' This echoed in my mind each time I had to leave her.

Slowly the harsh winter weather began to give way to early spring. First came the melting of the heavy icicles over the windows and at the edges of the Warsaw roofs. The snow melted and the ice over the Wisła began to crack. By the middle of March the wide river was open in some places and the ice had begun to move slowly. The slim trees in the streets, which had dressed themselves in snow and the black dress of winter, started to erupt in first blossoms. Once more it was daylight before six in the morning. Even the icy cold of the early spring mornings was somewhat easier to take than the winter mornings. On the Kiercelak the change expressed itself in its own way. After the defeat at Stalingrad the Swastika flags had been draped with black ribbon at the top for a number of days, and there was a flood of personal arms for sale, such as rifles and semi-automatics. Soldiers on leave in Warsaw no longer looked the victorious individuals they had been last summer. Some of them could have been mistaken for members of the Polish Underground. They wanted to spend their short time in the city living it up and for this they needed money. Selling either their own weapons or what they could steal from the stores was one of the ways of achieving it.

To my great relief, I had found that the people we had entrusted with our furs had kept their promise. Every month they delivered the allowance to Luba. It was small change compared to the value of the furs but under the circumstances it was an act of unusual honesty. Hundreds, if not thousands, of Jews had trusted Poles and ended up without a penny or had even been handed over to the police or the Gestapo. We had met all round with decent people. One single Pole could cause the death of many Jews. It needed the least effort to denounce a Jew. In a single day one *szmalcownik* could blackmail and in the end hand over many Jews to the Gestapo. Many young Poles made a lucrative living out of sending Jews to their death, and they did not mind in the least if it also involved the life of an entire Polish family, as long as they made a profit out of it. But to help keep one Jew alive it took a number of people.

The financial resources were a critical factor. But so were other factors, such as accommodation. To find a secure place to hide and to have another place in case of an emergency required considerable organisation. In our case more than ten families were involved in keeping us alive, beside those who provided for our financial needs.

I was outside the ghetto two days before the flare of the Uprising went up. It was Saturday 17 April. I had spent lunchtime with Luba and had, as always, left her without telling her where I was going or when I would visit her again. There was some unusual traffic in the streets. It was obvious that something was going on but it was not enough for me to discern if it was a Polish matter or something being prepared for us.

The police and Gestapo movement in Warsaw was not unexpected. I suspected that it had to do with the ghetto because the Poles moved along freely, feeling secure, and no military vehicles were parked at the larger intersections. I was right. When I arrived at the place where Jewish workers were cleaning bricks as usual, the tension was very noticeable, and three of my unit were missing. The foreman looked nervous. 'I have been waiting for you since the morning. You have to report to Muranowska as soon as possible.' I asked if I should go right away via the cemetery or wait until the group went back and his answer showed the tension. 'Better stay with us here. The others have gone to contact those who are living on the outside but are getting called up. I may need you to make up the numbers. If they all come back we have made arrangements at the cemetery wall. The Poles have put some sentries there. They will signal if it is safe to enter the cemetery.'

He was sure that the ghetto Action would start on the Monday. 'It is the eve of Pesach, and on the twentieth is the Führer's birthday. Besides, they always love to start on a Monday when they are rested and fresh for us.' I took off my coat and started work. It didn't take me long to realise why the foreman was so sure. The vehicles driving past seemed to slow down as they came close to us; some stopped completely for half a minute and observed us quite openly. An SS limousine stopped across from us. A uniformed German got out and began to cross the street. Our foreman ran out to the edge, took off his cap and stood to attention. Our thin blood began to congeal as the officer seemed not quite satisfied and called to another soldier in the car. The man came over and together they spoke with the foreman who was now standing stiffly. After a few minutes they left. We ran up to the foreman and found out that he had been warned to keep a strict eye on us. He was asked if he knew us all and he had said that he knew everyone. The German who came over later had told him that they were going to search us and the place for hidden weapons. If the foreman suspected that any of the group might be carrying hidden revolvers they said he had better tell them before they began their search. If he would point out those he suspected, he would not be harmed. But if he did not point out the criminals and they found a single bullet, everyone would be shot on the spot. The foreman assured the officer that he had been with the same group for nearly two years and to the best of his knowledge he had never had any of his group involved in the least illegal thing. 'We have been checked bodily,' he had told the officer, 'at least a hundred times and never was anything found on anyone in the group.' The officer asked him if he could be sure that no one had ever smuggled anything into the ghetto, such as bread or sugar. In his most humble way the foreman had answered, 'I am well aware that on my honesty depends the lives of the whole group. I cannot honestly give a full guarantee that never has anyone of the group smuggled something. But to the best of my knowledge and to the best of the record of the physical searches we have undergone, nothing has been found on a single person.'

They drove away without making the threatened search. If they had searched us, we would all have been shot. The place was full of forbidden matter, from food to dollars, and parts of a whole light machine-gun which had been dismantled to be carried into the ghetto on our way back. Of course the gate to the ghetto had already been made secure because the guard on duty had been bribed that morning.

By the end of the day it was no longer a secret what the large movement meant. The only thing that was clear to those of us who had been outside the ghetto throughout the day was that nothing would happen until the assistant murderers, the Ukrainians and the Latvians, arrived. They were the dogs who would be led on the leash by the Germans. So far we had not seen a single one of them. We came back to the ghetto uncounted, and as soon as we had cleared the gate and turned to the first side street I was off to our headquarters. The entire leadership was there but no one was giving any direct orders. There was a constant coming and going but nothing seemed clear. The ones who were stationed there permanently seemed better informed. One of the Łopata brothers stopped me and asked me where I could be found if I should be needed later in the evening. I was surprised by the question and asked why I had been called urgently to come to the headquarters.

'To tell us where you can be found from now on — immediately,' he answered.

'And if I go out tomorrow morning will you send somebody to find me on the Aryan side?' I asked.

'You will not go outside the ghetto tomorrow or the next day, or the day after, because we do not know if the moment of truth will be on Monday, on the eve of Pesach, or if they will start the Action on Tuesday, as a gift to Hitler. On Tuesday he will have lived fifty-four years too long. From now on I have to know every movement you make, even when you go to the toilet. Understood?'

Suddenly I knew where I belonged and who my commanding officer was — the younger Łopata. 'I am hungry,' I told him, 'and I am going to the restaurant on Szczęśliwa Street; you know, the one on the second floor.'

With a face that did not betray any curiosity he said, 'I am not asking what draws you there or how long you will be there, but remember you will be either here or there and nowhere else.'

There was nothing more for me to do at the headquarters. Impulsively I saluted and left. The restaurant I was going to was not just out of choice. For months I had been meeting there with my Polish friend Janek Kostański. He was the one who had delivered Luba's false documents. His family kept a Jewish family hidden somewhere outside the ghetto, and he had fallen in love with the girl of the family who was near his own age. It was a reciprocal love story under very unusual conditions. Young Kostański had grown up with many Jewish friends in the poor part of Warsaw. The family was liberal minded and, like many of the Polish working class, the friendship meant more than the religion. Janek had many old friends in the ghetto and he also made new ones. I remembered that some weeks earlier he had told me that he planned to spend the first two days of Passover in the ghetto; he loved the Seder ceremony. I also remembered that he had made plans to arrive Friday night and spend the Saturday and Sunday with friends. I did not know where he would be staying but I knew I must get him out of the ghetto immediately. This was why I was going to the Szczęśliwa Restaurant. I hoped I would meet him there and if not, somebody would surely know where he could be found.

This restaurant was the meeting place for all sorts of people in the ghetto. Like the Kiercelak on the Aryan side, the Szczęśliwa Restaurant on the Jewish side was the hub for everything and everybody. The Jewish Underground leaders met there and so did the Jewish confidants of the Gestapo. The smugglers came to buy and sell goods. Everyone knew who the others were. The place was both the battlefield of all and the neutral territory, with one odd exception: the Jewish confidants of the German authorities, the informers to the Gestapo at the restaurant, knew not only who the leaders of the Underground were but also that the leaders of the Underground were to be taken seriously and feared. They were not a commodity to be sold to the Germans for a price. The long arm of the Underground had already removed those who had in the beginning laughed about a Jewish resistance. Now the reverse was happening and the ex-informers who came to the Szczęśliwa were the first source of information about the plans of the Germans. The Underground fed them bits of useless information to keep them trusted on the German side. Like the rest of the Jews still in the ghetto, most informers had lately began digging bunkers for themselves and their families. Half jokingly, they invited members of the leadership of the Jewish Fighting Organisation as well as members of the leadership of the Jewish Military Union to come to their bunker if they should need a place.

The Germans who knew of many vital matters going on in the ghetto didn't know of the restaurant in Szczęśliwa Street. The Polish word '*Szczęśliwa*' means 'lucky female', and it was a fitting name for the place. Or maybe they did know about it and for one of their perfidious reasons they treated the restaurant the same way they treated the Kiercelak. Whatever it was, the Szczęśliwa Restaurant was the only place I believed I would find out about my friend Janek Kostański.

I had made no mistake. As soon as I entered our eyes met. He nodded and signalled not to disturb him. He was in the middle of his meal with one of the familiar faces I knew from the place. The restaurant was almost full as usual. In the corner known to our people as the 'seat of the 13', the Department for Fighting Against High Prices, created by the Gestapo as a front for their informers, two men and a woman were sitting around the table with a bottle of vodka and a dish of herring and pickled gherkins between them. They did not hide their curiosity about me. The man obviously in charge nodded to me and I nodded back. I ignored Janek's nod and went over to him. He turned towards me but I would not speak to him in front of the other man. He stood up reluctantly and we went over to the serving counter, where I told him he would have to leave the ghetto immediately. I can even reconstruct the conversation we had.

'Janek,' I said, 'you must leave the restaurant and the ghetto immediately. There will be no Passover celebration in the ghetto. It will be fire and death and the people need you more outside than here.'

'What makes you so sure?'

'What do you want, a bet?' I was impatient. 'I have just come from the other side. I saw only German vans and trucks. Plenty. But at the headquarters I have been informed that the Ukrainians and the Latvians have begun to arrive. Do you want me to remind you what they do? Get out of here and over the fence.'

Janek knew how serious I was about his leaving. But he had no intention of doing so and tried to put off the final step. 'I'll go as soon as I have finished my meal. By the way, that man there with me wants me to have a look at some silver stuff he wants to sell. I haven't got the money but let's see it.'

My agitation was beginning to be noticed. People at the dining tables began to turn their heads towards us. Out of the corner of my eye I noticed the people at '13' getting up from their places and leaving in a hurry. The place was close to breaking out in a panic. Training took over. Automatically I bent over the serving counter and picked up the phone from the other side. 'Janek, ring whoever you have to ring and tell them to wait for you over the cemetery wall. It is getting late and you don't want to be caught near the wall after the curfew hour. Do it!' He responded without protest. He had to move over to the other side of the counter to speak on the phone. People had come up to us and everyone wanted to know what was going on.

As Janek finished the phone conversation I grabbed him by his arm and together we left, without paying. The restaurant had been feeding its clientele for some weeks without asking for payment unless voluntarily offered. Four men from ŻZW who had been at the restaurant joined us as we made our way to the cemetery. In the short time since I had come to the restaurant something had happened to make the Jews in the ghetto realise what stood before them. The many young men and women crossing the forbidden areas were not there for romance.

We reached the cemetery wall and Janek whistled; there was a response from the other side. Quickly we put up the ladder kept in one of the open graves. Janek wanted to take us with him. One of the four there, a teenager, asked, more as a plea than a question, if he could go with him, and quickly we nodded our agreement: 'Go.' Kostański embraced each of us in turn. I reminded him to send up a Polish flag, telling him that I had the Jewish blue and white one to raise but no Polish one. He seemed to take this in as he climbed up the ladder.

A Polish policeman, known as the 'Navy blue uniformed', despised among Poles as a collaborator, was waiting under the wall. As he looked up to Janek we could hear a voice from the other side. 'One peep from you, pig's ass, and you'll be beheaded.' Within a second the same voice rose again. 'Stay where you are, pig's ass! You'll move when we are gone and not before,' and immediately after that came the order: 'Jump!' Janek jumped and we heard an outburst of laughter from the other side. One of our members had the presence of mind to quickly climb up the ladder. He still made it in time to see both Janek and the 'Navy blue' rising from the ground. Janek's colleagues were already helping the unfortunate cop dust off his uniform and telling him to stay and have a rest, and to forget that he had seen anything unusual.

The next day, Sunday 18 April, we were all called to ŻZW headquarters. For the first time I became aware that in all of the running around which had seemed so chaotic, there was some order and things were prepared. I was ordered to put on the black uniform of the German SS, and did so. I became the object of many eyes and many voices. The older Łopata raised his hand and as silence fell once more he said very calmly, 'You may scream like they do, but make sure that nobody understands you. Your German, if you try to use it, will give you away in two seconds.'

It was the best advice I was given during the Uprising. I

remembered it and it stood me by. Meeting a German coming my way I would give a signal making out that it was too dangerous to speak. I would then deal with my murderers when they came close enough to taste their own medicine.

25

A time to live and a time to die

SUNDAY 18 April was a warm, beautiful, spring day. Over the wall in the Krasiński Garden, the Easter Carnival was in full swing. The music of the merry-go-round's organ grinder penetrated into the desolate streets of the ghetto. Underfoot, the soil was giving forth new green life, which pushed up wildly between the ruins.

To keep us occupied, the leadership made us dismantle the rifles, machine-guns and revolvers, clean them and assemble them for a last time. A kind of unreal peace hung around the headquarters of Muranowska. Here and there women were preparing Passover meals for the spring holiday, which has always been the symbol of the time of freedom for our people. With death before our eyes, we tried to believe that we could last a little longer. The Underground radio gave out the news of the eastern front. The Red Army had begun its first real push against the Germans and their allies, the Rumanian and Italian forces. It was to take another two years before the Red Army would enter the gates of Berlin to end the Nazi regime, but to the dying ghetto it was an announcement of joy. As was the news from the western side, where the Allies had bitten off the toe from the foot of Italy.

In the afternoon, we sat in the courtyard and tried to relieve the heavy atmosphere by talking politics, reminiscing, and recalling friends who were no longer with us. Someone said that we would never use up the store of armaments we had. He believed the Germans would come and fight house to house, and all of us would be dead by the evening of the first day of the Uprising. To which the younger Łopata replied sarcastically, 'I don't believe God would suddenly become compassionate and let us die as heroes in a single day. I believe we will last out longer in order to satisfy Him with a final agony. If He is wise He will let us use up the last of our arms before He permits us to die.'

Our afternoon philosophy continued uninterrupted as we began transferring some of our equipment from the headquarters of 7-9 Muranowska Street to number 17 Muranowska. Once or twice during the previous days we had debated the wisdom of sitting in a building in the corner of the ghetto with the brick wall in front of us. It had remained nothing more that a theoretical point. Until, in the last hours, we received the order to move into the empty buildings in Plac Muranowski. It was a wise decision even if it came very late. From the square we had a better position to look out over the wall of the ghetto, and it would be easier to retreat deeper into the ghetto from there if it became necessary. In the evening the women prepared a warm meal and our discussions continued. When I asked if anybody had noticed the red sky of the dying sun one of the young women said, 'By tomorrow we won't have to rely on the red clouds. We will have the fires of the ghetto and the blood of the fallen.'

The telephone line to the Aryan side was still working. Late in the night Frenkel came out of the small command office to tell us that he had received a call confirming that the ghetto was surrounded. As far as the information went, the Germans and their helpers were stationing themselves some twenty to twenty-five metres apart all along the wall.

'I think we should send somebody out and tell them they are a night too early,' I said. 'Passover starts tomorrow.'

Frenkel responded dryly, 'They can't wait. On Tuesday it is Hitler's fifty-fourth birthday; they have to hand him a clean ghetto.'

One of our members arrived from the other side before dawn. He had been expected to report the previous evening but had been held over by his neighbours to help carry two elderly people from their apartment to a bunker some streets away. He had to carry them there on his back. As he was on his way carrying the old woman, he heard a girl's voice, 'Avoid the crossing at Zamenhofa and Muranowska, the Latvians have just stationed themselves there.' In the darkness he could not see the speaker. This latecomer also knew that the Jewish Council had transported their own families in a blue 'Star of David' ambulance from their private apartments to the Council building.

When dawn broke, Frenkel said to me in passing, 'We have also started our Night of Guard [the *Layl Shemurim*, as the first night of Passover is called] one night early.'

At around six in the morning the first German units had entered the ghetto. Clearly they expected that it would not be as easy this time as it had been in the past. They came equipped for battle, marching towards the centre of the ghetto island nearest to the *Umschlagplatz*, in the vicinity of Franciszkańska, Miła, and Gęsia along Zamenhofa. For some reason, we were told not to move out from our positions. We were probably no more that six to eight hundred metres away towards the north-eastern end of the ghetto and could have engaged the German column within a matter of minutes. Years after the war I was told that the policy of the ŻZW and of the ŻOB was not to fight in the open, as we would have had no chance to inflict even the slightest losses on the Germans. The explanation sounded reasonable in retrospect but I am not convinced that it would have been so during the first moments, when the Germans did not expect us in the open.

Within the next half hour all hell broke loose. The one hundred and twenty people in our group waited impatiently for an order but we never received one. The telephone rang three or four times. From the other side they told us that they had seen wounded Germans and Latvians being brought out of the ghetto and that whole units were running in chaos. According to the information coming from the Poles, a unit of the German Army, on its way to the eastern front, had joined the fight. It was not clear to our informers whether the soldiers were held over especially for the Action or simply had some free time and the chief hangman of the ghetto, Colonel Dr Von Samren, had invited them to join in hunting down the last Jews.

The greatest surprise we had on the first day was to learn that at last the Germans had begun to take us seriously. The Colonel had been removed and replaced by no less than a General. That information lifted our spirits enormously.

Only when the day ended did we have the opportunity to hear any details. In their first foray in the morning the Germans had come in fully dressed for battle, marching along the centre of Zamenhofa together with those Jewish police who were still left. As far as we could make out, the fighters of the ŻOB had let the Jewish police cross their hidden positions and when the Germans followed them the soldiers were met with a hail of fire from machine-guns and hand grenades. The sons of the super-race became disoriented and panicked. They left their wounded and dead in the middle of the street and ran away. They were gone within the first hour.

It was hard for us, who had been sitting doing nothing, to believe what had happened. We felt ashamed and betrayed not to have participated in that act. Could there have been a more messianic dream than the one in which a Jewish bullet killed a German in the open battlefield of the ghetto? And we had missed it on the very first day when it had become a reality.

As if to rub salt in our wounds, we had visitors in the evening — two young boys of sixteen or seventeen who did not belong to any organised group but had managed in the last days to get hold of rifles and bullets. They had joined the shooting independently. They showed us the rifles and revolvers they had managed to take from the German SS who had been left dead in the street. They told of the fighting and it sounded as if God had begun handing over the first murderers into the hands of their victims. We learned of the greatest triumph on that day from informants on the Polish side: 'Not a single Jewish fighter had lost his or her life.' We were elated, proud and unbelievably jealous and ashamed.

To our half-angry murmur of revolt Frenkel had a short answer, 'Tomorrow will be another day.'

He was right. The second day of the Uprising belonged to the ŻZW. Fate can be more sarcastic than the most caustic man. The day belonged to us less for the battles we led than for the shame which the organised German forces had to swallow from us, the last, most ill-equipped Jews of the ghetto who were already dead as far as they had been concerned.

The building at 17 Muranowska Street was four storeys high and faced the ghetto wall across to a lookout and a building that housed one of the groups in the Polish Underground on the other side. We had taken up our position there because it was one of the properties my family had owned before the war. It consisted of a whole complex of entries and staircases in different directions. And I knew every nook and cranny.

I had my own reason for choosing the building. I had made up my mind to raise the Polish and Jewish sovereign flags over the fighting ghetto. I could not fulfil my plan on the first day because I was waiting still for the Polish flag, which I had asked Janek Kostański to deliver to us. Raising this flag was both symbolic and a secret signal to the Polish Underground. It would tell them that the ghetto fight had begun and they could begin their uprising on the Aryan side. Sadly, we later found that the Polish organisations were not ready to fight. I had made up my mind to raise the Jewish flag alone if by the end of the second day the Polish flag remained undelivered.

I was overjoyed when early that morning a messenger came to tell me that a young boy had come through the tunnel at Muranowska 7 with a message which he had been told to deliver only to me. He had come through the sewers and stunk to high heavens when he was brought to see me. I was standing on guard, dressed in the black uniform of the SS with a machine-gun in my hand. From under his shirt the boy pulled out a packet wrapped in newspaper. I knew immediately what it was and understood why he had been told to hand it over only to me. The boy was about eight years younger than me. His blue eyes and the smile on his face told me that he must have lived with death for a long time and it no longer held any fear for him. He was living an adventure. When I asked him if he would be willing to raise the flag on top of the building he became elated. 'Do you really mean it?' I warned him that this would be unlike any adventure he may have had before.

'The Germans will see you and you will not be protected. They will shoot at you with all they have. You may be dead before you reach the chimney.'

'It's all right. Sooner or later we all have to die; all Jews have to die. I have seen how people die when they are shot; it isn't so bad. When do I go up on the roof?' I told him to hang the two flags on the lightning pole on top of the chimney, and not to stand in one place even for a few seconds but to keep moving while he hoisted up the flags. I also explained that he wouldn't be going up there alone.

'You will protect me from here,' he said eagerly, 'and if anything happens to me it would be better than to you, because I am only a boy and you are a fighter.' He did not comment on my SS uniform and I slowly realised that he must be closely involved with the Underground, otherwise he would have been shocked by my appearance. I knew I could rely on his own sense of survival.

On the second day of the Uprising the Germans watched with fury, the Poles with elation, the Jews with fire in their hearts, as the Polish and Jewish flags were raised by a group of children above the rooftops for the world to see. Two young boys paid with their lives for the audacity. They wrote a chapter of courage and bravery which remains a symbol of the Uprising. I can only weep that their names remain unknown. However, their leader, Jacek Eisner,* the brave young flag smuggler, a child fighting in the Underground, lives to this day to tell the tale.

The Warsaw ghetto Uprising belongs to the group of heroic battles which have surprised the pages of history. It belongs to one of those unusual chapters where the result was known at the beginning and the vanquished were the victors who did not live to see their victory.

But little is known about the way the fighting took place. Although the ŻZW was not part of the main fighting body, there was a united command in the ghetto, the ŻOB. It embraced the Zionist youth organisations, from the left to the right, except for our organisation, the Betar. The first sparks from which the battle arose belong without doubt to the youth of the Hashomer Hatsair, a socialist left Zionist body led by graduates from its own ranks. They were educated towards the Land of Israel and a life in a Kibbutz. Already during the great deportation of July–September 1942, they had begun to collect any armaments they could obtain for the planned Uprising. The group lost its leaders, Yosef Kapłan and Shmuel Breslaw, on the same day when it lost the few revolvers and hand grenades it had managed to obtain. The future leader of the movement, who was to become the commander of the Uprising, Mordecai Anielewicz, was not in the ghetto during the deportation. After it was over, an expanded united command was set up under his leadership. It comprised various units of Zionist origin as well as non-Zionist political movements such as the Bund and communists. The Bund was represented first by Dr Feiner and

* In 1993, David Landau was reunited in Warsaw with that same boy, Jack Eisner (Jacek) who remembered David as 'Dudek the Great', a fighter the children idiolised. Jack Eisner's account of the flag raising and his own history can be read in his autobiography *The Survivor of the Holocaust.*

later by Marek Edelman, one of the few surviving leaders of the Uprising.

The command was united but as the ghetto had been divided into islands it was difficult to assess the progress of the battles. Only the preparations that had been carried out before 19 April made it possible to fight separately but united at the same time.

The second day of the Uprising was the fifty-fourth birthday of the Führer, Adolf Hitler. In all German districts special governmental meetings were held and orders were given for the day. From documents that have been found it is clear the first day of fighting was already causing the Germans unusual worries. The Governor General of occupied Poland, Hans Frank, wrote about it: 'In the special meeting which we had today in honour of the Führer's birthday, we discussed the security developments that are taking place. In reality, security is developing under the influence of various factors in a seriously dangerous way. We are engaged, already for the second day, in a well-organised revolt in the Warsaw ghetto in which we have already made use of heavy guns.'*

The General who had taken over the Action against us had obviously not wanted to forego the celebration in honour of his Führer's birthday completely. There was no activity against the ghetto before noon, except for some sporadic, aggravated fire against the flags we had managed to raise, for the price of two young boys. But celebrating Hitler's birthday did not stop the murderers for the whole day. After midday, they came. This time they paid no attention to the main section where they had been given a fiery reception the previous day. They tried their luck in another island, and they turned to the brush makers' factory. So sure were they that they approached the gate of the complex in orderly rows, fully armed. The entrance to the closed section was through one of the gates in Wałowa Street. Precisely as the columns entered the gate a

---

* See reference in Yisrael Gutman, *The Jews of Warsaw*. Midland Books, USA, 1989, p. 427.

hidden mine was exploded by remote control and lifted the orderly columns from the ground. In seconds, order gave way to chaos, with Germans running for cover and firing their machine-guns, more out of fear than at targets. From a distance one could distinguish the German firing which came in quick, continuous bursts while the short replies from the fighters came in intermittent spasms.

Somewhere the hidden fight reached the open stage, as the leader of the group, Marek Edelman, told it. Edelman related a confrontation which should become a legend for all times. The fight must have had a tremendous psychological effect on the Germans. Three officers approached the lines of the fighters waving white signals. They proposed a fifteen-minute cease-fire to remove the dead and wounded. They were willing to guarantee the Jews in the sector a peaceful relocation to working camps in Poniatów and Trawniki, allowing them to take all their possessions. 'We replied with fire,' Edelman reported.

Less than a hundred metres across from us, on the other side of the wall, the Germans placed a small artillery gun. Unfortunately they positioned it in a way that made it impossible for us to attack it with grenades or machine-gun fire. Nevertheless, it was not a very good day for the German General. In his report to Berlin, he had to admit that of the four thousand Jews he had hoped to remove from the sector, only twenty-eight volunteered to come forward. He was ready to start a military action with anti-aircraft and howitzer guns to destroy the buildings but as twilight approached he decided to leave it for another day.

The Germans suffered considerable losses on the second day. It is remarkable that they were willing to lose face and ask for a cease-fire from the subhuman 'bandits' (as the General called them in his report) they had come to destroy.

We had our own fight on that day. Early in the afternoon we saw a group of ŻOB fighters moving across from the area where the fight had taken place the previous day, towards the section of the brush makers. There were some eighty to a hundred fighters, male and female, in the group. The road seemed empty from where we saw them. Then one of our guards noticed a column of Germans coming from the other direction. Soon the Germans were directly in the path of the fighters who were heading towards an open field. They would have mowed them down before the small group had any chance of action, but within a minute we had the order to open fire. The crossfire lasted some minutes before part of the German columns separated and moved away while the rest remained to do battle. It was not a very serious effort to fight us. Within another quarter of an hour they cut off and moved away from our position. It was, however, enough time and noise to alert the ŻOB to move out from the open field.

The Poles on the Aryan side were surprised how war-like the battle sounded. They could hardly believe what they saw and heard. German Red Cross ambulances were running in and out of the ghetto; constant firing rang out; artillery was being employed; once or twice they saw aeroplanes circling the ghetto. The fires had not yet started but here and there heavy smoke was hanging above the walls. In some historical documents there is mention of a diversionary fight instigated by the Polish Underground on that day. I know nothing to confirm it and I am not in a position to deny it. If it did take place it made little impact. We received help from both Underground armies, the Home Army and the People's Army, small contributions, but in the scale of things they were worthwhile contributions.

The chimney of 17 Muranowska Street did not give way on that day. The Polish and Jewish flags were left there overnight. They must have given the great German General real nightmares. At dawn on the third day came the first fire on our position in Muranowska. The order came for us to leave. Heavy artillery was being directed towards the building. By seven in the morning we had moved out. The German special units did not appear inside the ghetto until hours later.

26

A taste of action

FOR the first two days the ghetto fighters had it mostly their own way. The Germans had serious psychological difficulties in accepting that they could be killed by Jewish bullets in a straight out military action. By nightfall after the first day they had pulled out of the ghetto. The darkened streets on the first night of the revolt were safer than at any time since the Germans had entered Warsaw. Old and young came out of their bunkers to feel the euphoria. The change wrought by the fight of one day could have hardly been believed by any onlooker from the free world. Suddenly death had lost its hold on fear. A feeling of being part of the heroism filled the streets on that first night of Passover.

Unit leaders came to report to the headquarters for food, to replenish their ammunition, and to talk. Nobody could begin to understand how it had happened that not a single fighter was missing, or even wounded. While we at ŻZW were licking our wounds for not having shared in that great day, the rest of the ghetto was celebrating. A new order and discipline had come over the people, and the few young men who had rifles in their hands were now recognised and thanked for what they had done to lift the spirits of the many thousands. The fighters made good use of the hours of darkness to clean their guns; to plan. Orders for the next day were given out and by the following morning everything was as ready as could be to resume the fight.

On the first night the Germans had surrounded the ghetto only from the outside. During the second day they began to learn our tactics. They realised that the fighters were using the attics, which gave them a dual advantage. While the Germans were exposed, the Jewish fighters were hidden until the last moment. And they were fighting from a height. They could also escape through attics from house to house. On the second night the Germans undertook an experiment to counteract this tactic and were very successful. Dressed in civilian clothes, with blackened faces, small units of Germans infiltrated the 'wild' streets and silently stationed themselves in attics. They came in small groups of three to five and took up assigned places so as not to expose one group against another. Silently they managed to kill individual fighters, as they moved from attic to attic.

By dawn of the third day they had eliminated some eight to ten men and women. We heard about it in the early hours and felt enraged to the point of losing our senses. We had to match the German tactics. The opportunity presented itself so naturally that we did not need to plan it. For some unrelated reason Frenkel ordered us to return to the headquarters at 17 Muranowska Street. A small group of us was standing inside the building with Frenkel when the guard on the first floor signalled that two German officers were approaching with their machine-guns at the ready. They had stopped two houses away from us and were silently waiting while closely observing the surrounding area. The artillery shooting had stopped. Obviously there was some co-ordination between those who were trying to destroy the chimney with the two flags and the two officers. Frenkel gave me the order: 'Go and bring them here!' It came so suddenly that I was shocked.

'Me? How can I call them with my German?'

He was angry. 'You are wearing their uniform! Go and bring them here!'

The atmosphere was growing tense and the guard from the first floor came once more and said, 'They are still waiting for something.' When Frenkel repeated his order I knew what to do. I asked three of our men to wait behind the entrance, hidden from the outside. I went out and began to signal to the two officers by placing my finger across my lips and pointing above my head. It worked. They responded in a similar manner by asking with their fingers how many: two? I made the sign of four and encouraged them to follow me by going back into the entrance of the building.

Although my uniform was good enough to be accepted from twenty-five metres away, the hand-painted trims would have given me away if they had come closer. As I disappeared into the gate I signalled them to follow me. They came and stopped at the entrance. Nothing happened to frighten them. Slowly they moved in, following me as I made very cautious steps towards the staircase. Before they could realise their mistake they had wires strung around their throats. Their machine-guns didn't even fire before they were out of their hands. I turned around to see their eyes bulge out of their sockets and their hands held firmly by our fighters, while they convulsed in a useless effort to save their lives.

Frenkel's first words to me as he came down from the floor above were, 'If I give you an order you better pay attention to it the first time. Understood?'

I realised that his strain was no less than my own and with a sudden coolness I said, 'Yes, sir.' I still had to pay for having broken the discipline in the first place. I was ordered to stand on guard for double the ordinary time; two hours instead of being relieved after an hour. When I came down from guard duty a warm meal was waiting for me and while eating I took part in the planning of some action to trick our German tricksters. For some reason I had clearly become a reliable man. From the way those around me spoke about the two dead officers it became obvious that I was now some kind of expert at catching Germans.

The best idea came from a man who had been trained in the Polish Underground, and had served in the army before the war. His plan seemed well thought out. He suggested we organise groups of eight for the attic forays. He argued that the Germans surely would not go in large groups. He estimated then, and this later turned out to be correct, that they would be working in twos or threes at the most. They had the advantage of their machine-guns and a limitless supply of bullets. We could not match them in this respect. They would shoot whole rounds and we could reply only with single shots. Even if we could be successful, our gun-fire would give us away immediately. Should another group of Germans be close by we would have no chance to escape. We therefore had to work in silence. There had to be at least two or three of us against each of the Germans and we had to stop them from calling out.

The details were slowly worked out. We decided to station ourselves in an attic in a spot where the darkness would hide us. We would have to observe the movements of those who would be passing our position and make sure that we made no mistake before acting. I was placed with the first eight before I had a chance to volunteer.

Exhaustion took over. I would not have believed it possible, but I woke up on a straw mattress without knowing when I had fallen asleep. It had happened while I was sitting at the table with half the food eaten, concentrating on the plans for the night. I woke up because somebody was standing over me, calling to me. It was the younger Łopata brother. He was wearing a black outfit and held one in his hands for me. Miracles do happen in the oddest times. I was ordered to go up onto the second floor and wash before putting on the black camouflage. There I found a wooden tub filled with heated water. How it came to be there was a riddle to me, but it was heaven-sent relief. I hadn't had a good wash for God only knew how long. I removed my clothes, paying attention to fold the SS outfit correctly so that it would be ready for the next day. The hot tub did wonders. I was ready for anything.

By the time I was dressed I realised that the artillery was no longer firing on us. I concluded that the flags must have been shot down some time earlier. How the house was still standing and the people still in it I did not understand or worry about. The only thing that seemed odd was that I had seen only Łopata and one of the young women who passed me on the staircase as I went up to the second floor. The day was ending as I dressed and Łopata came back for me. Now I was told what had happened. Minutes after I had fallen asleep the woman on guard had told Frenkel and the others that a German car was cruising outside looking for someone. They must have been looking for the two Germans who had been killed. They cruised up and down the Muranowska and eventually drove away. Frenkel then ordered everyone to get out of the building as quickly as possible. Instead of waking me, Łopata decided to put me down on the straw mattress. I must have been out to the world, for I had not heard anything and, according to Łopata, hell had broken out around the house. It lasted for a good half-hour before the chimney gave way. With it the bombardment stopped. Łopata had come back with the woman and they had heated the water for me. The others were back at the headquarters.

Only when Łopata and I were outside did I realise how close I had come to being killed. The wall was pocked with shrapnel marks. We left the headquarters once it was completely dark. Our shoes were wrapped in rags to silence our footsteps. We had orders to move to Nowolipki and to take up our position there in one of the attics which had become a thoroughfare for the fighters. We lay crouched in one spot the whole night, hardly moving from our confined space. When the first light broke, our bones were aching, but we had not met any Germans. Nor had we seen any fighters moving through the roofs. By the time we returned to our quarters there was already a report about four men who had been killed in the night. There were no shots fired and they were not killed in any attic; they had been knifed to death on the ground floor in one of the houses in Franciszkańska. The sixteen men who had gone out in two groups were ordered to rest as much as possible, but first we were told that the failure to meet up with the Germans would have to be made good on the coming night. And so it was.

The order was to go back to the position we had occupied the first night. This time, fortune came our way. Late in the night whispers reached our ears. We froze. Three shadows were climbing up to the attic across from where we had taken up our positions. They stood behind the chimneys without speaking. After a few moments it became clear that they were not part of our group, and there was no reason for ŻOB members to take up guard duty in the attics during the night. The attics were only used for contact between the different positions. Although we were eight and they were only three there was no way we could jump them. The few metres were too great a distance between us. We waited without clearly knowing what we were waiting for. We knew who was to give any order and the way the order would be given; but nothing happened. It was sheer luck that came to the rescue of our impatience.

We heard one of the three say in the best German, in a voice that was hardly audible, 'Watch out for me. I'm going over to the other side for a piss.' Of all places, he came over to us and nearly stepped on one of our men. It was the last thing he did. With the speed of a snake, our commander was behind him with one arm around his throat and the other hand on his mouth, in total silence. In an instant he was sitting down again with his prey and with the two of us helping him. All this was happening in absolute silence, as if in some old silent movie. By the time the other two Germans began to call in whispers, 'Ulbrich', four of us were moving towards them. We stopped when we heard them shifting their guns to the ready. Again they whispered, 'Ulbrich?' The call sounded nervous. They made the mistake of moving from their secure places. It was enough for us. This time we paid less attention to the order of silence. Only four jumped them but the eight of us finished the job. The struggle didn't last more than a few seconds. When it was over, we thought we were the only ones left, but from another corner came a louder voice in Yiddish: 'Thank you, whoever you are. But you were lucky we did not jump on you. You were only shadows when you came out, but you were too far from us. We were forced to lie down. We too could hear the first whisper in German and realised where the greater danger was. You could have fooled us with your first action. We could neither see nor hear anything. Your second action told us that you are Jews. Thank you. Now we still have to get to Muranowska before dawn.'

I would be willing to pay with part of my life for the privilege of being able to capture the change in the spirit of the ghetto on the second and third day of the fight. We did not expect to be alive and fighting the German killing machine for so long. We had prepared to kill and be killed in the first encounters with our murderers. No one in the Warsaw ghetto had any doubt about the Germans storming the buildings from which the first fire came. We expected to be overcome by the sheer brutal force of that mass-murder industry at the end of the first day. But it did not happen.

The heroes of the blitzkrieg which had stormed nation after nation across Europe had to run from the last Jews of Warsaw in the first days of the fight. We were overcome by our own success and no longer feared the future, although we knew what it would be. When the second day of the Uprising met with similar, if diminished, success we became hardened. The euphoria no longer blinded us. Instead, we became focused and determined. We had to ration out every bullet, count every fighter, restrict every cup of water; all this to stay alive and kill as many of those who came to kill us as we could. Our lives no longer belonged to us; they belonged to the call of those who had already been murdered, or died of starvation, or succumbed to treatable diseases because they had no medication.

Up until the end of the third day our spirit to fight was growing and we were truly the victors, just as we felt it in our veins and in our emotions.

This began to change on the fourth or fifth day. No longer did the German units enter the ghetto in parade formation; no longer did they act openly and arrogantly. They had to resort to systematic brutality; they began to destroy the ghetto by fire.

It may have been something learned from the Jewish fighters. When the German units had used the mattresses from the Töbens factories as shields, someone from the Jewish side had thrown a Molotov cocktail and the mattresses had gone up in flames. It may have given the Germans the idea. On their way into the ghetto one or two would approach a building with flame-throwers, while others positioned themselves with light submachine-guns ready for those who jumped from the upper windows trying to escape the fire.

The success of this action was, according to the report of the General, so great that he came with a photographer to have his picture taken, with the black clouds of heavy smoke from the burning houses for a background. No longer was the Command of the ŻOB able to co-ordinate the details of each unit. No longer was there a report to be given every night. The General now felt secure enough to have night patrols stationed in the ruins to intercept anything that moved.

The toll on our fighters grew heavier. While some German units were engaged directly in fighting, others were engaged in sniffing out bunkers. Expert units were employed in this work. They were helped by sniffer dogs and here and there by the last Jews they managed to capture. They would leave one of them alive and make this unfortunate person follow them as they approached a bunker. The living sacrifice would be made to call in Yiddish: 'Jews, you can come out, the Germans have gone!' Sometimes the ruse worked. In this way they broke the back of the fight. Civilians, who had been elated on the first evening of the fight, became desperate when the bunkers in which they had been sheltering became living graves. The air gave out, the heat became unbearable, their water supply dried up, children and weak ones died, and there was no way to dispose of the bodies which began to decompose. The success at the beginning of the Uprising turned into a curse for the survivors waiting to be discovered by their killers. When the Germans found a bunker, the sapper unit would be ready to force an opening over it, through which they would throw gas-filled grenades. It was not unusual for those who were forced out of the bunkers to be ready with a grenade of their own, or a Molotov cocktail or even a revolver. A third of all who were discovered in bunkers died that way.

The open fights came to an end with the battle that took place at Muranowska on 25 or 26 April. Our group gave a strong account of itself. On that day we exchanged fire with the murderers from the early hours until late in the afternoon. As the houses in which we fought were directly against the wall of the ghetto, the Germans had obviously decided not to attack them with flame-throwers. By the time the battle was over on that spring evening we had lost a considerable number of our members. Many others were wounded. I went out into the street. The smoke filled my nostrils and the sky was aflame. Our medical workers were busy collecting our fallen comrades and during the evening we gave them a respectful burial, as much as conditions allowed. After that our commanders informed us that arrangements were being made on our side and on the Aryan side to evacuate our group through the sewers to join the Polish partisan units in the forests. We were told that each of us was now free to decide to go with the group that was leaving, or to remain. From that moment on, everyone was free to make their own arrangements for the future.

Only three or four members of the ŻZW left that night. At dawn we were told that we would not engage the Germans in any battle unless it became impossible to avoid it. That morning everything was completely quiet in our corner. We had strict orders not to go outside the buildings and contact was to be made only where it was possible to move directly through one building to the next.

Around midday two covered trucks came along from the other end of Muranowska. Two guards jumped down and took up positions with their guns at the ready. From the drivers' cabins two other guards got out at the same time as if in a rehearsed action. They went around to the back of the trucks and, with a flip at the corner, opened them up. They had brought a group of Jews in from outside, who were now made to leave the vehicles and stand to attention in a single long row. The trucks moved back some metres and an officer appeared from somewhere. With a move of his hand he ordered the unfortunate Jews to lie down in the middle of the road. There was some hesitation. A short burst of a machine-gun close over their heads explained what was wanted of them; they obeyed. As they were spread out on the ground — men, women and two teenagers — two men were called to stand up. They were given a rope. Each man had to take hold of one end and move to the end of those spread out on the ground. The rope was put out at the feet of the victims. Looking down from our hidden positions we wondered what it all meant. When the rope was lined up the two men were asked to line up the soles of the others straight against the rope. The exercise seemed slow but there was no hurry, as the two Jews pulled some individuals by the head or feet to line them up with the rope. Finally it was all done. The two who had performed their work so diligently were told to take their places at the end where the trucks were waiting.

Now the four Germans with their machine-guns ready came forward. We could not make out what they had said but it was obviously some order. They moved back and immediately the trucks drove forward. Now we understood it all. While one side of the trucks remained on the ground, the wheels of the other side rolled over the miserable victims, precisely over their knees. The screams rose up to us. Those at the end who tried to get up and run never made it. They were run over or died by the bullet. When it was all over the four soldiers and the officer climbed back into the cabins of the two trucks, the trucks drove in reverse to the corner and left, leaving their victims wriggling like worms. Two of us went down from our hiding place to see what we could do.

Our leaders stood at the closed gate. 'No one will leave the building. The Germans have not left them for nothing. They have left them alive to tempt us out of our hiding. Understood? No one will go outside!' Most of those in the building agreed with the commanders. Those who did not could only feel anger but obeyed. Once more our leaders proved right. After half an hour one of the trucks came back to the corner. Two SS guards stepped out and made their way slowly to the writhing group, of whom not a single one had managed to rise. Slowly, with measured steps, they went along the row and with two revolvers finished off their victims. We were close enough to kill the bastards. But realising that by doing so we would be giving away our position to the others who were waiting just around the corner, we held back.

During the night we moved the bodies from the middle of the road and piled them up in the gateway of one of the buildings. The next morning another group of Jews was brought to the same place. At first we thought they would be subject to the same cruelty, but we were wrong. The Germans must have been surprised that the bodies had been taken away, for the Jews never left the truck. The black covers were placed back in position, the truck reversed into the corner and drove out of the ghetto.

27

The end of the ghetto

I look back to those crucial days and wonder how nature makes the human being act according to its needs. Since the day I had returned to the ghetto, on 17 April, I had felt no remorse about my action. I thought of Luba often, even during the most dangerous moments, but I felt no anxiety for her or my family. Nor did I feel that I might be the cause of any. When the moment came and I no longer had any responsibility to the ŻZW, something in my mind switched my allegiance from the people of the ŻZW as a group to my wife, who was waiting to hear if I was still alive. I could feel it as I could feel the smoke hanging over the ghetto. I was as concerned about Luba as I was about life itself.

We had no specific orders any more, just to wait and hear when and how we would be taken out of the ghetto. I had already made up my mind not to leave with the group. One may call it a premonition, or a sixth sense; to me it was too dangerous. I could not believe that the Germans would not be on guard around the exits of the ghetto. It was their unholy duty not to leave a single Jew alive. The outcome for us did not depend on the outcome of the war. I had decided that if I was to stay alive it could only be as an unknown individual. After the first day of waiting I became restless. Once more I became attached to my revolver which I always carried tucked into my belt. No longer did I wear the black SS uniform all the time, although I had not given it away altogether.

On the second morning after the spectacle with the trucks, I was witness to a new horror. I could no longer feel surprise, but the method showed the special training these German beasts had gone through to divest themselves of any human emotions. Our kitchen was still functioning; now better than in the first days of fighting. Some tables had been brought together on the first floor of the half-destroyed building and a reasonable breakfast was being served up to our members. The bread was stale but edible. From somewhere somebody had found the ghetto coffee of burned grain. We even had vegetable jam for our bread. While a few of us were talking over our breakfast, all outside seemed quiet — and then we heard the trucks. Was it going to be a repetition of the previous day? I grabbed my rifle and ran up to the next floor. There, at the window, I could watch unnoticed. They looked like the same trucks with the same black covers. Even the ballet of the SS seemed to be similar to the performance two days ago. But this time the sadists had a new version of their entertainment.

The Jews climbed down; they were ordered to stand to attention like the ones before them. I watched the trucks reverse and leave, then noticed that there were not four but ten murderers. Two placed themselves at each end and the others went around behind the victims. This time they had come much nearer to our hiding place; I had the feeling they knew we were somewhere close by and this was meant to be a spectacle for our eyes. While some looked right up into the building, the two SS men at the side ordered the row to step forward right up to the ghetto wall across from us. They obeyed and were now all facing the wall, pressing their noses hard against it. The Germans who had stationed themselves behind the row came closer. With the butt of their rifles they touched some of their victims. I could not hear but those who had been touched turned around to face towards us. I thought of a chessboard: one Jew was facing the wall and the next out to the street.

Frenkel was suddenly by my side. 'I was looking for you

downstairs. If you are by any chance thinking of letting go on them on your own, don't! And this is an order! I wouldn't mind having a go at them myself. There are ten of them, but at the moment we are not alone. We have guests who arrived an hour ago from the other side to co-ordinate our departure. They are still with us. At any other time they would be with us to fight. But unless they go back later to the other side the whole operation will come to nothing, because they are the ones who co-ordinate the channels through which we will be crossing. Understood?' I was beginning to grow irritated by hearing his 'understood' all the time. He stood at my side and told me how important our visitors were, because the Germans had begun to flood the sewers and poison some of the passages with gas. If what the Polish guests had told us was true, the Police Commandant of Warsaw had been ordered to begin to weld the sewer covers in the centre of the city closed, to stop us from escaping. One of the men had brought a detailed plan that showed which sewers were still open, or rather which were still possible to cross in reasonable safety.

We stood and watched what was going on in the street, and Frenkel's words were streaming past my ears and accepted with divided attention. Now the murderers took their time. One brought out a thermos with some cups while others lit cigarettes, as if this game at the wall was nothing to them. After some minutes, Frenkel repeated his order, said that he must go back to his visitors and left. I could not tear myself away from my position. I was unable to act, but bound as a witness. I had to see the end. It felt like an eternity.

Finally their lunchbreak was over and they went back to work. An officer arrived in a command car which we knew so well from earlier times. One of the guards saluted him and the others lined up. Behind them most of the ghetto was burning; shots rang in the distance, but they stood calm, obviously feeling completely secure, while their victims waited to find out what kind of death they would receive. At last it came. The SS spread out near the street gutter and opened their fire. They shot only those with their faces to the wall. Not in the head, but at upper parts of their legs above the knees. Like toys, those shot slid backwards leaving streams of blood behind. Those facing the Germans stood frozen. I suddenly felt sick and threw up. I was torn in two. I was ready to gamble away everything to take on these animals who were within my range. On the other hand I now felt something I had not felt earlier. I wanted to go back to Luba. I wanted to tell her that I was still alive.

I had not realised how soiled my clothes were until I came down to the first floor. Somebody noticed me and asked what had happened. Only then did I realise how affected I had been by the spectacle that had played itself out before my eyes. On the advice of one of the women I took off my outer garments and stretched out on the floor. Somebody put something under my head and I was left alone.

It could have been a few minutes or some hours before I was brought to a state of full awareness by shots. I jumped up and went over cautiously to the window. The Germans were shooting those who had been standing facing them. Like their previous victims they too were shot in their thighs. They too slid down but forward and the blood pool became a stream. Three of us went out during the night to see if any of the wounded were still alive. They had all bled to death. I whimpered like a dog.

When we came back in, we found a great commotion going on. Some fifty members of the ŻZW were making their last preparations before leaving. Some Poles were present, waiting to give final instructions before moving out with our men. I was asked if I wanted to join them. I said no. I was not the only one to decline the invitation. I could not help visualising those who were about to leave lying in the streets in pools of blood like those I had just seen.

Before midnight the group left. One after another the weary fighters with blackened faces went down for the last time into the entrance of the bunker, to come out on the Aryan side. Those of us who remained could physically feel the emptiness which each departing comrade created as he or she disappeared into that opening. Nobody spoke. Nobody gave any instructions or last messages. The older Łopata stood and checked the forward movement. The last two to leave were Frenkel and Łopata. I had hoped to hear some words of encouragement or despair from Frenkel, but except for the speech in his eyes to those who had decided to remain, he did not say a word.

Like family members returning from a funeral, the few of us who were left turned our backs on the opening to the bunker, which had been our main artery to the world for so many months. Suddenly it was cold, lonely and we no longer felt the closeness to each other; the knot which had held us together had finally given way completely.

I was the first one to leave the ruin of the building and go outside. The ghetto was burning fiercely. The sky was light red from the flames and smoke and the thousands of sparks that moved across it — red points moving across a background of red, dying as they moved. The sound of fire in the chilly air was devastating. I turned around to see that some of the others had followed my footsteps. They too stared, entranced by the burning ghetto. Words failed us; only the sound of the flames was heard.

I remembered that in our apartment, my father had paved the attic with small gold bars. Never before had it held much meaning to me. It belonged, after all, to my father. Now I had become heir to it, maybe not the only living heir but the nearest one. I left the others and went towards the buildings. For the past four days, only five houses and a corner had separated me from it. The last thing we did in that building was choke two German officers to death. Yet those four days seemed like an abyss of time. I shivered from the cold that was coming as much from inside me as from the night. Was I a mourner? If so, why was I thinking of the gold? If I had such a great thirst for life, why did I feel totally resigned? I did not belong to anything or anybody anymore, yet I was going, of all things, to find gold bars in a desolated attic, in the middle of the night, in a burning ghetto, not clearly knowing why. As I came closer I saw that the building was no longer there. A huge pile of bricks and mortar lay in its place, facing the fiery night light like a huge animal that had lain down to die. Reflecting the sky, the skin of this dying animal was tinted pink. The flames made it shiver, as if in agony. I stood before the ruins feeling nothing inside — and then a wave swept through me. I had never before or since cried with such depth and pain; I wailed at the foot of that dying animal, which had only four days before been our family home — the building with the two flags that had mocked the Swastika before the eyes of the world. I cried for everything. For the flames of the ghetto; for the living Jews and the dead; for the Jewish Warsaw which had existed before the war. I cried for the children who had marched with us on that memorable day in August to the death wagons, and most of all, for the first and only time, I cried for me.

Finally, out of exhaustion, I stopped. Over the sound of the flames I heard somebody approaching. I had my hand on the butt of my revolver by the time I realised that those approaching were my companions in the lost fight. One of them spoke. 'What are your plans?' I had no plans and said so with a shrug. Then I found my voice.

'My father had hidden bars of gold somewhere in these ruins.' They looked at each other to confirm that I had lost my mind. I explained, 'This house belonged to my parents, the whole block. During the first year of the war we managed to remove all the leather from our tannery and sell it. It was sold for gold and my father hid the bars in the attic behind the floorboards.'

'Do you think we might find it if we dig?' one asked. The question brought me back to my senses.

'If you want the gold, start digging for it, but deep down. You can have what you find. And you too,' I turned to the other one.

Somehow this returned me to my faculties, and I knew I wanted to leave the ghetto. I turned back to the mountain of bricks and mortar, bowed my head and silently thought, I salute you, ghetto. It was a last gesture to all I was leaving behind.

28

Echoes of the valiant dead

THERE are major differences between the figures quoted by the SS chief, General-Major Jürgen Stroop, and the figures quoted by the Jewish fighters of the Warsaw ghetto, for the number of Germans killed and wounded during the Uprising. Official figures quoted by Stroop are fifteen killed for the whole period of the Uprising and none for the first day of fighting. It has, however, been established from the personal records of fighters — eyewitnesses inside the ghetto and observers from the Aryan side of the movement of German ambulances in and out of the ghetto — that a number of Germans were killed even in the first hours of the Uprising. It is not known how Stroop covered his losses, but according to his report no German lives were lost on the first day and only twenty-four of his men sustained wounds in the ghetto on 19 April 1943. The German records, however, admit the need to bring in two tanks and an armoured vehicle. One of the tanks was set on fire. The first German foray into the ghetto finished in fiasco, which Stroop could not help hiding in his first report.

In his personal report* he admits: 'In the first penetration into the ghetto the Jews and bandits managed, through a prepared fire attack,

* Stroop's typed report, page 4, presented at the International Military Tribunal in Nuremberg; USA exhibit 275, filed 13 December 1945.

to repulse the entering units, including the tanks and the armoured vehicles.'

It is unimaginable that the German forces which, together with their helpers, numbered over two thousand well-prepared fighters, would have retreated from the badly equipped, starved and untrained forces of Jewish 'subhumans' were it not for the losses they sustained as soon as they entered the ghetto. Stroop's official report is much more a cover-up than a record of facts. But ten days later he came closer to the truth. There was still much fighting to come but no longer could the Jewish leaders undertake organised actions, as had been the case in the first two to three days.

Having left Muranowska, I felt lonely, much more so than I had believed I would. Within hours I visited two bunkers where some of my friends were holding out. Suddenly I felt I was a Jew, a fighter with a revolver, in the midst of the most fateful field of battle — but I did not belong anywhere the way I had the previous day.

Late on that day I was told that Frenkel had gone only as far as the other side of the Muranowska tunnel but he and his offsider had remained in the ghetto. I was later to confirm that he had indeed returned to the ghetto.

I was torn in two for a number of days before I finalised my decision to leave the ghetto. I could not leave, however, without knowing that my departure was not as a stranger. I took part in a few skirmishes and battles between the day I left Muranowska and the day I finally left the ghetto. During the hours of battle, I was one of the fighters but as soon as the battle was over I could no longer emotionally identify as others did with feelings of satisfaction from the battle or feelings of grief for the losses. They fought on. Shots continued to be heard in the ghetto well into the month of May. Although all the major battles had taken place in the early days of the Uprising there was fighting for some time — perhaps in fact, for many months.

By 2 May I had fallen victim to a kind of resignation. I can recall eating, sleeping, washing and other such actions, but they were written with chalk on my slate of being. The instinct of wanting to survive was beginning to let go. Something in my soul asked me to decide if I wanted to go on living or not. Something inside spoke to me, telling me that if I wanted to live I must leave the ghetto. I obeyed that instruction with the same sense of resignation I had been following for the last few days. Somehow I found a telephone covered in dust and broken bricks. I picked up the handpiece not really believing that the phone would still work. It did. The sound of the dial tone shocked me back to reality. Immediately I recalled the number of Jadwiga Ziemska, one of the Polish women I had come to know in the early days of my Underground work. I dialled. I prayed that Jadwiga might answer the phone. My prayer was answered — I recognised her voice immediately. As soon as I spoke she recognised me as well. Only for a moment did she betray any excitement. Then her voice returned to full control. 'Janek, why haven't you been to visit us for so long? We are still friends and living close enough for you to see us sometime. Isn't it so?' Her words woke me from some long sleep. I cottoned on out of old habit.

'Jadwiga, I have been very ill for some time. You know I live alone. This is the first time in weeks that I have gone out to a telephone. I wanted to see you very much and soon.'

She was cautious. 'I too would love to see you. I thought you must have been offended by something I may have said but I did not know how I offended you. I thought you may have found another, better looking girl. These days one cannot trust anybody. Janek, can you come up to see me or do I have to come to you? You know I still love you.'

We arranged to meet 'at our usual place' on Nowolipki the next day around midday. 'Our usual place' was near the sewer cover on that street. By some miracle this was one of the few canals that the Germans had so far overlooked. It had not been flooded or poisoned by gas candle. I was beginning to feel alive and wanted to go on living once more.

Stroop had, by that time, closed the water supply to the ghetto, but somewhere I found water to wash decently and some reasonable clothes so that I would not look too suspicious on the other side. In the morning I shaved and dressed with an expectation which surprised me. I had to run the gauntlet of a fire exchange between a small unit of Latvian guards and the people with whom I had spent the previous afternoon. Eventually I made it, reaching the entrance leading to the Nowolipki exit.

In the early days of my work, I had learned a code to discern if the person I was expecting to meet had arrived or not, if I could not see them directly. It was actually a series of codes for different situations. In this case, when I wanted to know if it was safe to lift the lid of the canal I first had to knock in a particular way to receive an answer that Jadwiga had arrived. After that I would still have to wait for the second signal of safety. Whoever arrived had to give the sign. I knocked on the metal cover but obviously I had come too early. Either I had been too eager or something had held her up. I waited at the top of the ladder. Some time later the signal came. I was awaiting the second signal to begin lifting the cover when somebody did the work for me. By the time I lifted my head to see who had done it, I could only make out a man with his back to me walking away quickly from the opening. Jadwiga was walking on the footpath hardly looking in my direction. A tiny nod told me that it was safe to come out. I quickly put the cover back. Nobody seemed to have taken any notice of my action. I walked away as if crossing the street. Only then did Jadwiga join me.

We had passed only two or three buildings when a Polish policeman, in the company of two young gangsters — *szmalcowniks* — stepped out of the gate we were approaching. They came face to face to meet us. I pushed Jadwiga away from me and she began walking the other way. The policeman and his two leeches couldn't care less about Jadwiga. I was to be their victim.

The policemen spoke while the others just observed. 'Where have you come from?' he asked with studied quietness. There was no use prolonging the situation.

'I have come from the ghetto,' I answered, mimicking his voice. He looked away for a second as if making up his mind whether to involve Jadwiga. He decided against it.

'Your documents.' I had none. 'You'll come with us,' he said, and his two sidekicks took up their positions on either side of me. They had not suspected that I was carrying a revolver. I was too fast for them to react: the policeman held his hands to cover the open hole in his belly. Before I managed to turn on one of them they were running away and others were running with them.

I also ran, back to the sewer. I knew that within minutes the Germans would be there and the street would be closed off. It is still a riddle to me how the cover I had put back in its place was once more moved away. I jumped down into the canal and the same mysterious hand that had opened it for me covered it again the instant my head disappeared from the surface. For a moment it was too dark. When my heart had stopped pumping blood into the pupils of my eyes and the wheels of many colours stopped turning in them, I began to make my way back to the ghetto. I reached the bunker at the Nalewki, where I had been only two or three days before.

The first man to meet me was a fighter who had told me some days earlier that no fighter would live long enough to leave the ghetto. I had asked him at the time if he believed in fate. His replied seriously but with a cynical smile, 'Our fate has already been decided by the Germans. But to leave the ghetto one needs to change the colour of his skin more than his Jewish looks. We have burned faces which would fit well with the August sun, except that it is hardly the beginning of May.' The fighting had dried all emotion from his voice. 'So, you went out but you couldn't find a second-hand clean face anywhere. Right?'

Later in the evening, when we had found a place where the air was less poisoned with smoke, somebody brought slices of bread and hard-boiled eggs out from the bunker. I was offered a portion like the others. We ate and I told them my story — how the hand of some unknown Pole had stretched out to help me.

'You have always been one of the lucky ones,' I heard someone say. In the dark it was hard to recognise the woman who spoke. But she had recognised me. It was one of our ŻZW members. She had scavenged two rifles from the ruins of Muranowska and used them and the ammunition to pay for the privilege of joining the group of the Nalewki. She took over and told the others that I was the man responsible for the two flags that had caused the bitter fights around Muranowska before the Germans overcame us.

Before I was given a place to lie down for the night, I was told that I would have to leave in the morning, as no armament or food could be spared for me. I was advised to find my way to the living quarters of the factories. 'There,' they said, 'you will find everything you need, just make sure to arrive alive.'

I did not wait until the morning. The flames of the burning ghetto were enough to help me find my way to the factories. I knew it would be safer to move in the dark, although the German General had begun to post guards in the burned-out skeletons of the ruins. They remained there throughout the night, sniping at anything that moved. I would strain my memory trying to remember if the place I reached was the Többens factory or the one that belonged to Schulz. Neither was working, although it was obvious that the German owners were still interested in continuing to save their Jewish workers, not out of love but to protect themselves from having to leave the millions they had accumulated so quickly and even more to save themselves from being sent to the eastern front. A few Jews were engaged in crating machinery while the greatest number were living like moles underground. Compared to the rest of the ghetto the German factories had been quiet and the evacuation which had taken place had been less brutal than it had been elsewhere. Their rations were reasonable even now. I was told that until a few days ago the German owners had tried to convince their Jewish slaves to believe that they would be protected from the fate of those who had started the Uprising. But in the last day or two the owners had not been seen and it was now only a question of time before Stroop would turn his attention to these workers.

We lasted another week, an eternity, before our turn came. By then we no longer had the drive to carry on the fight and the sniffer dogs made it impossible to even think of resisting without a gun or a hand grenade.

The Germans came to us with loudspeakers, promising that those who walked out voluntarily would have nothing to fear. We would be sent to the factories which had already been prepared for us at Poniatów and Trawniki. Those who would not come out voluntarily, they warned, would be dealt with in the same way as the bandits who had begun shooting at German soldiers.

I could not tell if anybody in the other bunkers volunteered or not. From our group of some eighteen to twenty people, not a single one left the bunker voluntarily. First we heard the dogs barking, then one of the entrances gave way to the search of the Germans. Standing hidden from the opening, the German voice commanded: 'You have one of two choices. You can come out with your hands up and be transported, or you can remain in your stinking grave. In less than a minute from now we will let the dogs in to eat you alive and when they have almost finished with you, it will be gas grenades.' We began to move. I was blinded as I came up from the bunker, but not for long. Each one who came out was pushed to the ground by the butt of a German rifle, with the sniffer dogs being led along the rows. Lifting one's head or any other movement meant being immediately mauled by the dogs and finished off with a bullet. After a considerable time we were ordered to stand up. By then I had regained my senses.

The air was full of the sweet and sickening smell of burned flesh and timber mixed with an odour that was hard to identify.

Surrounded by a heavily equipped unit of guards we were led through some strange world of half daylight, half darkness, filled with smoke. There was no path under our feet. Here and there buildings were still smouldering and Germans were passing by without paying any attention to us. We walked and tripped. Along the way the heavy guards would ask some individuals to step out of the columns. They were shot and left.

We reached the *Umschlagplatz* from the side of the ghetto at the same time as the train entered the closed-off area from the other side. Thousands of people were already there. Within ten minutes they were loaded into the box-wagons; we were still waiting. Not far from us some civilian Germans were debating something with the SS and pointing towards us. The discussion went on for some time. In the end the SS officer in charge moved his head and hands signalling 'No' and turned from the civilians who moved away, obviously disappointed. He gave the order that we be loaded into the last empty wagon. As soon as the doors were closed behind us I turned to the others with a voice which showed clearly that I was taking command of the situation. It was a gamble — and it worked.

'Comrade fighters! I don't know if you all understood what went on outside just before we were ordered to enter the wagons. My guess is that the civilians wanted us to be spared for their factories. They would not have come to save us otherwise. They had let all the others go quite calmly. They must have known that we came from the shops and they may have considered us as trained workers. The SS did not agree and so we are here. To me it is absolutely clear that we are going to Treblinka. Some of you may still try to fool yourselves that this is not certain, but those who have a clear mind know that the last chance of trying to stay alive a little longer is not to be in this wagon when it reaches its destination. Some of us may have had enough and have resigned themselves to the end. I am not ready, and I hope there are others who may be of the same opinion. I am asking those who do not wish to try to escape the wagon before it reaches its destination, not to make any unnecessary difficulties for those who want to try to leave the train earlier.'

I was immediately surrounded by a few who, like me, were not yet ready to give up. Before the train began to move we had shifted those who could not help much due to weakness or lack of willingness to one side of the wagon. Those who, like me, had decided to jump from the train, moved over to the small wired openings, which were high up on the side wall. Others who had been brought this way since July 1942 had jumped the trains. In the ghetto I had known many individuals who claimed to have done so successfully and a few who I knew for a fact had jumped the death train on its way to Treblinka. They belonged to our movement or to some other organisation. I had not given a minute's thought to the possibility that one day I would be one of them, so sure had I been that I would either die fighting or survive on the Aryan side.

As soon as the train began to move we went to work. From the experiences of those who had done it before us the most successful way was to get the small windows free and roll out through them. Some had got out of the wagons by breaking open the side of the box, while others had even managed to get out through the floor. We decided to try to get out through the window. One ray of hope was on our side: the death train pulled around sixty cars powered by a single old-style locomotive. This meant that the train moved slowly all the way and particularly around the bends. After an hour of hard work we had managed to open a gap big enough to let one person through at a time. Then they would roll down to the side embankment of the line.

When everything was ready I took charge of who went first. I had brought one man who had worked hard to the window, when somebody called out, 'Stop! Before you let him jump make sure it is safe to do so!' For a moment I looked at the caller and did not understand what he wanted. He didn't wait for me to ask him.

'This will be my second time. I have already done what you are going to do, once before. Take a bundle of clothes and push it out the window using one of the bars we have cut out. If we have a guard on our wagon he will shoot at it. Then we will have to create some diversion. If not we will know that it is reasonably safe to jump.' We did it. There was no guard at the back of our wagon.

Six people, including the woman who had spoken up for me at the bunker at Nalewki, made their quick exit one after the other. I was left with the last two who were ready to jump. By this time we were some twenty kilometres from Treblinka. Before we jumped we agreed to hide and meet close to where we landed. From one person to the next it took no more than two to three minutes. As I was the last I became concerned about who would help me up to the window. An elderly man who I had not noticed before offered to help me and immediately there were others willing to help, in spite of the fact that they had decided not to join us.

Everyone who jumped heard the same words: 'Don't let go of the window until you hang with your feet close to the ground. Start moving your feet as if walking. Not running, but fast walking. Let go of the window and keep the movement of your feet. You will go forward and fall, but if you move forward the fall will not be heavy.'

I felt a mixture of so many emotions I cannot try to express them. There was the man who had come forward to help me. He was saying to me the words I had repeated to the others. I stretched my arms and pressed him to my heart. Tears found their way into my eyes as I turned my back to him and the others and lifted myself out of the broken opening.

I came out of the wagon swinging heavily against the wall of the cattle box. Immediately, I began to move my feet as instructed; the train was going around a bend and had slowed down. I let go my hold on the window and rolled down the embankment, concentrating on staying low to avoid the notice of the guards on the carriages following our own. The first carriage behind the locomotive was the guards' wagon; we were in the next car, followed by more than fifty box-cars.

I rolled down at a lucky spot, where I could crouch behind a large rock. It seemed an eternity before the train passed. Only after it had gone more than half a kilometre down the line did I move. My legs were hurting badly. I tried to stand up and succeeded. I was bleeding but grateful not to have broken my leg. For some seconds I felt a kind of panic, how am I going to walk back to meet the other two? I started walking and to my great relief found I could manage, although with great pain. I remembered we had passed a small cluster of trees not far back and I started walking towards them following the bend of the train line.

The cluster turned out to be a small forest and was much closer than I had thought. Nobody was coming towards me and I began to fear that I might have lost my companions. I entered the forest and was relieved to hear a whistle, low and very cautious. They had not left me. They had noticed me limping but had been afraid to come out to help. The cuts on my legs had to be treated immediately against possible infection. And while I was wondering what to do, one of my companions acted. He took off my jacket and, taking hold of my shirt, tore the back off it forcefully. He handed me the cloth and said, 'Piss on it and wash out the wounds!' I did not feel well enough to tell him to leave me alone. I did as he ordered. The open wounds smarted like hell, but this was not the end. My friend had by this time taken off his own shirt and torn the back out of it; again he handed the torn rag to me. 'Now repeat your great work,' he said seriously, 'and bandage the wounds as well as you can.'

We rested in the protection of the forest until late in the night. My cuts throbbed but they hurt less than earlier. I was not sure that my companions would want to risk their own security because of my position, but they did. 'We can only walk in the night,' one of them said, and suggested that it would be better to walk slowly, even if this should mean staying out in the open for an additional night or two. I knew that this proposal was made solely for my benefit. With a good walk the two, without me to hold them back, could have reached the outskirts of Warsaw at dawn, or at least come close enough to arrive an hour or two after the next night fall. I accepted the proposal with gratitude.

We did not walk very far the first night. At dawn we found an old wooden ruin outside a village and moved in for the day. During the day we heard some movement outside but nobody came to disturb us. The days were growing longer and before dusk we were already very hungry. One of my companions suggested that he go and find food. He returned with a handful of flowers, some spring onions and three potatoes. It was a meal.

During the second night we picked flowers and ate them. We dug up half-ready carrots, but the best food we found was the lettuce, soft European lettuce, which tasted to us like nuts. We had to warn each other to be careful not to overdo the eating, which could in our case be dangerous or even fatal if we got diarrhoea.

During the second night we reached the outskirts of Warsaw and by around six in the morning we were in one of its outer suburbs. The end of the curfew for Poles was still two hours away and all the gates to the houses were shut. We decided to wait in the gateway to a building, in the hope of moving on when the city came to life at eight.

Like most of the gates in the apartment buildings in Warsaw, this one had a small opening just above the height of an average man. Through it, the caretaker could see anyone who rang the bell asking to be let in during the night. After some time the voice of a boy came through the gate opening, 'What do you want?' I answered for all. 'We are from the country, we have received work in Warsaw but we came early. We have decided to wait here until the curfew hour.' It worked; the boy didn't ask anything more and when my friends looked inside he had gone. But a few minutes later we realised our mistake — we should have left immediately after we had been challenged by the boy. A *dorożka* arrived, with a German guard and two Polish policemen, the collaborators in their navy blue uniforms. The *dorożka* stopped in front of us. Without asking any questions we were invited to join the three. As the *dorożka* turned around, the questions started. We were interrogated in Polish and the policeman who asked the questions translated our replies into German. His German was reasonably correct.

As we had no documents, we admitted to being Jewish. Otherwise we would have to submit to the degrading spectacle of having to drop our trousers to establish if we were Jews or not. We knew that we had reached the end. Here, some kilometres from the ghetto, the smoke was still visible. The sunlight was tinted brown as we were driven into the city. We could not talk to each other and the German and his policemen ignored us after obtaining our confession. The only thing we had not revealed was that we had jumped from the train carrying us to Treblinka. I had spoken up first and said we had been hidden in Otwock (some thirty kilometres from Warsaw) during the days when the Jews there were deported. The others had agreed, and that was enough for these officials.

There is a limit to an individual's strength of endurance. When the limit is reached nature takes over. With me it expressed itself at that moment in anger. Instead of analysing our predicament, I was angry about matters which had nothing to do with our situation. I was angry with myself for not having left the ghetto earlier, on my own. Throughout the war I had held on to my own conviction, that I had a much better chance to stay alive on my own than joining with others. In senseless anger I could only punish myself with the thought that I deserved what was awaiting me, because I broke my own rules. Only for seconds at a time could I spare a thought for Luba. She would never know how I died. After nearly four years of avoiding death I was to finish up with a bullet in the neck and not in a fight. I was sure we would be taken to

Aleja Szucha, the headquarters of the Gestapo. There we would be tortured for hours or days, for as long as those animals in uniforms believed they could find out something useful from us for their death industry. I began to make all sorts of unrealistic plans that had more to do with my state of mind than with reality.

But it was our fate to face a different situation than we had imagined. Instead of the Gestapo Headquarters we were brought to a collection camp in Warsaw, at Kolejowa 3. The Germans had calculated that it was cheaper to collect escaping Jews at one place and send them off to the death factories, than to shoot them and bury them one by one. We had landed at such a collection point.

First we had to be interrogated; then we would be accepted to wait at the camp for the collection date. Of course we did not know any of this at the time, and we were surprised when the *dorożka* stopped at the gate of the camp. The three who had arrested us asked us to walk over by ourselves to the Ukrainian guards who were standing near the gate. For a moment it was so strange that we remained standing at the *dorożka*. The driver and the three officers ignored us and drove off. With irritation one of the camp guards called us over — in Polish. We came to the gate. As if we were a nuisance more than a danger one of them tore himself away from the others, opened the gate and called us to follow him inside. We obeyed, dumbstruck.

29

A miracle by mistake

THE lone Ukrainian guard seemed quite sure of himself. 'Follow me,' he said in Polish, not afraid to walk in front of us. The eyes of hundreds in the camp watched us. All the guards in the camp were Ukrainians and all the inmates Jews. I noted that the barbed-wire fence was a simple construction, like the fences used to keep cattle from escaping. The strings seemed stretched on wooden poles; only the two rows on top were bent inwards and close to each other. As always I was still carrying my gun. The Polish policemen had not bothered searching us and the guard seemed just as uninterested. At the *Umschlagplatz* the soldiers were more concerned with herding thousands of Jews onto the death train than looking for arms.

We came to a halt outside an old brick building, guarded by another two Ukrainians. The guard who brought us did not bother to salute and the others did not seem offended. I could not hear the exchange between them. One of the guards went inside the building and after some time he returned with a fat, middle-aged, red-faced civilian not fully dressed for a formal reception. Clearly this German was the boss of the camp. He wore no coat, just a pair of trousers held up by braces in which he had put his thumbs with two big red palms facing towards us. No one spoke while he looked us over. After feeling that he had done his duty he turned to the guard who had brought us. 'Have they lice?'

'No. They were brought here by a *dorożka* sitting close to two Polish policemen and a German officer. They must be clean.'

'Put them up with the others,' said the fat German, 'and find out where they came from. I want it all in writing.' Having made his declaration he turned and went back to finish his private business. Obviously we were of little interest to him. The guard took us to one of the wooden huts and said, 'This is your barrack.' With this he considered his duty done.

Over the next two days many other Jews were brought to the camp at the Kolejowa. There was no visible administration in the place. The ration was handed out in a chaotic manner and only the strongest managed to get hold of the bits of food distributed; the others starved. My two companions had shared with me whatever food they managed to get hold of on the day of our arrival. They were gone on the second day. In the chaos of the camp I did not waste time and energy looking for them. My wounds had begun to form scabs without infection; this was at least a good sign but I still had pain when I walked. In addition I had found a place in the sun where I felt warm and unbelievably comfortable in resignation to my fate.

It must have been on the third or fourth day after we arrived: I was sitting on the ground alone, warming myself in the sun with closed eyes when someone gave me a gentle kick in the side. I opened my eyes and saw two guards, Ukrainians of course, standing over me. 'Get up,' said one of them, but in a surprisingly decent tone. I obeyed with some difficulty. 'Are you a Pole?' he asked me.

'Yes,' I replied, without adding that I was also Jewish.

'I said so to my brother. He wasn't sure that I was right. I saw you sitting here yesterday. I was wondering what brought you here?' Alarm bells rang in my mind: this was the opportunity. Even if they discovered their mistake I had nothing to lose. The old fighter in me was back to attention.

'Thank you for asking. To be completely honest with you I must say that I have no clue myself. They were leading a group of Jews along our street and the gate to our building was shut. Like some stupid idiot I didn't think and opened it and walked out, right into the arms of a German. I was pushed off the footpath into the middle of the road and here I am.'

'I told you that he doesn't belong here,' one said to his brother, and turning once more to me he began in a most friendly way to tell me that they had already arranged between themselves to help me get out of this place before the collection. 'They will all finish up in the death chambers of Treblinka in a few days,' he said, looking around at the others. 'You are lucky you have met us in time. In two or three days there will be enough of them to fill the train and the camp will once more be free for a while. The first Jews who come afterwards will have to clean out the shit and the stink and wait for the others. But you will be back home.'

'We will see you here later and give you the details after we have found a way,' said the other.

'I thank you both very much for your understanding,' I replied. 'A Slav should stick to his brother Slav, particularly a Pole with a Ukrainian. We have a lot in common.'

'That's what I have said to my brother. We'll help you, today.' And with this they left.

I sat down once more and began to think. It was true that my features had never betrayed me outside the ghetto. Never before had I been challenged by the *szmalcowniks*. So maybe these two Ukrainians had really taken me for a Catholic Pole. Or was the whole thing a trap? Were they going to shoot me as soon as I was outside? Would that make them look good in the eyes of the fat German? Why, then, would they have chosen me? No, they said they had recognised my features as a Pole, maybe they meant it. But why should I mean so much to them? Why would they want to risk their own freedom and maybe their lives for me? Why? They may have been good Christians. There were tens of thousands like them who thought that killing Jews was not a sin, but they believed that I was not a Jew, and that's why they wanted to help me.

My brain did not rest. I worked out a thousand reasons why I should trust them and a thousand and one reasons why I should not. I could hardly rest, but I had again fallen asleep in the sun when I was once more gently kicked. This time only one brother had come to see me. He came straight to the point: 'When I leave, go over to the bin standing near the wire to your left. Don't go right to it, or you will be shot by the guards. They don't know what my brother and I are going to do. Just go close enough to see where we have left a small hand-shovel for you. It is one used by grocers to weigh flour and sugar. You'll use it to dig your way out of here. You'll dig behind the bin. I'll be back soon to tell you the rest. But now stand up after I have gone and see if you can see the shovel. And don't be afraid, nobody will go near it to take it away. It lies in the forbidden zone.' He left and I stood up and made my way leisurely towards the bin he had pointed out to me. I could see it from a fair distance. Once more a chain of thoughts started turning in my mind like wheels. But the optimist in me had the upper hand. I decided to take the chance with them.

Some time late in the afternoon the other brother arrived. This time I had been waiting for him. He called out from the distance in an angry voice, 'Hey you! You there!' He pointed to me and ordered me over to where he was standing. His voice was so sharp that I became worried but obeyed the order. As I came closer he said softly, 'Stand to attention!' The way he said it made me relax. 'Now listen. I have the final arrangements for you. You know that we have put the shovel next to the bin. Behind the bin you'll also find a railway worker's cap. It will protect you, as you will be walking out during the night. But don't go far away in the night. The caps are not a hundred percent security. We have orders to ignore the railway workers around here if they disobey the curfew hour. But this is only near the camp.

'My brother and I will be patrolling this area together, walking in opposite directions. We will meet right where you have been standing just now. As we separate we will have our backs to you.

When you hear one of us sing, follow the one who will be walking towards the bin. Pick up the shovel and dig deep enough under the wires to give yourself room to get out under them. Pick up the cap and put it on as soon as you're on the other side of the fence. Walk over to the other side of the street and turn the first corner away from this cursed camp. From there you'll be on your own. By the way, you're in luck: we have our orders for tomorrow — we'll do guard duty on the train to Treblinka. The camp will be cleaned out tomorrow lunchtime.'

He suddenly gave me a hard push and it took me some seconds to reorient myself and realise that he had done it for my benefit.

Before sunset we were driven into the huts where we each had to find a place to lie down, as best one could. While I was lying on the hard ground my doubts returned. I kept questioning the reason for their offer. Did he tell me that the camp will be moved on tomorrow in order to entice me tonight? What if they meant every word they said and my doubt becomes my own death sentence? What did I have to lose? If I didn't get out of this camp I would surely go to Treblinka. I might even be shot on the way to the train. I was gambling my death which was a certainty here, for the possibility, no matter how slim, to live. To live! How much longer? Long enough to see Luba.

By the time it was dark I was once more the fighter I had been at Muranowska during the first day of the Uprising. I didn't know where the strength came from but I knew that I had to carry out my part of the arrangement. If it turned out to be a trap I would have to act according to my instincts at that moment. I rolled out of the barrack quietly. Once outside I avoided the patrolling guards by crawling on all fours and on my belly. I reached the agreed spot and knew there was no way back. A guard passed close by and signalled by coughing. I responded with a slight sound and immediately he turned towards me. 'We will be here in a few minutes,' he whispered, 'be ready.'

Within minutes I saw two shadows approaching from both sides, as they had promised. They met precisely in front of me. The one walking towards the bin began to sing a well-known Ukrainian song and I followed him on all fours. Near the bin he whispered, 'Good luck!' and turned around. In a final moment of doubt I stopped until I saw him going away without turning back. I had no difficulty locating the small shovel in the dark. I found that the soil behind the bin had been moistened to make the digging easier. Within minutes I had dug enough to let me slide under the wires. The railway cap was where it was supposed to be. For a moment I wanted to thank my two guardian angels but the thought didn't last — the Angel of Death was also an angel. Tomorrow they would sit in one of the boxes on top of the cattle trucks taking a few thousand Jews to their death in Treblinka. If anyone tried to escape they would shoot. I had nothing to thank them for. They had performed a miracle for me, but by mistake.

I slid under the barbed wire and was on my way very quickly. Around the corner I found the ruins of a house. I went inside and lay down. Apparently I had made no noise in doing so, for I soon heard a couple on the other side of the room in intimate action. I felt a sense of relief when I heard them get up and leave before the break of dawn. I sheltered in the destroyed house until the end of the curfew hour. With the first daylight I discovered that the building had been used by others before me: the corner where the couple had been so active was fitted out with a straw mattress. Papers, wrapping and other signs told me that I was lucky not to have been found by the regulars who came here for night visits.

At around eight in the morning the street came to life. Without any difficulty I joined the throng of people, making sure that I was moving away from the Kolejowa. Some of those going in the opposite direction looked at me for a second or two but turned their eyes away when I met their gaze. I entered a nearby gate and took stock of myself. My clothes looked poor, like those of a working-class man in Warsaw. I removed my cap and checked it out; it was the standard railway worker's cap. Everything was all right but there was no doubt that something was giving me away, or at least making me look suspicious. When I realised at last that it was my burned dark face, I knew that I had to take my chances one way or another. I pulled the cap on lower than before and went back out to the street. At the next corner I came to a tramline and recognised the surroundings. I could take the tram in the direction of Ceglana Street where Luba was living with a Polish family.

I stepped off the footpath and went over to the tram stop to wait. As a Pole I was not allowed in the first half of the first carriage, which was reserved for Germans. I made my way to the place where the rear of the second carriage would stop. My heart missed a beat. Right in front of me stood the fat, red-faced German who had welcomed me when I was delivered to the collection camp. This time he was properly dressed in a smart sports coat, with the swastika button in the lapel, a tyrolian hat with a feather in it and an official case under his arm. I was not sure if he would recognise me but I took no chances; I turned the other way. Again, my mind had begun to work quickly. I knew that my clothes were smelly but I was a working-class railway man — I could not care less. If others didn't like my smell let them move away. This worked beautifully. No one wanted to have anything to do with me and I was left in peace.

As the tram moved on I recalled the last four days. I was surprised at my own resignation during that time. I had actually met Luba's sister Helena on my second day in the camp. I had spoken to her about the possibility of trying to escape, but she wouldn't hear of it. I had not tried to convince her otherwise and now, in the tram, I remembered that I had actually thought that she might have been right. 'It is over now,' I kept telling myself sharply. 'Forget it for now. Think of the future. Maybe that way you'll live long enough to tell it. But not now.'

I got off the tram and walked to the building in Ceglana Street. I rang the bell, and it was answered by the lady of the house. She opened the door and let me in but her face was full of fear.

She closed the door quickly and in a strange voice called, 'Pani Zosiu! Pani Zosiu!' In seconds Luba was standing in the doorway of the other room, and like some far off dream I recall embracing her and thinking that she was with me standing not on the Aryan side but somewhere on Muranowska. The thought was so real for some moments that I even imagined hearing explosions.

'Pani Zosiu! He can't stay here very long,' I heard the lady cry. 'His face! You know that this is called the Jewish ghetto face. He can't stay with us, it is too dangerous.'

Luba wiped her tears as she calmly replied, 'First of all he must wash and change his clothes. The smell alone could have given him away.' The woman started to protest but Luba was unusually calm. 'Pani Irena, we won't stay, but let him wash, change into human clothes, eat and sleep at least. He has come here unnoticed so give us a chance.' Grudgingly, Irena calmed down. Luba, now Zosia as she was called in her Polish documents, prepared the bath and laid a shirt and an old suit out for me. 'We will have to get rid of these,' she said as she picked up my clothes.

Not with one single word did she express what must have been going on in her mind. She did not ask where I had been since the day I told her I was going back to the ghetto; she did not ask what I had done or how I came to arrive in such a state with a railway worker's cap. The only sign she had was my brown face — it told her that I had been in the ghetto. Pani Irena was not unreasonable in her fear. The *szmalcowniks* made no distinction between Jews and their protectors. Nowhere was the saying 'the walls have ears' more true than on the Aryan side of Warsaw. Luba was known to most people as Zosia, a Polish woman. Only the closest members of the family she was staying with knew who she was. To keep a Jewish man in the house was much more dangerous, particularly one who had come out of the ghetto during the Uprising. In the end Irena was willing to let her husband decide. He was at work and would come home close to the curfew hour.

I was kept out of sight when he came home while Irena prepared him in her own way. Luba did not interfere. He came into the room where I was waiting and without the slightest hesitation he gripped my hand with all his strength, saying, 'Good to see you alive!' Irena looked shocked and disappointed, even more so when he asked me to take my place at the table. For the first time in many months I was sitting at a normal table with normal people partaking of a human meal. There was very little talk and the little that was spoken seemed from another world. It was all domestic and daily. When the meal was finished and the plates removed, the question of our staying on with the family was raised. Wacek, the husband and head of the family, opened up the problem. 'Panie Janek,' he said, 'I hope you'll understand the position we are all in with your sudden appearance. Please, don't misunderstand me, we will not ask you to leave right now, or tomorrow, but we cannot accept the danger for the long run. We will badly miss your financial help but I have a family to protect. Not only my family but you and your wife as well.' With this he had said everything there was to be said.

'Does your remark mean days or weeks?' I asked.

Before he had time to reply Irena spoke her mind. 'Not weeks, Panie Janek. If Zosia stays by herself, well, I don't mind if you come to visit her from time to time. Not too often, you understand. But if you want to stay together, then a week should be long enough to find yourself some place.'

'A week, at most ten days,' Wacek put in. Somehow it was better than I had expected, we had just been given ten days to find some other arrangements. That night I asked Luba about Feliks, the man who had worked for her father before the war and was now entrusted with the furs we had smuggled out of the ghetto. It was an immense relief to hear that he was paying the money every month as we had arranged. I was even more relieved when I heard that he would be coming in two days time to see Luba and hand over to her the monthly pay. We had a start. I also had Polish friends from dealings on the Kiercelak and the contacts with Bystry, although I did not believe he would still be at his old address.

Irena seemed much calmer on the second day. She tried to make up for the sharp tone she had taken the previous day by asking me what I would like for dinner. 'You deserve at least to be well fed for the few days you are with us,' she said with a forced smile. I responded in a similar way as if we had made up some friendly misunderstanding. Luba had already left to buy the provisions for dinner. I was to learn how independent my wife had become in the few months she had been away from the ghetto. With her hair dyed blonde she was relatively safe and her features were the best evidence of her 'true' Aryan origins. When she came back from the shops she smiled at me. 'Come and listen to what I have to say to Irena. I have everything fixed. We will be out of here in three or four days.'

I followed her into the dining room where Irena was sewing. She looked up as we entered and Luba said, 'Pani Irena, your worries will soon be over. We will probably be gone long before the ten days are up. I am expecting to have our accommodation fixed in three or four days.'

I was puzzled at first by the way Irena had smiled at this news. Later Luba explained and it all made sense. 'It was not only your burned face that worried her. She has a lover who visits her during the day when her husband is at work. She was willing to provide one for me as well. Your arrival spoiled it all. Now she will be able to have him back again.' I could only smile in surprise.

30

Natolińska Street

I was willing to pay our hosts up until the end of the month, which would have been two weeks after we had left, but Luba thought otherwise. She said that we should discuss the matter with Wacek. After all, he had told us that we had only ten days in his house and no more. Our monthly payments to him for Luba's board were equal to six times the monthly earnings of a Polish worker in Warsaw. But I had the feeling that there was something else involved, not just money. I accepted her reasoning without knowing the details.

In the evening some guests arrived, so Luba and I had to stay hidden in our room. After a day of conversation we had to sit in complete silence since we did not know who the guests were. Normally Irena or Wacek would have called for Luba to join them; this time they did not. Obviously they had good reasons. When the guests left, Wacek came to our room and apologised, explaining that Jews were not the only ones who were forced to lead underground lives. Having said his piece, he came to the point of our departure. Irena had already told him that we may move very soon, and of his own will he explained that as he had given us notice, we would not owe them anything more than what would be due on the day we left. He said it with sincerity, wishing us the best for the future. 'By the way,' he added, 'I believe that within three days you may be able to show your face in the street without any danger of being picked up. We had visitors today at the place where I work, and I found this out through them.' He offered me a vodka which I wanted to accept but Luba thought it would be better to avoid alcohol for a few days.

When the people of our new abode came to take us there it turned out that the two families knew each other from Underground work but for security reasons had not known each other's addresses. It was dangerous for four people to travel together in one *dorożka* in Warsaw. For the same reason it was also better not to ask the driver of the *dorożka* to come to one's house, or to be dropped off at a precise address. Luba went with the woman to the corner of the street where they waited near the tram stop. I was to follow on my own. As I came to the corner I saw a *dorożka* stopping for them. The driver lifted his cap and I heard him ask, 'Aren't you two the ladies from the butcher shop? If you are I am here to drive you home.' Our new hostess took Luba by the arm, helped her up to the seat and followed her in; then the *dorożka* drove off.

Our new address struck a chord, but I hoped that I was mistaken. I was to make my way to 10 Natolińska Street. In my memory it was a short street very close to Aleja Szucha, the headquarters of the Gestapo in Warsaw. Reluctantly, I had to make peace with reality. I had not been mistaken. It was the short street I remembered and number 10 was only five houses away from the most dreaded building in the whole of occupied Poland. It was rumoured that only one in five arrested ever left the building alive. It was also rumoured that those who did leave it alive should no longer be trusted, even if they had once been the most faithful of Underground workers.

Our new place was behind a shop. Before the war it had been a shop and a dwelling together but now the door between the two had been sealed off. The shop was run by the uncle of the owner of the dwelling. Both sides of the family were involved in Underground work which had to do with hiding Jews, mostly for some reward.

During the first week our host gave us some important instructions, concerning matters of life and death. 'Many Jews lose their lives because they act out of habit. Take for example such a small thing as washing your hands. If you are invited to a meal, be very careful that when you are asked to the table you don't ask if you can wash your hands first. More than one Jew has given himself away by asking where he could wash his hands. And never throw the towel over your shoulder. This would be enough to have you and me shot.'

At another time we were warned to be careful with the boys selling cigarettes at the corner of the street. 'Those ten and eleven-year-old boys are more likely to read your mind than professional mind readers. They survive by their instinct. Some of them are Jewish kids. They buy and sell cigarettes from Germans. Some of the Gestapo agents know which of them is Jewish and who is not. There is a lot of dirty business going on with those boys. Don't ask me why they are still alive, make up your own mind about it. So be more than just careful. Sooner or later, when they see you coming and going they will stop you and start some conversation. Don't immediately dismiss them. Listen for a few minutes and then tell them in no uncertain terms to be careful, because selling cigarettes in the street without a licence is a criminal offence. Add to it something like, "the Gestapo is only a few steps away". They will soon leave you in peace. Always remember to be on your guard, because your guard is the only thing between your life and death.'

I did not get to know Irena and Wacek well in the four short days I was there, but it felt as if Luba's life with them was a pure financial arrangement in which no emotion had been involved. I had the feeling that she was considered as an inferior tenant whose payment was not quite as generous as it should have been. Slowly I began to understand why my wife had been so eager to move, and why she did not want to pay to the end of the month.

Our new landlords were Jurek and Zosia. My name in hiding

was Janek and Luba was Zosia. The Polish names Jurek, Jasiek and Janek are all the same, like the English John and Jack. The couple were much closer to us in character than our previous landlords, but the name Zosia sometimes caused funny situations. They were also much friendlier. We paid them well but each time we paid we heard something like: 'Are you sure you can afford it?' or a reminder that the war might be going on for a long time yet and we should consider what we may need.

Jurek quickly became my friend. He was a straightforward character who could fit in with anybody and any situation. Zosia was the same, but much more worldly. Before the war she was on the staff of the Polish semi-dictator Józef Piłsudski, commonly called the Father of the Reborn Poland, which had regained its independence after more than one hundred and twenty years under Czarist Russia. She spoke four or five languages, which had helped her to become the public relations person for the Polish Government at the International Airport in Warsaw after Piłsudski died.

Unlike the couple at Ceglana Street, Jurek and Zosia introduced us to people. As well, we were invited to take part in discussions which had to do with conspiracy and the Underground. We could also read all the leaflets that appeared through the Underground network. In one of them we found that although the official Uprising had ended some time ago, individual fighters were still roaming in the ghetto. We read that two girls had managed to escape the ruins at the end of July. Another leaflet told of Greek and French Jews who had been brought in to clean up the area. They were separated from the local Jews who had been left behind for the same purpose.

We learned to trust our landlords as much as we could. I had only one secret which they didn't find out about for some time — my revolver. Until one unfortunate incident, they did not know that I always carried it with me when I left the house.

This particular revolver was not only my protector but also something of great emotional value. I had, long before the ghetto

Uprising, bought a very strong Belgian revolver at the Kiercelak. It was the envy of many fighters in the ghetto. Two days before the Uprising, on the evening I had sent Janek Kostański out of the ghetto, somebody asked me if I wanted to meet Mordecai Anielewicz. I had been surprised by the offer and wondered why it had been made. I was nothing more than an ordinary low-ranking soldier, and on top of that I was not part of the ŻOB but of the ŻZW. Of course, I jumped at the chance. The invitation to shake the hand of the Commander of the ŻOB had its reasons. While talking about the situation in the ghetto, Anielewicz avoided anything that touched on the split between the two fighting groups. As I was about to leave, he made a side remark: 'I heard you have a Belgian gun. I have just this,' he showed his simple revolver. 'Would you care to change with me?'

We did exchange guns and made a pact to keep spare ammunition for each other in our bunkers, mine in Miła, his in Muranowska.

So now, months after the Uprising had ended and the Commander of our great revolt had died in his bunker, I was carrying his gun in my belt. I called the gun Ania, in his memory. Once, the revolver nearly killed me. Carrying it tucked into my belt covered only by my shirt and coat, I went out of the gate of the building where we were staying to be met by the butt of a German rifle being pushed right on top of the gun and a German in full battle dress looking straight into my eyes. 'Where do you think you are going?' he asked. Of course I was not supposed to understand the question and made some funny signs, saying, '*No Deutsch sprechen*.' He repeated his question slightly more menacingly. This time I understood. In sign language I put my hands up as if to pray, crossed myself and lifted my face towards the sky. At first he said, 'No.' When I repeated the signs and indicated that I was preparing to attend Holy Mass he became softer. 'What is the name of your *mädchen*?' Of course I did not understand and waited. The German changed his mind. He signalled for me to come into the street where he spoke to a guard who was standing opposite the Gestapo building. 'Let him through. He is probably a priest or something. He is going to pray. Let him through.' The soldier moved his hand, and as I passed him he said quite audibly, 'I am also a Catholic.'

I noticed that the street had been closed off at both ends with soldiers. The boys who sold cigarettes had disappeared and the restaurant owned by the *Volksdeutsche* (a Pole of German ethnic origin), was full of police and soldiers. I decided not to return until some minutes before the curfew hour, and I approached the street cautiously. It was quiet. I entered our apartment to be greeted by a very anxious reception. A neighbour from above us had seen through the curtains that I had been handed over from one German to another, and had notified the family. They had all gone into hiding in the wall behind their large oven, awaiting the arrival of the Gestapo. They had waited there for some hours before they dared to come out.

The incident which had sparked the street closure illustrates the situation in Warsaw under the German occupation. A Pole had entered the German restaurant and ordered a lavish breakfast. The trouble began when he could not pay for the food he had eaten. The German owner tried to hold on to him as he called the police. The Pole was strong enough to tear himself away, break up furniture and other things, and make a successful getaway. They were searching for him.

I must have been more shaken by this incident that I had realised at the time. When I removed the gun I felt some pain. My shirt was smeared in blood. The revolver had cut into me and the blood made the shirt stick to my skin. It was a small price to pay under the circumstances.

Both Jurek and Zosia liked the bitter drop slightly more than was good for them. They were, however, sufficiently intelligent to drink only at home and mostly when they had visitors.

Their visitors were from the Underground, ordinary people and members of the occupational forces, mostly from the Gestapo. Jurek and Zosia sometimes became tipsy with their guests but they never got sufficiently drunk to forget the information they collected from their German friends. Entertaining the Germans was part of their information service to the Polish Underground.

Luba and I had the freedom of the house when nobody was visiting. When guests came the situation changed. Some of them knew me and some of them knew Luba. Only relatives knew us both. According to who the visitors were, one of us had the freedom to move around while the other had to sit quietly in the kitchen. The kitchen was considered a private sanctum and was closed to guests. One morning Jurek and Zosia were entertaining a junior officer of the Gestapo. So that he would drink enough to talk they got slightly tipsy themselves. Luba and I sat in the kitchen like mice, not daring even to whisper, while we listened to the laughter from the dining room. Suddenly something went wrong with my insides and made me feel very uncomfortable. I needed the bathroom urgently. But in order to get there I had to pass through the dining room. Very carefully I opened the door slightly and made a noise that would not attract the attention of the Gestapo officer but would be audible to either Jurek or Zosia. It was Zosia who got up from the table and came into the kitchen. I could not tell her of my predicament in words, so I rubbed my hands over the front of my stomach, accidently revealing the handle of my revolver. When the half-drunk woman saw it she ran out with a scream: 'Jesus, he is going to shoot me!'

I felt forced to react just as wildly, and this ultimately saved all our lives. Without waiting another second I had my revolver drawn and was in the dining room with the gun in my hand. The German officer was standing already with his hand on his holster. 'Drop the gun!' I pointed to him. Luba was also in the dining room. Jurek and Zosia stood frozen. The officer was somewhat younger than I. He slowly removed his revolver and dropped it. Several bullets dropped out of the gun. 'Pick up the revolver and run!' I screamed to Luba. In her haste to do so she picked up the loose bullets and ran away leaving the gun on the floor. I dared not bend down. I kicked the German revolver to the door and told the three of them to stand back near the kitchen. 'I will be leaving now but I warn you, if any one of you open this door too soon after me you will pay with your life.'

I opened the door, kicked out the revolver, shut the door after me, and picked up the German gun. In order to escape I had to run through the courtyard. With revolver in hand I came face to face with the caretaker of the building. He must have thought I was from the Polish Underground, which was nothing special in Warsaw. 'Have you seen anybody coming out of this building?' I asked.

'Nobody has come out since I have been working in the yard.'

'How long is that?'

'About fifteen minutes.'

While I was talking the Gestapo officer came running out. He looked at me with the fear of death in his eyes. The caretaker disappeared quicker than the words could report it. The German ran towards the gate and I ran after him. I had no intention of shooting. Outside the gate he turned towards the Gestapo Headquarters while I turned away from it. I managed to hide his gun as I turned the corner and began walking slightly faster than usual. I took stock of the situation as I made my way from our building as quickly as I could. If the caretaker had not seen Luba running out she must have run up the stairs. There was little I could do except hope that she would not be found when the Gestapo arrived to take Jurek and Zosia away. I could not go back there. Nor could I hide with Wacek and Irena in Ceglana Street in case Jurek talked while he was in the hands of the Gestapo. I remembered Luba's brother's address and went there. Abraham and his wife Lodzia had never left their hiding place, and the people who kept them knew us. I used to visit them before the Uprising.

I was accepted with the same friendliness I always received from their landlords. Abraham and Lodzia were also pleased to see me. When I told them what had happened, Lodzia went to ask them if I could stay with them for two or three days. They agreed reluctantly. Close to the curfew hour Luba arrived. It is hard to describe our stress and joy. To satisfy the landlords we agreed to pay them a considerable sum. After everything had been reasonably settled Luba told us that she had run up to one of the higher floors in the apartment building and wait there for some time. A neighbour saw her and asked her what she was doing, to which she answered she was hiding from her husband who was drunk and had threatened her. She left just before the start of the curfew and she had not seen any police or Gestapo coming to the building. She had watched Zosia leaving and coming back and that was all.

In the middle of telling her story Luba turned pale and frightened. 'Oh God! The money is still at their place!' There was good reason to be worried. We had no income or earnings. Our daily needs were provided for by the monthly payment we received from Feliks. He was decent and his regular payment allowed us to live in reasonable comfort. But we also had to consider the possibility of being exposed and needing to carry on without his commitment for one reason or another. For this purpose we had a special reserve of some gold and American dollars. At Ceglana Street, while Luba had been alone, she had carried it on her body. At Jurek's place I had taken out one tile from the large oven and built in a primitive kind of safe. Only Luba and I knew about it. Always after opening it we would put the tile back in place and draw around it with white chalk. Nobody could notice the difference between this particular tile and those surrounding it. In our haste we had left the reserve in our makeshift safe. There was little we could do at the time, except hope.

The whole night I tried to work out why the Gestapo had not come to arrest the couple, particularly because taking a gun from a Gestapo officer was such a serious offence. Then it dawned on me. They were waiting for nightfall, as they usually did, when Jurek and Zosia would be at home. Having come to that conclusion I began to wonder how we could get our money back. In the morning we made all sorts of plans which came to nothing. Luba decided to go back and find out from the uncle in the store what had happened. She returned an hour later looking radiant and showing us the treasure she had managed to rescue from the hiding place. Nothing had happened after the incident with the Gestapo officer. Both Jurek and Zosia were shaken but obviously the vodka had made them feel secure when they should have weighed the danger and left immediately. By the time they came to their senses they wondered why they were still in their own home and not up at Aleja Szucha. After speaking with the uncle in the shop, Luba had decided to go to the kitchen and retrieve our money and jewellery from the hiding place. Of course, we had no key to the apartment. She went to the door and knocked. Nobody answered but the door was unlocked. Zosia was asleep in the dining room. Luba passed her silently and entered the kitchen, removed the reserve from the safe and left without Zosia hearing a thing.

Four days later Abraham's place was 'burned', which meant that someone had found out that the family was harbouring Jews. We all had to leave, immediately. Now we were four without a roof over our heads. After I parked the others with an acquaintance on the promise that they would be gone before the curfew hour, I made my way — of all places — back to Zosia and Jurek's apartment. I had worked out that the place had become secure once more. I was right. The Gestapo officer was afraid to report the incident; doing so would have forced him to answer questions that could have endangered his own hide. He would have to give some good reasons why he was so friendly with Poles as to get drunk with them, to such a degree that he might have given away state secrets. He would have to answer for his lost revolver which was now in the hands of a Jew. It was better under the circumstances to forget the place — for good.

We had left the apartment four days earlier only a single couple. Now we wanted to come back as two couples. Jurek did not hesitate to have us stay for the night but thought it would be too much for all concerned to have four people together for any time. Zosia wanted to know how much additional money they would get from us. When she found out that we would pay one thousand five hundred złotys a month per person, she became excited. It was too good a deal to let go. Six thousand złotys was some two years wages in Warsaw. She was willing to take it on herself to provide the necessary food from the black market. Under the prevailing conditions this solved the greatest problem. We sat talking late into the night until we found a solution regarding our hiding place. In times of danger there was sufficient room four people to hide in the wall behind the big stove. Of course we would have to make the place habitable. Abraham and I decided to start on the work the next day and Jurek promised to provide the materials and the tools. There were now four of us living in hiding with Jurek and Zosia on the famous Natolińska Sreet.

31

A Jewish face

We spent over a year with Jurek and Zosia. Luba's brother and his wife never left their hiding place, but we dared to venture out of the house very occasionally, and only when we had to. Luba was more daring than I in this respect, but then she was in much less danger if challenged than I would have been. But there was an incident, the details of which I no longer remember, when I went out with Jurek. He needed my presence, or my assistance. Whatever it was, I reluctantly agreed to go with him. I had tried to persuade him to go alone but when he insisted I could hardly refuse.

It was a nice sunny day and we walked over to the tram. Jurek was in a particularly jovial mood, which made me nervous. He joked in an unusual way and I wondered if he was not a little bit drunk. We caught the tram and sat in the last available seat at the back of the second carriage. At the first stop some people got on and one rather rough-looking type stood in front of us. As the tram moved on I noticed that the man was staring at Jurek in a rather strange way. I became concerned but did my best to avoid drawing his attention to me. I wanted to signal to Jurek but knew that it would only make matters more tense. After a while the man bent down and asked Jurek, 'What is a fucking Jew like you doing in a Polish tram on the Aryan side?' Jurek's reaction brought me into the picture.

He turned to me and asked in a loud voice, 'What do you say to this so and so? Does he want to get screwed?'

The stranger turned to me. 'Are you with him?'

In the most polite way I could manage I said, 'May I know what your interest is in this man?' I was sure the man was a *szmalcownik*, but I thought it was better to be careful in such a dangerous situation.

The stranger nodded and said, 'See for yourself the difference between the way a Pole speaks to a Pole and the way a fucking Jew speaks. He still thinks Poland belongs to him.' He took his identity card from his top pocket and showed it to me. 'I am from the police. Would you both please leave this tram with me at the next stop and accompany me to the police station.'

Around us people reacted in various ways. Some showed open interest while others tried their best not to get involved. Others began to make comments about Jews. The most interesting remark came from a middle-aged woman. She looked at me with surprise and asked, 'Why should you, such a kind proud Pole, have any business with a Jew?'

'I want to talk to you, too,' the policeman said to me as we stepped onto the footpath, 'but first let's see this man.' I was ready to go to any length to avoid going to the police station. I had already realised that I was taken for a Gentile. I had also impressed the policeman as being of good character. Once more I used my best language. 'With your permission, officer, may I help you to avoid making a ghastly mistake? Please.' The policeman toned down his arrogance.

'What mistake?'

I smiled as sweetly as I could. 'Officer, this man is as much Jewish as you or I. He is the grandson of one of the first Generals who fought for Poland in 1920. His grandfather was one of the Marshal's Generals at the "Miracle of the Vistula", when they trounced the Bolsheviks. So far it is only a funny mistake, but at the station it may turn into something none of us would have wanted.'

The policeman became tongue-tied. He looked at Jurek and then at me and once more at Jurek. In a changed voice he asked Jurek in a civil manner, 'Have you any documents on you?'

'Of course I have,' Jurek replied, less flamboyant than he had been in the tram. Jurek's family name was the same as the well-known General, but there was no relationship between them. The policeman handed back the document without addressing himself to Jurek, but turned to me. 'Do you mind showing me your papers?' I had false documents. The officer hardly glanced at them and handing them back to me tried to give us some fatherly advice. 'In these days one is always wiser to be cautious and behave with more restraint. I am glad that you, Janek, have shown such presence of mind. If your friend had told me simply that I was mistaken I would have asked him for the documents in the tram and the matter would have ended then and there. Wouldn't it?' Of course I agreed. 'So, next time please, I speak to both of you, let an officer of the police do his duty in a polite manner. We are all Poles in a most difficult time and situation. I know how any decent Pole feels through a mistake like the one we have just avoided. He is brought to the police and has to drop his trousers to prove that he is not a Jew. Whenever I am forced to witness such a situation I feel embarrassed not only for the individual but for Poland. So thank you once more Janek for stopping a mistake that would have been very regrettable and remember my words in the future.'

When the policeman was out of earshot Jurek began one of the most profane bombardments of swearing I had heard for a long time. I could not help but smile.

I persuaded him to go back home and wait for another day to attend to whatever the business was. When Luba and Zosia heard what had happened they decided that Jurek owed me something for saving him from the indignity the policeman had described. Zosia could not help from joking, 'You should have brought the policeman here. I would have told him what a penis you had.' Thus ended my last voluntary excursion out of the house.

32

The art of survival

According to historical documentation, the number of Jews hidden on the Aryan side of Warsaw with the help of Gentiles varies between twelve thousand and twenty thousand. It would be hard to be more precise because the statistical information could not be kept in a reliable way. Many Jews, like ourselves, were never in contact with any organisation that assisted Jews in hiding. Many died on the Aryan side and were buried as Gentiles. The number can therefore only be estimated by an intelligent guess. But even if we accept the figure of only twelve thousand, we are forced to conclude that the number of incidents and miracles by which those Jews survived must be beyond the comprehension of the present generation. Only when one considers that I am speaking of one single large city in occupied Europe, may one begin to understand why the dimensions of our Jewish tragedy are beyond the faculty of human understanding.

Our two families, the Gutrajchts and the Landaus, were financially well situated to be able to survive by their own means. This, however, only partially helped us. We had good contacts with decent Polish people from before the war. We had reasonably Aryan faces which escaped notice. In spite of this, not all members of our families were willing or able to take their chances outside the ghetto. Luba's mother and my father fell in the ghetto. So did my brothers and sister and several of Luba's siblings. Her sister

Helena was murdered either on the way to Treblinka or in the gas chambers there during the time I was united with Luba. Her other sister, Esther, whose child, Noemi, I had carried out of the ghetto, was murdered by Poles who wanted her to tell them where she had hidden her daughter and where the other members of her family were hiding. A witness said she would not give away the address of the nanny who had taken the child under her protection. Noemi survived and now lives in Mexico. Whoever reads these pages should take good note that after everything I have described, compared to thousands of other Jews in hiding in Warsaw, our survival was comfortable. Here and there survival was a toss-up of fate but our survival was not a continual struggle for food or even a roof over our heads. Our danger lay in those small, banal situations which in normal life would not even be noticed but for us could mean instant death.

Often, such simple matters were the catalysts that forced us to abandon one hiding place and seek a new refuge. Sometimes we had to leave a hiding place before another one was available. In spite of the best intentions of our landlords, Jurek and Zosia, it became impossible for four people to be kept permanently at Natolińska Street. One of those reasons was fear.

Across the street from us lived a man who was completely paralysed from the neck down. Every morning as soon as the curfew hour was over the caretaker was seen pushing this man out in his wheelchair into the street near the entrance of the building. The paralysed man was always well dressed, with a quilt covering the lower part of his body. There, in front of the building, he sat the whole day long without being able to move any part of his body except his head, which he could turn only partially. Mostly he sat for hours in a catatonic state hardly moving his eyes. For some obscure reason I began to believe that this man was not paralysed at all. I started to imagine that he was a Jew who had taken on this appearance as his personal disguise, hoping that this way he might escape his Jewish fate.

Once, returning from a forced outing close to the curfew hour I noticed a passing Gestapo officer turning the wheelchair around and wheeling it back into the building. My gut reaction was, would he be so kind to this man if he knew his real identity?

From that day on I was sure that my suspicion was correct, and that as well as being a Jew he was also a spy. From there I progressed to the point where I was convinced that he was observing us, and when he was sure that we were Jews in hiding he would go to the Gestapo and denounce us.

Of course I did not tell anyone this, but with every passing day I felt a stronger urge to get away from the place. My brother-in-law and his wife spoke openly about their desire to leave. They were upset by the unhygienic conditions, which were unavoidable. The toilets were not in the individual apartments but were shared. Zosia was also getting tired of having to provide food for six people and the neighbours started asking uncomfortable questions about the amount of food she brought in each day. It was all discreet, but very dangerous.

Through friends of friends who knew someone who had connections, I was introduced to a civilian German by the name of Heinrich Ebel. He had come to Warsaw in the mid-1920s as a supervising chemist for a Polish industrial complex. He had become a Polish citizen when Hitler came to power. By the time the German Army occupied Warsaw he had identified himself with the Polish people sufficiently to declare himself a Pole. For this he suffered certain deprivations which he accepted. As the war progressed he became increasingly concerned about the German atrocities and became involved in anti-Nazi work. Ebel was more than willing to help the four of us. He lived with his wife and their seven-year-old daughter in Praga, on the other side of the Wisła, which was less under the observation of the Gestapo than central Warsaw. They often had German visitors who were friendly with them because of his German origin. Although they considered him to be politically naive for not having reclaimed his German citizenship, they never suspected that he had gone so far as to work with the Underground against Hitler.

The only place he could offer us was the cellar of his home. He lived on the ground floor and, as with all Warsaw buildings, the dwelling had a cellar under the main room with the entrance consisting of two trapdoors in the floor. Normally the two wings were covered. Ebel prepared a dugout for us in the cellar where we could hide in moments of danger. But there was very little fresh air and we could only last in the dugout for half a day at the most. It was, however, a very secure place, even when the cellar had to be opened for inspection. In less threatening times, we could hide in the small timber storeroom which adjoined the main living room. Ebel had built this addition before the war and it was a primitive structure. Except for the naked boards it was totally exposed to the elements. The cracks between the boards were large enough to let us look out into the yard, although it was almost impossible to see in from outside.

When visitors arrived we were usually dispatched to the storeroom. At all other times Ebel and his wife gave us the freedom of the house. The four of us slept in one room together with his daughter, who knew that we were the invisible people about whom nothing was to be said to anybody. She kept to this rule with absolute responsibility. When her mother asked her one evening, in our presence, if she knew who the people in the room were, she turned with her back to us and said, 'Which people, Mother?' When her mother pointed towards us the young girl once more asked in a very serious voice, 'Do you feel well, Mother? There is nobody in the house except you, me and Father.'

Ebel treated us like guests in his house. He had stated the sum he needed to keep us reasonably fed; it was less than we had paid at the two previous places. Luba and I eventually went back to live with Jurek and Zosia. But not once throughout the time we were with him did we feel threatened.

The German Governor of occupied Poland once boasted to his colleagues: 'If I were to put up announcements for every Pole I am hanging, there wouldn't be enough forests in Poland to make the paper for it.' Poland was in many ways treated differently by the Germans from any other occupied country in Europe, and the Polish population behaved differently from the other nations that fell under the German swastika. Poles who were caught helping Jews in any way, be it only with a meal, were often shot without trial. If they were found hiding a Jew the most common punishment was the death of the whole family. Yet thousands of Poles gave Jews succour; even if it was for payment, it was still desperately needed help. On the other hand, Polish organisations like the NSZ (Narodowe Siły Zbrojne), the National Armed Forces, which were supposedly fighting the Germans, concentrated their forces on murdering Jews. There were also countless incidents where those who took in Jews for payment handed them over to the Polish police or the Gestapo after having obtained the Jews' money.

There was a special Jewish Department at the Polish Underground Home Army which dealt with the question of helping Jews. It had an authorised representative known by the name of Wacław, whose real name was Henryk Woliński. He represented the official Polish Underground, which took its orders from the Polish Government-in-Exile in London. Before the Uprising, he headed the committee for supplying arms for the Jews of the ghetto. At the same time, the leadership of the Home Army held back any significant help. They feared that the Uprising might spread to the Aryan side and cause damage to their own interests, which were to wait for their own Uprising at a later date. The Home Army officially welcomed Jews in their ranks. However, as history was later to prove, a secret order was sent out early in 1944 to eliminate the Jewish Underground fighters because they were suspected of helping the advancing Red Army, which was politically against the interests of the Government-in-Exile. These and many other paradoxes were part of daily life under the Germans.

I have to say that the Church in Poland did not, on the whole, look on us with a Christian spirit. It has left its anti-Jewish residue in the psyche of the Polish people to this day. Individual priests and religious orders extended help to individual Jews or even small groups, but only on their own decision. The Church leadership, which was to a large extent itself the victim of German atrocities, not only ignored but actively justified the tragic fate of the Jews. To this day, whoever speaks of the Polish people as a unit, 'the Poles', does them the same injustice as the anti-Semite does to the Jewish people when they speak of 'the Jews'.

As one who has had extensive experience of the general behaviour of the Warsaw population I would make a calculated guess that for every Pole who made any kind of an effort to help a Jewish individual, there were at least three others who made a living out of our bitter misery. In the smaller towns and villages the Polish people were the beneficiaries of the economic leftovers after the Jews had been liquidated and the Germans had taken anything that was of value to them. Of the remainder, some were indifferent or apathetic to our fate, and others feared to express themselves one way or another.

I do not want to sit in judgement on Christian and Jewish relations during those dark years in Poland. To do so, one has to be an historian of some great measure. To evaluate what happened one would have to weigh the destruction of Polish Jewry against the fact that every third Gentile who has received the honourable title of 'Righteous Gentile' from the Jewish Memorial Headquarters of Yad Vashem in Jerusalem, was a Pole.

I must also record the risks the Polish people took to hide us in their homes. I recall an incident when, in a matter of less than three minutes, I endangered the lives of our friends Jurek and Zosia and probably also the life of Luba. In peaceful times the incident would hardly have warranted a mention. The Polish people rarely celebrate a birthday; instead they celebrate on the day of the saint after whom they are named. Jurek and I, 'Janek', celebrated our

Name Day on 24 July. During wartime, when Poles had so little to celebrate, the Name Day became a good occasion for festivities with friends. Of course such festivities had to be held sometime during the afternoon as invited guests had to be in their own homes at the start of the curfew.

On 24 July 1943, I was forced to leave the security of the house to meet with Zygmunt, who had some new identity documents for me. As a Jew I did not know that this was the day when all Jureks, Janeks and Jasieks celebrated. Zygmunt, although a native Pole, obviously gave it no thought.

We met outside a bookshop which had a large glass window. From the Underground I had learned that if I had to select a meeting place in the street the best place for it was near a shop, in particular where one could look at the goods in the window and observe in the dull mirror of the glass anyone approaching from the other side. In time I came to recognise that not all large windows were good for such observation, but a bookshop was ideal. If approached unaware, I could always make out to be reading the book titles.

Zygmunt gave me the documents and I made my way home. I pressed on the door-handle, then realised I should have knocked or rung the bell, as the door was usually locked to give us time to hide in the kitchen. But the door opened. An army of eyes turned on me. The table was fully extended and around it sat twenty guests partaking in a huge feast. I knew that I had better catch the festive mood quickly, but first I had to know what was being celebrated. I might have got away with it if Zosia, who was always slightly dangerous when tipsy, had not called out, 'Ah, Jasio, you are just in time to celebrate Jurek's Name Day with us.' The moment she said it her face changed — if I was Jasio it was also my own Name Day. Obviously I should have been at my own celebration. None of the guests knew me and the situation became, if not tense, at least stiff. The air of suspicion was heavy enough to spoil the celebration. I was sure that at least some of those present had already cottoned on to my real identity. When Zosia mentioned the reason for the celebration it threw me for just long enough to give me away as somebody who could not be what he appeared to be.

Luckily Zosia also had a quick mind, which she had developed before the war when she had mixed with all sorts of people and had learned how to quickly change the subject and the atmosphere in situations like this one. She pointed her finger at me and said, 'Remain where you are for a moment.' Her voice was very friendly. She went over to Jurek, bent down and whispered in his ear. Jurek seemed to agree with her. He looked at me, smiled, leant over and whispered something to the woman on his right. As the woman smiled and bent to whisper something to the man next to her, Jurek repeated the same thing to the man on his left. I began to grow nervous. I was thinking of leaving but two things sprang to mind, forcing me to stay: the first was Luba, who was hiding in the kitchen. The second was more ominous, although I could not read its meaning: I had the feeling that those who had heard the whispered message had changed their expressions from suspicion to something more like awe or admiration.

Zosia stood at Jurek's chair and looked at me and at her guests. To every turn in her direction she nodded her head in agreement. When everybody had been told the secret she turned to me. 'Now you can come here. They are all people whom you can trust. They know now that you have come from the forest. We don't know why you have risked coming to Warsaw but obviously you know that the risk was worth it.' Then she said to the guests, 'Please fill your glasses and let us drink a toast to our boy. Ladies and gentlemen, let's drink to *Jasio z lasu*' (Jasio from the forest).

As a smile crept across my face, Zosia came over to me and quickly unbuttoned my closed jacket. Pointing to the bulge in the front of my belt she spoke triumphantly, 'This is the way our boys in the forest live. Never without a firearm.' The glasses were filled all round. Jurek rose from his seat and I was physically forced to sit down in his chair, while he sat on one side and Zosia on the other, each with a hand on my shoulder. Then, together with their eighteen guests they sang the traditional Polish song *Sto Lat*, 'May he live a hundred years'.

Of course they all wanted to know what was going on in the forest. I had regained my confidence, and I made out as if I was ready to answer any questions they asked. Some of them were innocent and could be answered with a quick invention. Most, however, were obviously too risky for a man from the forest to reveal. I listened to them all. When they had finished I smiled, stood up and very demonstratively removed the revolver and put it down. They all fell silent as I began with a joke.

'My friends, I did not remove the gun only because I trust you. I can assure you that when you carry this thing as I do day after day in the place where I carry it, you get to know what a woman feels when she is pregnant.' The joke succeeded beyond my wildest expectation. The lady who sat next to me grabbed my face and kissed me. I waited until they had all settled down once more and continued. 'I am sure the Germans would also like answers to some of the questions I have heard at this friendly table, otherwise they would not have so many jails filled with our people. But, seriously speaking, I am asking you to understand the way my forest comrades look on it. Let me first of all tell you truthfully, that if Zosia had asked me if she should reveal to you my position I would have strongly recommended that she kept her beautiful lips closed. And, we must admit that she has a very beautiful mouth, which I am sure Jurek knows how to use and appreciate. But to come back to your questions. When I decided to move out of home for the forest I only told my parents what I believed I should tell them. They too asked questions: when had I joined up? who had convinced me to take such a step? and so on. I said to them the same as I say now to you, "If you don't know the answers you won't be tempted to brag about them and, may Christ protect you, if you will be forced to answer you will not be in a position that may endanger not only our own lives but the work for which we have dedicated ourselves."

'I hope that one day we will be sitting around this table and together we will celebrate in a free, prosperous and peaceful Poland. At that time I'll be able to tell you the full story and answer your questions in a manner which will explain why I am avoiding them today. Then we will laugh and cry with tears of joy, together. Until that day, all those who do not carry guns should do three things and consider them as their personal contribution to the battle against the German swines. One — they should help with whatever they can, be it clothing for the winter cold of the Polish forest, or food or money to pay for every bullet which we spend on our national enemy. Two — those who have the privilege of being able to go to church, please pray for us with all your heart that we may survive. And three — this is the easiest thing to do, keep your mouths shut even when you are among friends. There are enough subjects to talk about without touching on anything that has to do with what goes on in places where guns are used.'

When the guests left, Zosia called Luba in from the kitchen.

'From this day onwards,' she said to me, 'I won't believe a single word you say, because you are the greatest actor and liar I have had the honour to know. In the beginning I was ready to kill you for the bragging you started. But as you went on you became brilliant.' And turning to Luba she added, 'If he were not your husband I would steal him away and make him the propaganda speaker for the whole Polish Underground.' She went over and kissed me on both cheeks and said to Luba, 'You may kiss him on his lips. Do so and remember they are his best feature.'

33

The false dawn of liberation

OUR way of hiding was in many respects different from the majority of Jews who never came in touch with the daily life in the streets of Warsaw. We lived partly open, as Catholic Poles. Our landlords could not admit that they had us as tenants; this would have been too dangerous. But we came in contact with the non-Jewish environment sufficiently to know and observe the reality of Warsaw under the Germans. We also knew something about life for the Polish people involved in the activities of the Polish Underground organisations.

The two Underground armies, the People's Army on a small scale and the Home Army on a massive one, were each preparing for the liberation of Warsaw on different bases. The People's Army was making preparations to help, from the inside, the Soviet armies take over Warsaw as soon as they reached the Wisła. The Home Army was making preparations to liberate Warsaw through an Uprising which would establish free Warsaw as the capital of the Polish people, according to the exiled Polish Government in London.

The Home Army was by far the dominant force of the Underground. During the five years of occupation it had established an army which was better prepared than the Polish Army had been at the start of the war in September 1939. While lacking in heavy military hardware it had managed to establish Underground factories with a sizeable production of light machine-guns, rifles, hand grenades and all sorts of light fighting equipment for local use. The line of command was reasonably disciplined under the prevailing conditions and the spirit of the Home Army was growing, as the eastern front moved westward. A strong administration was being prepared to run the necessary ministries until the Government-in-Exile returned.

From the beginning of warm weather in May 1944, people began to hoard products for their own needs, particularly food and soap. As if on some secret order the Polish people seemed to feel their day of liberation approaching and behaved accordingly. It is hard to say what caused this change in behaviour in Warsaw. It may have been the news of the summer offensive of the Red Army, which had begun some time in June, or the effect of that offensive which expressed itself in the movement of the German Army, mostly westward. The mighty German Army, which had entered Warsaw nearly five years earlier in the most modern vehicles, was beginning to move westward in horse-drawn wagons through the streets of Warsaw. The trains arriving in the capital carried the wounded from the approaching eastern front. No longer was it the mighty German Army, but a beaten, dispirited, morally capitulated mob which could not stand up for its honour. While the subjugated Poles spat on them as they passed through the streets of Warsaw, the German soldiers could not bring up sufficient spirit to react to the insult; preferring to ignore it.

During the second half of July it became obvious that the civil administration of Warsaw was packing up, ready to move out as soon as the Soviet Army reached the Wisła. Most striking was the lack of reaction when the propaganda arm of the People's Army published a leaflet announcing that a Polish government had been established in Lublin during the last days of July. It called on the population of Warsaw to prepare for the liberation which the Soviet Army would soon bring to the Polish nation. The Gestapo failed to activate its usual machinery to suppress the dissemination of the leaflet, even when it was carried in trams and found on tables in some restaurants. The Polish police force, which had been the long arm for German orders during the years of occupation, turned its coat and became the instrument of Polish resistance. In the main political jail, the Pawiak, the Polish guards were all agents of the Home Army, since any who had not been so had already been eliminated. It was the same in all sensitive areas where it was vital to have the right people working at the right moment.

The Germans in Warsaw were making their preparations for departure, believing that the local population would not react. A very thin defense unit was spread across the western bank of the Wisła, which divided the suburb of Praga from Warsaw proper. They were equipped only for information to the rear and not to fight even a holding battle. Their full equipment consisted of a few small cannons, like the ones they had used during the ghetto Uprising the previous year. Polish workers who served in the military airfields around Warsaw were saying that the bombers and fighters were moving to the west, leaving only a handful for the defence of Warsaw. It did not look as if the Germans had any will left to fight for the half-destroyed city.

The Polish capital would have avoided total destruction and would have been liberated some six months earlier if not for the Polish Uprising. The proclamation of the Polish Government in Lublin came only two days after an unsuccessful attempt on Hitler's life. The attempt had failed but the establishment was still reeling from the very possibility of such an act. A few days earlier the Allies had successfully landed on the western front and were moving forward towards Paris. Even the fanatic followers of the regime could see the writing on the wall — Hitler's Germany was coming to its deserved end. Warsaw was no longer worth fighting for.

Militarily there was no need at all for an uprising. The importance of it lay in politics. While the Government-in-Exile was fully aware that the western Allies had handed over the eastern part of prewar Poland to the Soviet Union, the Polish people remembered that the war had begun with the German–Russian non-aggression pact and that the Russians had stabbed Poland in the back during the autumn campaign of 1939. The history of this Russian–Polish antagonism dated back centuries. The Home Army was not ready to accept the liberation of Warsaw handed to them on a Red Army silver plate; they were not willing to pay the price for such a liberation.

On 1 August 1944, the Soviet front reached the eastern bank of the Wisła without any substantial resistance. The Polish Underground on the western side of the river began its uprising in an unusual way. It started during the afternoon rush hour, and those who had no part in the secret preparations were caught completely unaware. Around five o'clock, young men appeared in many parts of Warsaw, wearing red and white armbands and carrying rifles. They took over various key buildings of the Warsaw administration, including the phone exchange on Warecka Street. The Uprising came as a surprise to the Germans who were ready to leave the city anyway. During the first hours of the chaos which enveloped Warsaw they failed to react. The Underground army was on the verge of winning Warsaw's freedom within a day or two, as the area of the old city fell to the Home Army without a single shot being fired. The red and white Polish flags began to fly on city buildings and the Underground administration began to take some control before the Germans noticed what was happening around them. They were busy making their own preparations to escape the Russian onslaught.

It took more than a day before the situation began to change. The thinly spread German military unit on the edge of the Wisła, which was expecting the first fire from the advancing Red Army, was very surprised. The soldiers could not believe what they were seeing. At a distance of only a few hundred metres, right across the river, the approaching army had stopped, as if halting for a picnic on peacetime manoeuvres. The enemy, which was close enough to open its attack on the city with rifle fire, had called a halt to the war. It made no sense to the Germans that the advancing liberators of Warsaw had stopped in the suburbs of the city. The Underground army had started the Uprising expecting military support from their allies on the other side. The Polish military units which had reached the other bank together with the mighty forces of the Red Army were called upon to come over and help to liberate their capital, but the call of the Uprising remained unanswered on the other bank of the Wisła.

A unit of the People's Army was stationed near our apartment. As soon as the Uprising began I presented myself, gave them my Polish name and showed them that I had a gun. For the moment it was enough. The whole organisation seemed to be founded on young teenagers, the *Szare Szeregi* (the 'Grey rows'), the runners between the various units across different parts of the city who were in need of some kind of organised communication. When some twenty recruits had assembled we were marched off in a semi-orderly military column to the nearest barricade. Across from us was a street with tramlines but the line was deserted. A single carriage had already been turned over and placed across the corner, stopping any traffic the Germans might have wanted to bring up against us. Polish women came along and handed out thick slices of bread with dripping and thin slices of sausage, which we ate while guarding our positions.

For the first three days nothing happened where we were stationed. The streets in our area were in the hands of the Poles. From time to time we had some visitors who told us that very soon the first units of the Polish Army attached to the Red Army of the Soviet Union would be joining us in our fight for the liberation of Warsaw. But still nothing happened. We spent the time on guard duty smoking, talking, exchanging anecdotes and killing time in any way possible. The civilians who provided us with meals from some unknown kitchen brought news about bombardments, fights and people dying in other parts of Warsaw. They also brought news that the Red Army could be seen across the river, peacefully going on with their daily duties. Not a single shot had been fired at the German units on our side of the river.

On the morning of the fourth day we experienced the first German raid close to our positions. Two German planes flew very low over our barricades; we could see the silhouettes of the pilots in them. As soon as they passed the barricades they began firing machine-guns. The second plane came towards us, releasing a huge bomb which fell five or six buildings away from the corner where we were stationed. For the first time the war had come to us. People began running out of the surrounding apartments. Smoke and dust rose towards the sky and soon bodies were being laid out less than fifty metres from us.

An hour later we had a partial change of defenders in our barricade. Among them was a new recruit who was introduced to me as Mietek Czarny. I introduced myself as Jan Cegielski. Neither of us showed the least emotion as we recognised each other. We had lived in the ghetto close to each other and had many times gone out in the same working group. When Luba went to live on the Aryan side Mietek had also disappeared; now we met in a barricade of the Polish Uprising. We managed to take up our positions away from the others and were joined by a third man who I did not know. Before I had time to react to the stranger, Mietek (whose Jewish names I cannot recall) calmed my worries. 'It's all right; he is one of us.' We exchanged a few words and then Mietek began to explain.

'I have told my friend who you are and we decided to tell you our plans. We tried to join the Home Army and went to the local headquarters. While we were standing in the queue to register somebody tapped me on the shoulder. I turned around and recognised a Polish neighbour from before the war, who played football in our Jewish club. He was wearing his red and white armband. He asked me and my friend Jasiek to leave the queue and follow him, which we did. When we were out of earshot from the others he expressed his joy at seeing me alive and advised us to leave without joining. When we asked him why he said in a rather sad way, "We have been friends since childhood. If I would have heard your name mentioned under other circumstances I would have thought you were dead already. I am honestly pleased to see that you are still alive. I presume that you both have documents as Christians?" I assured him that we had original documents given out to us by the town hall. He was pleased. "But the situation is not normal," he said. "While the Uprising is in full swing there is some discipline. Not fully, mind you, but there is officially an order to protect Jews, take them into our lines and treat them as citizens of equal rights. Yet I have heard already of three incidents where Jews have gone out with non-Jewish soldiers on patrol duty and somehow each time, the Jews were killed while the others came back without a scratch."'

Mietek continued, explaining that his Polish friend told them they should use the time on hand to prepare a hiding place for themselves. 'It does not look as if our Red Army liberators are in a hurry to come to our rescue and without their help we will not get rid of the Germans. The time may come when Jews will have to go into hiding once more.' From Mietek's story I found out that they had begun to build a bunker for themselves not far from Natolińska where Luba was living, although no longer with Zosia and Jurek. The men had wanted to join the Home Army because they were short of food and hoped that the army would feed them. However, they had heard that Jews were more secure in the People's Army and had come to this group. After the duty hours they were going to make their way back to help work on the bunker. They invited me to join them if I wished, provided I had something to contribute.

Once more we were bombarded, just as we were handed our meagre sandwiches. This time people were killed at our very position. We spent the afternoon pulling out the dead and the living from the rubble. The barricades were left unattended. Late in the evening we slipped away and disappeared under darkness into the ruins. On the city map, we had only some two kilometres to walk to the place where the bunkers were being built. In darkened Warsaw, where streets were no longer recognisable and the rubble was piled up, the short walk was a nightmare. Jasiek was our guide and knew the way we could pass. It took us close to three hours, crawling, climbing over ruins and journeying around, to reach our destination.

We entered what looked like the opening of a cave and saw a faint flicker of light coming from the depths. A group of men was busy enlarging a basement room. I was introduced to the others and Mietek told them all he knew about me and that I had come to join them. I corrected him, pointing out that I had a wife who would also have to be accepted if we should ever need to use the bunker. The man who seemed to be in charge quipped, 'Do you think that God has forgotten that Jews have to live in bunkers? We will be here for sure. First while the Germans remain and later because . . . because . . .' he did not finish the sentence.

The three of us were too tired to do much work. I lay down on some old rags. I can still recall the few hours sleep on that first night away from the barricades. There we had slept pressed together like sardines and here in the unfinished bunker I had a straw sack all to myself. Not even the dirt and the lice could disturb my rest.

In the morning I confirmed with the others that I would be busy each day. Only during the night, when the work went on, would I be able to come and do my share. The others, it turned out, did the same thing. We could not accomplish much during the hours of daylight anyhow, as every step of the plan had to be kept secret from undesirable eyes. Having arranged to return in the evening to do my share, I left to visit Luba. The house was untouched and the water supply had so far remained undamaged. It gave me the long dreamed of opportunity to have a decent wash. Having slept well and after a hot bath I felt revived. Our landlady brought out bread and a hot thick soup for me. I ate and talked with Luba and the landlady. Her husband had left home on the first day of the Uprising and joined the Home Army; she thought I should do the same. Somehow, I finished up taking her advice despite what Mietek had told me. The army quarters were close to Natolińska and since nobody was sent on guard duty or any other mission outside the local perimeter of their unit, I thought this would give me the opportunity to be close to Luba.

The local headquarters of the Home Army were a far cry from the drab and impoverished establishment of the People's Army. The building was guarded outside by four men in semi-military attire; civilian trousers but military jackets. Two were guarding the entrance, while the others were attending to the queue of men and women who were waiting to enter.

Once people reached the front of the queue they had to present their documents, identify themselves and answer some questions. If they passed the first examination they were guided to the other side of the building where their documents were then handed over to another soldier. When the name in the documents was called the individual was asked to join a short queue waiting to enter the building. It was all very orderly. In less than a quarter of an hour I had reached the front of the queue. I presented my documents which stated that I was Jan Cegielski, and showed my revolver. I was asked why I had not joined earlier. I had already prepared my answer: I had gone to the city of Łowicz where my sister was to be married on 5 August. Having heard that Warsaw was fighting for its liberation I made my way back to join them because I was a son of this city. It had taken me the last three nights to get myself into the city through the German ring, without falling into German hands. My reply was accepted.

Unlike others who had to wait in the second queue, I was taken to one of the guards; a few words were exchanged between the two men and I was told to enter and present myself to the officer outside the last room on the left. I walked into a long corridor with rooms on both sides. At the last door, a soldier in civilian dress with the red and white armband sat at a table. He asked what kind of weapon I had and I showed him my revolver.

'How many bullets have you got for this thing?'

'Plenty.'

'And how much is plenty? Ten, twenty or a few hundred?'

'I have two full boxes but not on me,' I answered.

He asked me to wait and went into the room, then returned and asked me to go in. The room was empty except for a table and two chairs. An officer sat at the table with his name and rank of captain written in neat handwriting on a small board. Some documents were on the table. As I entered he asked me to sit down, without lifting his eyes from the paper he held in his hand. I obeyed.

While still reading he asked, 'Have you been sworn in already as a soldier?'

I was surprised by the question. 'No, sir. I have not been told anything except that I have to come to this room.'

'But you have your own weapon, right?'

Again I agreed. He lifted his eyes, looked at me, and then back at the paper. Then he muttered a word which would have had no meaning to me if I were not Jewish. If I were a Pole I would have thought I had misheard. '*Umchu*,' the officer said as if addressing the papers he was shifting.

'*Umchu*,' I repeated. The word is Hebrew for 'Thy People', and it had been widely used between Jews during the Holocaust years to recognise each other in uncertain circumstances. He put down his papers and looked straight at me. He did not say anything about the exchange we had just had. He asked for my identity document and ordered me to stand up. 'Repeat after me: "I"'

I repeated, 'I.'

'Now state your name.'

I hesitated. Having told him that I was '*Umchu*' I was not sure if he wanted me to state my real name, David Landau, or the name in the document. For a moment there was complete silence. I was afraid to ask which name to give. Finally, with a sigh, he helped me: 'I, Jan Cegielski . . .' Relief flooded through me. After the ordeal was over he rang a hand bell. The guard at the door came in and stood at attention without saluting. 'Corporal,' the Captain addressed him, 'make out the papers for Private Jan Cegielski who has been sworn in at this office, to our military hospital, stating that Private Cegielski is to be stationed as the military guard until a full contingent is available. Address the papers to the hospital chaplain, Franciszek Młody, and bring them back to me.' I was ordered to sit down and wait. There was silence in the room while I was waiting. The Captain was absorbed in his papers. Only once did he speak, not even looking up at me. 'Father Franciszek Młody is *Umchu* but don't say anything unless he speaks about it first.'

The Corporal brought back my papers and handed them to the Captain saying, 'Captain, I am reporting that Private Jan Cegielski has at his private address two boxes of bullets which are now army property. I have made out the papers for Private Cegielski to report to the hospital late this afternoon, to enable him to go home and take the two boxes to the hospital and hand them over to Father Młody'.

The Captain looked slightly concerned. 'Did you say in the document that he has to hand the boxes over to the chaplain?'

'No, sir. I am only reporting that the Private has property which now belongs to the army.'

The Captain seemed relieved. 'Thank you, Corporal, you may go.' As the Corporal was leaving the Captain spoke to me, 'Private Cegielski, I am leaving the military property of two boxes of bullets for your revolver in your care, as a guard at our military hospital. You are to remove them from your private address and place them in a secure place at the hospital where you'll be stationed. You'll be personally responsible for their safekeeping. Should you in any way fail this order, you'll be court-martialled in accordance with the army rules governing the Army of the Polish Republic during wartimes. The court would be empowered, if it would see fit, to have you shot for disobeying a military order which may endanger the safety of the soldiers you have been ordered to care for. Do you understand what I have just said?' I understood and said so in my best military language.

I had just received my first order as a soldier. I was dismissed and *Umchu* was never again mentioned.

34

Hospital days

DURING the first week of the Uprising I learned little about its extent. Living, working, eating and sleeping in the confinement of four buildings didn't allow for much information to pass through to me. The only news I had heard was that the Red Army was expected in Warsaw at any time. Then, after the first three or four days, I was told that we could not expect any help from the other side of the Wisła, where our 'liberators' had decided to camp and relax. Warsaw's besieged state was unlike anything since the days of September 1939, when Hitler gave the order to make Poland his playground.

Once more the German bombers had begun to sow their terror. Once more whole streets had been devastated in the city which had once won the name 'The Paris of the East'. Turned over tram-trolleys were everywhere. Here and there I came across horse carcasses in the middle of the road with the flesh cut off them. The atmosphere of the streets had changed. They were nearly all empty except for young people, the fuel of the insurrection. The few civilians walking around outside wore the immediacy of the war on their faces.

I walked from the local army headquarters back to Natolińska Street feeling change with every step. I turned into the street at the opposite end from the Gestapo Headquarters. They must have left in a hurry or been overrun. Not a single German in uniform was to be seen anywhere. The man from across the street who had always sat paralysed in his chair was no longer sitting outside the gate. Like some satire I saw him the moment I had begun thinking about him: he came out from the building opposite ours, walking like any other person. He had a red and white armband and a light machine-gun hanging across his breast. Our eyes met for a second. I was ready to greet him but as quickly as he had seen me he looked away. I realised that he was also *Umchu* but he was not sure about me and he didn't want to risk being recognised.

I hadn't much time to spend with Luba. She had not expected me to stay with her for very long and had prepared for our separation as soon as I had appeared. She had packed shirts, socks, a change of underwear and some warm clothing for me. The landlady produced half a dried salami as a departing gift. In all of these preparations I nearly forgot the most important thing — the bullets. The landlady left us alone for the last few minutes and I said an emotional goodbye to Luba. Her words remain with me to this day. 'David, I don't want to lose you now, when we are so close to our deliverance as Jews and as human beings.' With those words ringing I left without turning back to her.

As I went out into the street a young man of the *Szare Szeregi* came towards me. He had an envelope in his hand and he signalled to me. He looked down at the sealed document and asked, 'Are you Private Jan Cegielski?' I identified myself and he gave me the sealed document. It stated that the courier who brought it would guide me to the hospital, as the direct way had been overrun by a German unit soon after I had been assigned to my post.

We were stopped twice before we reached the hospital. Twice we had to identify ourselves and twice I had to show the military order. Since the time in which my guide had received his instructions the Germans had encircled the area to split the different units of the Uprising. They made no effort to destroy them at this stage. We had come close to the front of the action. We crossed many demolished courtyards and deserted streets; apartment blocks where only a couple of walls were still standing. As we made our way slowly towards the hospital, I began to understand the dimensions of the catastrophe taking place in the city. Everywhere there were small markings of fresh graves which had been dug as provisional resting places for the many who could not be buried in the cemeteries. A few field flowers had been placed on some, others carried primitive wooden crosses, with or without names on them. Over one grave an old woman had spread herself in an effort to cover the body of whoever was buried there. As we passed near her she lifted her head towards us. She looked more like a black bird dying over the grave, than a human being.

I was late in coming to the hospital and it was now evening. My guide saluted as he left me at the door and I walked up the steps alone. I remembered the building from before the war. It was one of the well-known hospitals and seemed miraculously untouched within the destroyed surroundings. I wondered why it was showing its light in such an unguarded fashion and decided to bring it to the attention of the priest, but first I had to find him. The information desk was working. An invalid, with crutches near his chair, was on duty. I asked him about the open lights and he just smiled. 'You'll know it in time. It's all right. The light is on for our protection.' A nurse wearing a starched white apron as if there were no war going on, led me up the few steps near the reception desk. From somewhere above our heads somebody started to scream. We both looked up towards the direction of the cries. Then the nurse continued and I held my step behind her until we reached the hospital's chapel. I thanked her and went in.

The chapel was dimly lit. In front of a small altar a priest was kneeling. I wondered if Franciszek Młody was kneeling before a Christian altar or if there were some other priests as well. I sat down in one of the pews and waited. When the priest rose from his prayer I recognised him and knew he would not know me. He was Jewish but he had converted to Catholicism long before the war. I knew him as one of the priests who had been serving in the ghetto church to the converted Jews, whom the Germans would not exempt from their Jewish heritage. He was *Umchu* only as far as the racial laws were concerned. I had not been brought up in any religious sense but this much I had learned already in my childhood: one could be Jewish or Christian, but not both at the same time, not even under the Germans.

I gave him the papers and he was pleased to have me. While still in the chapel we started to talk. Father Franciszek was of the opinion that the hospital could have been an island of happiness in the midst of tragedy, but for two things: it should have had plenty of medicine and no patients. Unfortunately the reverse was true; there was no medicine and plenty of patients, nearly all surgical and too many of them without hope. 'In the last days,' he told me, 'we have averaged about thirty new patients a day and an average of twenty-five deaths. This should give you an idea about the state of the hospital.' I asked about the lights being left open to the outside and the priest became animated. 'The lights and you are part of us being left in peace. I am glad that you are here, because up till now I have had nobody to look after our most precious patients who have been here since we took over the hospital. I had been praying for a man like you, just before you came in. You see how quickly God sometimes answers our prayers?'

I did not have the heart to correct his illusion, however I had to say, 'Father, I am not a doctor. The papers state clearly that I am a soldier.'

'I know, I know. I can read the order. You are what I need here, a soldier. You see, we have here five German soldiers. They were wounded in the first skirmish during the earliest hours of the insurrection, at the telephone exchange. The Red Cross let the Germans know that they were in our hands and are receiving the best medical care we can give them under the circumstances. Now you may understand why we keep the light on. The five Germans and the light are our best insurance against being attacked.'

'And where do I come in on all this?'

'It will be your duty to guard them like the eyes in your head. If anything should happen to them we would be — like this,' he put his hand across his throat. I understood.

Before I began my guard duties the priest showed me around the hospital. It had sufficient linen to keep running for a while. The basement laundry, I was told, was working reasonably well and so was the kitchen. The representatives of the Swiss Red Cross had used the German soldiers to obtain a delivery of basic foods, but when it came to medicine the Germans had nothing to offer.

We went into the first-floor operating theatre which was being cleaned following a limb amputation. It was the source of the screams I had heard earlier. The nurse explained that there was some chloroform available but only for serious internal operations. Limb amputations were performed without anaesthetic. The wounded were strapped in a cradle which was bolted to a special frame, and they were given some alcohol before the amputation began. I could not hold back my astonishment. 'But I heard the screams from downstairs. How do you stand it?'

'We have enough cottonwool to plug our ears and carry on with sign language. Besides, the saws make enough noise,' he replied.

By the time Father Franciszek had taken me around the wards and I had seen the yellow faces of the dying and the critically wounded, I was sorry for not having stopped the priest showing me so much hospitality. The German prisoner–patients were the hospital scoop of the Uprising. While we heard the sounds of war around us, the hospital was protected by both sides. Once a single bomb fell outside the entrance but to our good fortune it did not explode. When I asked the priest why no other German patients had been delivered after the first five, he smiled and said, 'Other places also need some protection.'

A few times I had to defend my enemy patients from being attacked by people who had good cause to hate them. Each time I did it more through explanation than by lifting my revolver.

During the daytime I was at the hospital and three nights a week

I helped build the bunker. Only God knows how I had the strength to accomplish it, or how I found my way from the hospital to the bunker and even more so, my way back to the hospital. But obviously I had not yet reached the end of my energy.

The hospital atmosphere became increasingly morbid as the situation of the fighters became more desperate and the flow of wounded and dead slowly overwhelmed the hospital's resources. It began with beds appearing in the passages and continued with wounded lying on the ground without even straw sacks to insulate them from the stone floor. Three or four times a day the medical arm of the army brought in the wounded and removed the dead. No civilians were admitted to us, partly because we were a military hospital and partly out of fear that something would happen to our insurance — the Germans.

When I first appeared the German patients had been frightened. They were sure that the hospital would eventually deal with them the way their people had dealt with us. It took a few days and the handing over of Red Cross parcels to calm their fears. They never knew the reasons for our behaviour but they began to ingratiate themselves to the Polish people, believing that I was a Pole. Sometimes it was sickening the way they tried to acknowledge how human the Polish people were. They were full of 'ifs'. If only they had known before how decent the Poles were, if only Hitler hadn't, if only they could in some way make good. I kept my mouth shut but often, after such compliments, I thought, if only I could cut your throats.

During the six weeks that I spent at the hospital I saw Luba only once. It was the one free day I was granted throughout the whole time. I was given the day off to save the life of Jurek's wife Zosia. Luba had been in contact with Jurek and Zosia throughout the Uprising. During one visit Polish soldiers arrived at Zosia's house and read her an accusation that she had been friendly with the Germans throughout the occupation. She was accused of having been a collaborator with the enemy and had been, according to the rules of martial law, sentenced to be shot. Luba was with her during the whole procedure and the reading of the sentence. The two women could not believe their ears. Both explained that their husbands were taking part in the Polish Uprising, both were fighting as soldiers. It was Luba's presence of mind that held back the execution of the sentence. 'You are soldiers and our husbands are soldiers,' she pleaded. 'We don't know the whereabouts of Zosia's husband, but my husband is guarding the military hospital. He is a Home Army soldier and we have been friends and coming to their place for more than two years. Zosia knew that my husband worked in the Underground. She often hid documents and arms for the Underground. There must have been some mistake or false information.'

I was contacted at the hospital. The soldier who brought the information gave me a one-day release from duty, requiring me to appear at the local military quarters near Zosia's home. I was glad to repay her for all she had done for us and also for the opportunity to see Luba. Zosia had been taken into custody and her head had been shaved already. But before I saw her I was thoroughly interrogated. I was walking a tightrope, not knowing what they knew about me and where I could make myself sound more important than I really was. But the questions, although thorough, did not touch the points I was afraid of, namely how long I had been in the Home Army. When my identity was accepted I was asked about Zosia. I made it sound the best I could. 'It is true that Germans came to her house, often. Before the war, she had been a public relations officer at the airport and she speaks fluent German, French and some other languages. She had once worked for Marshal Piłasudski as his personal secretary. I was present twice when German guests visited because I had come for military matters and they came for entertainment. Of course, they did not know who I was. Under the oath I made as a soldier of the Polish Republic, I say with a clear conscience that the accused used the Germans for the benefits of our cause. I do not deny that she received gifts from such visits, but I wish to state that with those gifts she helped many who were Underground fighters for the same cause that you, gentlemen, and I, are fighting now. Her association with Germans as such, never existed.'

After that speech Zosia was brought to the room. I wept when I saw her with shaven head. She did not know how things had gone and believed that I had come to say goodbye to her before the execution. She embraced me and thanked me for coming. The officer in charge waited for a few minutes and then told her in a most friendly way that she should thank her lucky stars for having me as her friend. We could leave after my statement was written out and my military number quoted. I had to sign it and was asked to take Zosia home, as she could have been attacked by strangers because of her shaved head. Zosia, Luba and I sat at her place for the rest of the day. We laughed, cried and retold the incident with the German Gestapo officer I had threatened with my revolver.

The next day I was back at the hospital, where I continued to fulfil my duties until it became necessary to look after Luba and myself.

35

In a bunker again

THE Warsaw insurrection had begun at the peak of summer, in August 1944. It ended in the first grey days of autumn, when the cold rains arrived. Our mood changed with the season. By the beginning of September it had become clear that the Uprising was a lost cause. The official number of people dead and wounded during the month of fighting was given as forty thousand, mostly civilians. Freshly dug graves studded around courtyards became a common sight. Provisional hospitals sprang up everywhere, lacking even the minimum of medical facilities. The smell of death was hanging over the doomed city and the mood of the people was dark.

The Soviet Army maintained its position across the Wisła without firing a single shot. The Germans were able to take their time and revenge on the inhabitants of Warsaw for having dared to rise up and attempt to bring their own deliverance an hour earlier than the final German defeat. The beaten German Army, which had two months earlier begun to retreat from the western bank of the Wisła, now made a turnabout, not in order to build the defence of the city, but to satisfy its bloodthirsty greed for murder, destruction and revenge. Even at our hospital, which had better provisions than the rest of besieged Warsaw, the situation had become very difficult, if not desperate. I considered my duty there as a blessing in disguise. Luba could come from time to time for a relatively decent meal and I had been spared from fighting in the ruins, or worse.

By the end of September our German patients no longer spoke of the decent Poles. Their talk began to fill with the favours they would do us when the Uprising was crushed and their army once more brought order to Warsaw. They spoke of the protection they would give me by telling their superiors that I, although a soldier of the Uprising, behaved decently towards them and should be spared from the fate of the others. Each time they told me of their gratitude I asked myself silently the same question, 'How would you sons of bitches behave if you were told that I am a Jew?'

It was a day at the very end of September: I had finished my night duty, the nurses had washed the Germans and had fed them their gruel. I became aware that my relief had not arrived. I began to grow concerned. I became even more worried when, half an hour after the end of my shift, no one came to relieve me. Angry, tired and worried, I closed the door from the inside, moved the chair over to it and sat down. My patients began to show signs of fear and I calmed them by telling them the truth, that I was tired, my replacement had not yet arrived and I would like to rest for a short while. They understood and became very considerate.

I was awakened by the noise of a megaphone which had started up right outside the window. Within seconds I was wide awake and listening to its announcement.

'Attention, attention! Soldiers of the Polish Uprising and inhabitants of Warsaw, attention! The Uprising has ended. A document of surrender has been signed by the Commander of the Polish forces. In accordance with the Geneva Convention all those who have taken part in the Uprising will be regarded as prisoners of war and will not be treated in any way other than that established by the Geneva Convention for prisoners of war. The civilian population of Warsaw will present themselves to the German authorities together with the Polish soldiers, to be evacuated from

Warsaw, which has been declared a military closed area. The area is to be cleared in the next seventy-two hours beginning at six o'clock this morning.

'Soldiers of the Uprising and inhabitants of Warsaw! No harm will come to you for what has happened in this city during the last two months. The soldiers will present themselves with the civilian population, handing over their weapons at points which will be given at the end of this announcement. No fighters are to present themselves to the German forces in military formation. I repeat: fighters will present themselves with their personal weapons, as individuals together with the civilian population and not in any military formation. The evacuation will begin today at ten o'clock. The German authorities expect the evacuation to pass peacefully. They will receive the civilians and the soldiers at the following street crossings . . .'

I had to translate to the Germans what had just been proclaimed. I assured them that no harm would come to them as the Polish soldiers would have to remain with them in the hospital. They then started to assure me that I would be protected from anything that might go wrong and that I should stay with them. I thanked them for the goodwill but rejected their offer.

I went to see Father Franciszek. He had heard the proclamation and was not surprised when I told him that my replacement had not turned up for duty. He showed great understanding when I told him that now, without a Polish military command, I no longer saw myself duty bound to continue guarding the Germans. As if to underline his understanding he said, 'If I were not a priest who has to keep faith with my flock, I would also leave, rather than stay here and present myself to the Germans, but I cannot leave those who depend on me for their faith. I'll pray for you as long as I'm able.' He opened his arms and embraced me. As he released his embrace he added a single sentence: 'You understand why I would also leave if I could do it with a clear conscience; but I can't.'

On my way out, I remembered that in one of the drawers in the service room we kept the armbands with the official stamps of the guards. In a moment of impulse I put them all in my pocket, justifying my action by thinking that they would no longer be of use to anybody at the hospital and somebody might misuse them. I had no other clear idea why I was taking them. With my bag, the armbands and my revolver tucked under my belt I left. I never saw Father Franciszek again and, although I made inquiries about him later when Warsaw was in the hands of the Soviet Army, nobody could give me any information about his fate. He probably died, because he was the son of Jewish parents. But did he consider himself a Jew?

We had finished preparing the bunker only days before the insurrection finally collapsed. We had dug a well in the centre; it had been my idea and in the end also my own work with the help of one man. The opening I had seen during my first visit to the bunker had been replaced by a small camouflaged hole through which we had to slide horizontally, one person at a time. A similar opening had been prepared at the other end. Through our bunker we had an entry to the sewer canals of Warsaw, which had been used successfully during the ghetto Uprising. We had planned to tap the electricity cables but the whole city was now without electricity. For illumination we had collected candles, which according to our calculations would last us a week or even longer; enough to see us through until the population had left and the Germans were gone. The bunker was large by any standard and well fitted out. We had knocked out walls from basement to basement until we had a number of connecting rooms. The floors had been covered with boards over which we laid carpets we had taken during the night from destroyed buildings. We had fitted out one of the larger rooms as a sleeping room on three levels. We had also selected the driest room and covered the walls and floors with furs and good bedding; again taken from bombed buildings which had been abandoned. The accommodation was organised to give everyone a small space but sufficient privacy. There was enough room for the fifteen men and five women to stay together in the bunker for some time without getting on each other's nerves. Something we could not provide were flushing toilet facilities. We had to use buckets which we intended to empty each night. The camouflaged entrance to the bunker could be closed from the inside, and it would not be opened for anybody who didn't know the secret signal. Everything was prepared as it should be and ready for us.

The curfew had been enforced once more and the streets were cleared before nightfall. A few hours later, during the first night of the evacuation of the city, we arrived silently to take up residence in the bunker. We felt a strange kind of security in our cave. We lit a candle and, sitting close to each other, we began to analyse our situation. We had ignored the most important thing we needed for our survival: weapons to defend ourselves. I was the only one who had a revolver and bullets. We had all brought some food to last us for three to four days and knew that after the people living above us had left, we would find all the food we needed for our survival.

We were concerned, however, about arms, and began to make plans to obtain some. One after the other we came up with ideas which turned out to be impossible to realise. We had all been living under stress for years and during the last two months the strain on our nerves had been multiplied many fold. By the time the candles allotted for the first night burned down we had not come up with any feasible ideas. We decided to sleep on the problem and come up with something the next day.

The answer came to me in my sleep and I awoke filled with adrenaline. I woke four men and took them silently to the other room where I put my plan to them. 'By tomorrow we can have all the arms we need if my plan is right.' I had brought with me the white and red armbands which identified Polish officialdom. The population of Warsaw had begun to leave the city. At eight in the morning they were going to renew the exodus, civilians and soldiers alike, with the soldiers carrying their arms to hand them over to the Germans. I proposed: 'We will put on the official armbands and place ourselves at the side of the road, some two streets before the German control, as though we are part of the army. When somebody comes along with an automatic or even semi-automatic gun we will ask them to give it to us for our collection, assuring him that he is leaving it in the right hands. If we play our roles well we will collect more than enough arms and be thanked for it.'

By the time we had refined the plan we were sufficiently excited to start immediately. It was already near dawn when we slid out of the bunker one after the other. The streets were deserted; neither Poles nor Germans were to be seen. We made our way to the point where we had decided to take up our position and hid inside a bombed-out building. A few minutes before eight an announcer came along the road, calling for the population to begin to assemble for departure. The caller issued the same demands as the day before, adding that all Poles were bound by the same national fate, the stronger should help the weaker and that those who believed they could keep order should try to do so. The men who carried arms were reminded to hand them in to German control.

To our astonishment and delight we heard the announcer add: 'It is desirable to declare oneself a soldier of the Uprising even without arms, as representatives of the Swiss Red Cross will be present at some points to accept you.'

The streets came to life. People appeared from buildings, mostly in family groups with parcels in their hands, or on homemade carts, in baby carriages and slung across bicycles. When the queue began to snake in front of us and back for some hundreds of metres we made our appearance, armed with our white and red armbands. People in the long queue began to notice us.

We asked the first man carrying a semi-automatic gun to leave it with us but he hesitated. In response the civilians around us encouraged him to do as we wanted. 'Leave it with them, give it to our boys,' they said. The man following him put his rifle down next to it. We were in danger of collecting an avalanche of weapons we did not want. I walked back a few rows and began to speak to those who were carrying arms and had noticed our action. 'Give your rifle to the Germans,' I advised those who had simple rifles, 'they are of no use to us.' Where I saw a light machine-gun or some similar weapon with bands of ammunition I told the man discreetly, 'I am Lieutenant Jan Cegielski. In the name of the Polish fighting forces I ask you to put down your weapon and the bullets at the feet of the soldiers there in front of you and move on with the others.'

The ruse worked far beyond our expectations. After the first five minutes I had to order two of my 'soldiers' to carry the arms to the nearest building. Within half an hour we had collected enough to fit out a whole platoon with semi-automatic and automatic arms. Together we saluted the marching people as we gathered the last arms and disappeared into the building. With two or three pieces of our substantial collection we made our way back to the bunker. Making sure that we were no longer observed we managed to get back into the bunker in daylight together with our arms. It was the first and last time that anybody moved in or out of the bunker during the day.

While the Soviet Army, apparently on Stalin's orders, stopped on the eastern bank of the Wisła to watch with shameless indifference, the Germans, deadly enemies of the Soviet Union, murdered the Union's allies, the Polish people of Warsaw, and step by step destroyed their capital. The people were forced to abandon the city until the Soviet Army took control.

Except for a few Christians, the bunkers were practically all occupied by Jews. Joining the exodus of seven hundred thousand Poles was, in practical terms, equal to committing suicide. Jews had experienced the Warsaw ghetto, and those who had been in hiding on the Aryan side were familiar with the system. With the option of going to the bunkers or joining the Polish exodus, Jews in general believed they had a better chance of survival in the bunkers. Everyone knew that the bunkers would be of no value if the Germans were to remain for weeks on end. However, we were sure that once the people were taken out of Warsaw the Germans would abandon it and let the Soviet Army take over, which would happen in days. For such a short time bunkers were the better choice.

Under these circumstances it was inevitable that we would know of each other's plans. In our group, more than half had been receiving assistance from the Jewish and/or the Polish Underground. Through such contacts we knew of many places where other Jews were living underground, and an informal organisation came into being. Although only the closest and most trusted friends knew the precise location of each other's bunkers, we had sufficient knowledge of where and how we could keep contact to exchange information and goods. As time went on the net of contacts grew to such an extent that we used the boxes of the electricity system as post boxes.

By the second night of the exodus the city was nearly empty. We went out to collect the arms we had left hidden. We also began to search the basements for food. The population of Warsaw had been living for some weeks in the basements of buildings for safety, and they had stored in them most of their staple food, both for use and to prevent it from being stolen. On our first night out we managed to bring back all the weapons and a good supply of food. We had attached pipes to one of the chimney openings in the walls of our bunker. After dark we lit a fire in the stove and cooked our first meal in the belief that the smoke would not be noticed. Unknown to us, the smoke was visible and could have given us away. We waited two or three nights before we dared move out of the bunker again. We could observe outside movements from our hiding place without being detected.

Our careful observations were important: after the second night we noticed that movement in the street above had decreased as the exodus continued. On the fourth day, when we had expected the deportation to have ended and the Russians to have crossed the Wisła, we were astonished to see German military uniforms through our lookout. Dressed in their long green winter coats, they led a row of horse-drawn carts with Polish drivers within metres of our bunker. We froze as we heard the carts pass practically over our heads. By nightfall they were gone. As we slid out of our bunker we could see the flicker of flames; two tall buildings near us were on fire. It did not take us long to realise that the Germans had brought in the carts and the Polish workers to remove bedding, furniture and anything else of value that could be taken from the empty buildings. After a few nights we found out how they set the buildings on fire; in each case the fire had been ignited in the basement, fed by loose bedding and old furniture, which the Germans must have considered not worth stealing.

A man in our group offered to build a crystal radio if we could supply the necessary crystal. We had no crystal, but somebody offered to hand over a diamond if it could be used instead. Our radio man said he had never built a crystal radio with a diamond but he was willing to try. In two or three days he had built the most expensive crystal radio in Europe. We attached a thin antenna and listened to the first broadcast as if it was magic. It was a limited radio and we could only hear the Raszyn station which was some thirty kilometres from Warsaw on the German side. The radio remained our closest contact with the situation around us for a long time. The station went off air on 12 or 13 January 1945, and caused us some serious problems in the last days; but that is a different story.

There were many curious, tragic, comic and dangerous situations connected with our life as moles. At one stage, a few nights after the city had been emptied of its population, we went out to look for food. We walked with our feet tied in rags to dampen our footsteps. We came across a paddock with some goats and cows in it. After a quick debate we decided not to touch the sleeping animals. Some fifteen minutes later I thought I could hear somebody calling for help, but the others could not hear anything. As we walked I became convinced I was hearing somebody calling faintly. It was a cold but dry night and on my insistence we separated. I went on alone in the direction of the call and the others went on their way. As I walked the call became clearer. I reached a destroyed house and could now hear the faint but clear call coming from close under the ruins. Carefully I began to remove the rubble and to my relief I found an exhausted man buried not far from the surface. He was truly on his last legs. I managed to pull him out. All he could say was, 'I am Eddy Jagodziński. My brother is buried among the ruins.' He believed his brother was already dead, as he had not heard him call out for some time. Jagodziński could not tell me how long he had been buried. He did not know about the evacuation or the end of the Uprising, so he must have been there for at least a week. I put him on my back and carried him like a pack all the way to the bunker. By the time I reached it those inside had begun to worry about me. I gave the appropriate signal and they opened the entrance. From the outside I could hear the reaction: instead of watching me crawling in they faced the head of a stranger who looked more dead than alive. They heard my voice and pulled him in.

Eddy Jagodziński looked gravely ill. I was wondering what we might be able to feed him in his state. I remembered the paddock we had passed; without telling anybody anything I decided to give him goat's milk. The next night I went back to the paddock. There was a German sentry hut but it was empty. The Germans were confident that nobody was around to steal the animals; they were wrong. I had brought a length of rope with me. I checked out the sleeping goats, and when I found one with a full udder I dropped hard on it and grabbed it by the muzzle to keep it from making any noise. It took some time to subdue the animal. It fought for all it could while I fought for my life — any noise would have given me away. I learned a very valuable lesson from that experience: an animal will fight for as long as it believes it can escape. Once it knows it cannot get away it stops struggling and lets itself be handled. After a struggle which it nearly won, the goat gave up. It let me tie its feet and let itself be lifted onto my shoulders without resisting. I carried it on my shoulders all the way back to the bunker just as I had carried Jagodziński the night before. For a few days we kept the goat for milking. The milk did wonders for Jagodziński. But it was impossible to keep the faithful animal for long in our circumstances; we slaughtered it after ten days.

It was quite a problem as nobody wanted to kill the poor animal. When the first meat meal came to the table one of the women said, 'We feast like ancient cannibals, to gain strength from our murdered goat.' We did not know whether to cry or laugh.

As it turned out, we had to live in our bunkers for three and a half months. A great number of Jews died during that time from starvation, frost, disease and unforeseen circumstances. And many were discovered by the Germans.

Eddy Jagodziński survived. He came in 1993 to Warsaw with his children and in-laws to greet me at the fiftieth anniversary of the ghetto Uprising commemoration.

36

Freedom

THE word 'eerie' in English could have been invented for the desolated ruins of Warsaw after its remaining seven hundred thousand inhabitants had been removed. The only people left in the Polish capital after the expulsion of its legitimate inhabitants formed the two illegitimate extremes. The streets of the city were inhabited by dogs — the Germans, who systematically emptied the buildings of anything valuable then put them to the torch. Berlin had decreed that Warsaw was to be erased from the map of Europe before the Germans left.

Under the ground, Jews inhabited caverns and bunkers, like moles, eking out a wait which stretched into three and a half months. A few hundred Jews were daring to defy the fury of the Germans.

Our large bunker was one of the better ones: comfortable, roomy, but ultimately unsafe. We had become concerned about the escape facilities. Whenever we heard conversations taking place over our heads, only metres from our camouflaged entrance, we became afraid even to breathe. Loading our weapons, we waited. For a whole day the noise went on without interruption. Before dusk we heard carts move off in the direction of the entrance and then drive further away. Late that night two men went out through the front entrance to inspect the rear escape way. They found it buried under tonnes of rubble. They returned very concerned;

there was no way we could move it all away without it being noticed by the Germans. The next day the noise was back and that evening when we sent the two men out again, they came back to tell us that although there were buildings on fire not far from us, the cooking smoke coming from our chimney could still be distinguished. We decided to enlarge the bunker by the same method we had originally built it, by tunnelling and going from one basement to another.

That night three of us went out to look for an empty ruin where we could begin to dig from the basement towards our bunker. The nearest suitable place was approximately a kilometre from our exit. We chose it because three quarters of the distance consisted of basements. The general opinion was to start working the next night and to dig from both ends.

I offered to go to the other end with a man I liked as company; we got on well together and had many common interests. We knew that we would be separated from the others for many days. During the day we packed up tools, food and a stack of candles and carbide. In the afternoon the weather changed; the first snows began to fall. Through our spy-opening we watched the snow pile higher and higher. It was coming down like soft bedding; the bedding of death. How could we leave the bunker without our footprints being noticed? Somebody was of the opinion that footprints wouldn't matter, there would also be the footprints of the Germans, the Poles and the horses going in all directions. It was plausible but not convincing. Our footprints would lead straight back to this bunker and to the other end, which was an empty building where nobody was supposed to be living.

It appeared that our plan was lost. But one of the women came up with an invention. She suggested making flat-board soles with long nails attached to them, which we could tie to the soles of our shoes. At first we laughed at the idea. But having nothing better proposed, we found some suitable board and made two shoes with long nails pointing downward towards the snow. I was impatient to see how they would work. As soon as it became dark I volunteered to go outside. Taking some rags to muffle my footsteps I slid out through the front and found it hard to stand up on my platform of long nails. But having stood I was pleasantly surprised at how easy it was to disperse the snow and cover my footprints. I took a few steps and found that I had to lift my feet high to avoid leaving scraping marks in the snow but otherwise, the invention was perfect.

Snow began to fall again soon afterwards and the sky looked heavy. We had no worries; by dawn our prints would be covered by fresh snow. With two bags of tools and food we began by walking away from the opening in the opposite direction to the one we wanted to take. The falling snow was also a wonderful blessing because we could see much better by its glare than on other nights. We entered the first building on our way, climbed over the rubble and retraced our way in our new shoes. To our great joy the steps we had taken only a few minutes earlier were no longer visible. After a while we became used to the nail soles and reached the empty basement where we were due to begin work.

Before leaving the bunker we had made an arrangement to do something which we did not really believe would work. An ex-coal miner in our group believed that we could stay in touch with the bunker even if we were a full kilometre away. He kept telling us that we could hear each other's digging because there were hollow areas in the basements between us. 'The hollow basements will be like drums,' he kept saying. On his insistence we had arranged a signal of three knocks from our side when we arrived, to be answered by the same three knocks from the bunker. When we arrived we placed a heavy piece of board against the wall in the direction of our bunker. My companion held the board as I lifted the sledgehammer and knocked three times. For some seconds nothing happened. Then, like the knocking of a ghost in the dark, three knocks came back to us. In the cavernous basement lit by a single candle we shivered with fear and excitement. With all that we had gone through over the years, the hollow sound coming to us was like a message from some dark world we knew was our own.

We began to work towards the direction of the sound and could hear those at the other end doing the same. By the morning we had knocked through the first wall and had gone through to the basement of the next house, which was on a street corner. We found a small sack of sugar, a bag of winter potatoes and jars of dripping. We started digging through the soft soil towards the next basement. We were now under a street fifteen metres wide and across from the basement we had reached in the night. We spent a large part of the day arranging our residence for the next few days. Judging by what we found, the people who had lived there before the deportation had been well off. They had established a fully fitted-out dining room and a kitchen stove. The beds had mattresses and covers, and they had even left some chairs. We began to wonder if, or rather when, the Germans might hit on the building and destroy our hard work. If they came down to the basement they would be right in the middle of our extended bunker.

We rested well for a few hours and before nightfall we had an answer to our problem. We went up and looked above ground. We had decided it would be necessary to start a fire, like the Germans, but on the ground floor. However, our plan was not necessary; our rich find was already under a huge amount of rubble and across the street, where we were going, was a ruined shop with half a building hanging over it.

Sometime during the night we reached the other side of the street and the tunnel we had dug came up to the bricks of the basement under the shop. My friend knocked out the double bricks and stretched out his hand with the carbide lamp to illuminate the dark opening. As he did so he screamed, moved back quickly and nearly got stuck in the earthen tunnel. When we reached the basement we heard our bunker end signalling desperately. We answered with three knocks and it became quiet. My companion looked as white as the snow outside. He was shivering and trembling, and his words came out in a stutter. As he had stretched the lamp into the opening, a huge squad of rats had begun running in all directions, one jumping right over his hand. He had glimpsed them gnawing on a half-eaten human body.

I boiled some water and we drank real, sweet coffee to steady our nerves. We sat and talked a little and I slid into the tunnel holding my loaded revolver in one hand and pulling myself forward with the other. My friend was behind me with the lantern. As I reached the end I stretched back and took hold of the lamp. I brought the light forward, then fired the revolver. Rats screamed and ran in all directions. Some began to run up towards the light and I fired again. In seconds they were gone. I looked into the basement. The sight of the half-eaten body was not pleasant but unlike my friend I had been warned, and I had perhaps become more hardened than he. I told him I was going to look around, but my companion began to whimper, begging me not to leave him alone. I told him to follow me but he was too shocked to do so. 'The rats! There are hundreds of them there,' he said. 'They will eat you alive!' He had become hysterical and we were stuck in a tunnel, in the dark. I decided to ignore him and jumped down into the horrid basement. As I did so he jumped after me and quickly settled. Like the first basement, this too had been well prepared. In the far corner on a small table, covered with a tablecloth, stood a kerosene lamp with kerosene in it. I went over and lit the lamp and the place became bright with light. We could make out that it had been used by a single person, who had, judging by the smell, died some days ago. We had a messy job, cleaning up the place, removing the half-eaten body and getting rid of the dirt the rats had left behind. But when we finished and went in to the next room attached to the basement it all became worthwhile. The place had belonged to a jeweller. We found a safe with the key in the lock. Inside it was a small box containing gold coins, a gold-covered cigar box, ladies' watches with wristbands and on chains, and a considerable number of smaller pieces of jewellery. In ordinary times such a safe would have made one very comfortable.

It took my friend a day to regain his balance. I made him promise not to speak about the rat incident to anybody as we had five women and thirteen other men on our hands, and it could have caused a catastrophe if any of them decided to run from the bunker because of it. The contents of the safe were later divided more or less equally between us, but we soon discovered we had a thief among us. We had a suspect but we could not prove anything.

Our life in the bunker took on the character of permanence. We had more than enough staple food, so much so that we began to grow choosy. On arrangements with other bunkers via the boxes on the electric poles, we exchanged sugar for coffee, a dog carcass for a jar of dripping. As the winter cold set in we cut down drastically on our outings unless they were absolutely necessary. Luba and I were the exception; we knew the whereabouts of other bunkers and went visiting once or twice.

Carbide was considered a luxury. It was one of our finds while digging the extension. With good management we could last with candles and carbide until the spring. But for many others carbide was a problem. On one particular night people from a nearby bunker who had gone to look for food found a bag of it. On the way back with their precious find, somebody called out in German, '*Halt!*' They dropped the parcel and ran. While running they realised that not a single shot had been fired and nobody was chasing them. They stopped and waited. After some time they turned back to retrieve the bag; it was gone. After that we used our post-box system to make it clear to all concerned that for calling 'Halt' the caller would be shot. It never happened again.

On New Year I said to our people, 'This year we will either die or be free.'

Luba replied, 'We will not be free as long as we live. Only after we die will we be free.'

Radio Raszyn, our only German station, transmitted the New

Year's speeches of the Führer who boasted of the new revenge rockets, the V2, which would bring a turnabout in the war and England to its knees. Again, he raved about the Jews and the Bolsheviks. Someone else addressed the American 'Jew President' Roosevelt, telling him that soon not only he but the whole mongrel race of Jewish America would be paralysed by the new German weapons. They played lively military songs and we felt like joining in the New Year celebration out of boredom.

Luba and I had a few friends who sheltered in a bunker close to one of the entrances to our enlarged cave. On the spur of the moment, Luba had told one of them the location of this entrance. I was angry with her at the time but it turned out to have been a master stroke of luck. Halfway through January we began to hear heavy artillery and bombing. We hoped to learn details about the action from Radio Raszyn but just at this critical time it went off the air. After two days everything became silent again. We discussed the situation, guessing at what could be happening. On 17 January we heard Russian songs outside. We agreed that it could be Ukrainians who had been brought to the Warsaw front to repel the Russians.

The snow had covered up our spy-hole and we could no longer see through it. So two young men were sent out to climb up the building and report what they could see. They came back soon afterwards, to tell us that the Germans had returned and were laying out the ground with red and white markings with the swastika on them. Somebody remembered from army days that this was the sign around the perimeter of the front line when they went on front manoeuvres. The news devastated us. Luba became desperate; she begged me to shoot her to save her from falling into the hands of the Germans. A new panic gripped the whole bunker.

We moved from the front of the bunker to the rear. Somebody began knocking on our secret entrance desperately telling us that we should come out, the Germans had fled. Of course, we knew that it was a German trick; they had used the ruse already during the ghetto Uprising. The caller kept on for some time but finally left. We became unnerved and nobody went to sleep that night. In the morning the same voice came back: 'The Russians are here! We are free!' As we did not answer, the caller seemed to become fed up. 'I won't come back again to call you if you don't believe me. But before I go, open and let me slide in. Have your revolvers ready. If the Germans follow me you may shoot me first, I'll slide head in first, just open the entrance.'

We risked it and the man slid in. It was our friend to whom Luba had entrusted the secret location of our entrance. He had brought us a page of a proclamation in Polish and in Russian as evidence. We were indeed free.

The weight of that freedom is something Luba and I and a fateful few have carried with us ever since.

The first Jewish Committee of Warsaw was already established on the Praga side of the Wisła when the Polish–Soviet Army entered Warsaw proper. After a few weeks it had a register of over three hundred Jews who had survived the last three months like us in Warsaw bunkers.

Suggested reading

Bartoszewski, Władyslaw, *Warszawski Pierścień Śmierci, 1939–1944*. Second edition. Interpress, Warszawa, 1970.

Eisner, Jack, *The Survivor of the Holocaust*. Kensington Press, New York, 1997.

Gutman, Yisrael, *The Jews of Warsaw 1933–1943: Ghetto, Underground, Revolt*. Midland Books, USA, 1989.

Jankowski, Stanisław M., *Emisariuz Witold*. Bicentennial Publishing Corporation, Nowy Dziennik, New York, 1991.

Kostański, Jan, *A Gentile in the Ghetto*. Puma Press, Victoria, 1998.

Lazar, Chaim, *Muranowska* 7. First edition, Hidekel Press Ltd, Tel-Aviv, 1966.

Ringelblum, Emanuel, *Kronika Getta Warszawskiego (Chronicle of the Warsaw Ghetto): September 1939–January 1943*, S.W. Czytelnik, Warszawa, 1983.

Wood, E. Thomas & Janowski, Stanisław M., *Karski: How One Man Tried to Stop the Holocaust*. John Wiley & Sons, Inc., New York, 1994.

Maps

WARSAW AND ENVIRONS, 1940

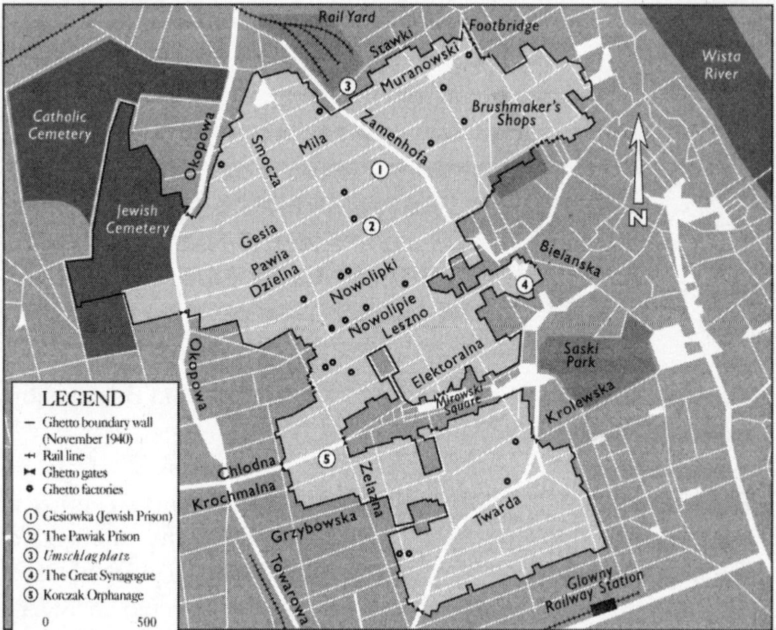

WARSAW GHETTO, 1940

These maps show the boundaries of the Warsaw ghetto as they were in November 1940. The boundaries changed over the years that the ghetto was in existence.

Acknowledgements

David would have liked to thank certain people and organisations which provided inspiration for this work.

Professor Jan Karski, Professor W.B. Bartoszewski, Jack (Jacek) Eisner and Janek Kostański encouraged him to write. The joy of their reunion provided some of the most wonderful moments of his life. Other friends throughout the world also encouraged David to write. All thanks to them and to his relatives who so eagerly awaited the manuscript.

Jeffrey S. encouraged David by lending him a book about Warsaw. (David later repaid the compliment by assisting Chaim Lazar and his daughter, Sarah Ozacky-Lazar, with details and information about the Warsaw ghetto Uprising.)

Tess, Alan, Anna, John and staff at Currency Communications gave us sympathetic patience.

Brendan Cohen, Abraham Cykiert and our cousin Robin Goodrich provided assistance. Robin and Jason Jones did the cover design. Brendan Cohen helped edit the final sections of the book with my mother. Thanks to Tony Ingram for final work and István Bronowiecki for his painstaking data work; to Mark Stern for his critical assistance and to Krystyna Duszniak for putting it all together. Thanks also to Julian Duszniak for the entertainment.

Thanks to Debbie and Colin Golvan of Golvan Arts Management Pty Ltd; and to Tom Gilliatt, Bernadette Foley and the staff at Pan Macmillan Australia for their enthusiastic support and sensitive understanding.

Faye and Sue from our office spent much time and effort typing and retyping the manuscript, filing documents and keeping track of all related details.

Thanks to the many friends of David in his private and business life — people with whom he had a special bond and became a much-loved part of his home and life.

Thank you to David's wife, his beloved Luba. Their love and friendship brought happiness and peace to many, healed divisions, and was a beacon to friends and family alike.

Thank you to the world for Israel, sovereign and restored. May understanding on the basis of equal rights provide inspiration for every nation and to all people.

Thank you, too, to Australia, you vast, spiritual land, where so many war-torn, tortured souls have found healing and solace in an environment that allows them to be free. May you remain forever thus and may we all assist towards healing their hurt and the hurt of the Indigenous people, and continue to champion a 'fair go' for people of the world.

The Landau Family
On behalf of David John Landau

A prayer

As Jews
we were supposed to be
the chosen people.
Chosen for what, I ask?
To be murdered, laughed at, scorned,
to be misunderstood, to be objects of jealousy,
to be shut out of our previous homes where
we were peaceful and to which we gave so much,
from Iraq and Iran, from Germany, from Jerusalem,
from Poland, England and France.
To be expelled from Spain, from Egypt, from Switzerland.
We are tough because we are
of the desert, then of the heat,
the snow, the ice and the mountains.
We are fair because of our teachings,
our prophets and our judges and because
we fear and respect the Almighty.
We are peaceable because we know
pain and fighting and war.
We defend because we value
the life of every living creature and respect
the earth that sustains us.
We survive because we are
humans just like you,
because we love
and because of you.

History shows us that where all people live in peaceful environments, those free societies flourish.

Wherever Jews have lived in those societies they have brought strength, generosity and innovation to areas as diverse as medicine, the economy, the arts and defence.

Where people have been harmed and freedom lost, those societies have fallen into chaos and eventual collapse.

One can only conclude that 'live and let live' is the way for all people, woman and man, innocent child,

'We are all in this world together,'

. . . and to wonder if perhaps, just perhaps, the Jews are really the good luck charms for each society they inhabit.

'Treat everyone well and you may be blessed.'

Rest in peace, my beloved father.

‘Those beasts who perpetrated the Holocaust perished. David Landau and the people like him didn’t perish. They won the war. They have lived to tell the tale and build new lives for themselves and their children.’

Jan Karski

‘We dream of a better life with truth and justice, a life that is not but will some day be.

My aim is to love and be righteous instead of being loved and adored.’

Janusz Korczak

Index